William Faulkner's Legacy

Florida A&M University, Tallahassee
Florida Atlantic University, Boca Raton
Florida Gulf Coast University, Ft. Myers
Florida International University, Miami
Florida State University, Tallahassee
University of Central Florida, Orlando
University of Florida, Gainesville
University of North Florida, Jacksonville
University of South Florida, Tampa
University of West Florida, Pensacola

UNIVERSITY PRESS
OF FLORIDA

Gainesville · Tallahassee

Tampa · Boca Raton · Pensacola

Orlando · Miami

Jacksonville

Ft. Myers

WILLIAM FAULKNER'S

LEGACY *"what*

shadow, what stain,

what mark"

Margaret Donovan Bauer

Copyright 2005 by Margaret Donovan Bauer
Printed in the United States of America on recycled,
acid-free paper · All rights reserved

10   09   08   07   06   05   6   5   4   3   2   1

A record of cataloging-in-publication data is
available from the Library of Congress.

ISBN 0-8130-2854-X

The University Press of Florida is the scholarly
publishing agency for the State University System
of Florida, comprising Florida A&M University,
Florida Atlantic University, Florida Gulf Coast
University, Florida International University,
Florida State University, University of Central
Florida, University of Florida, University of
North Florida, University of South Florida, and
University of West Florida.

University Press of Florida
15 Northwest 15th Street
Gainesville, FL 32611-2079
http://www.upf.com

This one is for my father, Carl W. Bauer,
whose support and influence I appreciate,
even as I re-vision and revise;
and for my mother, Jane Colvin Desonier,
whose support and example give me the courage
to re-vision and revise.

The wagon wound and jolted between the slow and shifting yet constant walls from beyond and above which the wilderness watched them pass, less than inimical now and never to be inimical again since the buck still and forever leaped . . . out of his instant of immortality the buck sprang, forever immortal.

Faulkner, *Go Down, Moses*

Contents

Acknowledgments

I begin these acknowledgments with Dorothy Scura, my mentor, whose support and influence continues. And posthumous acknowledgment goes to the late James D. Wilson, of the University of Southwestern Louisiana (now the University of Louisiana at Lafayette), whose class (and book) on the romantic heroic ideal most certainly influenced my response to Faulkner's romantic idealists. Thanks as well to those who have read and offered suggestions for revision over the years: Fred Hobson, Jeff Abernathy, and Matthew Guinn, in particular. I also recognize my colleague and friend Sally Lawrence's contribution to the last chapter: she called my attention to the echo of "A Rose for Emily" in Tim Gautreaux's "The Piano Tuner."

I thank, too, the East Carolina University Thomas Harriot College of Arts and Sciences for the spring 2002 College Research Award that gave me reassigned time from teaching and thus allowed me to make substantial progress toward finishing this study. I also appreciate the editorial staff and board members of the University Press of Florida, especially those who have worked with me on this book: Amy Gorelick, acquisitions editor; Michele Fiyak-Burkley, project editor; Susan Brady, copy editor; and Casey Woodling, marketing assistant.

Finally, I thank all of the students in the various classes in which I've taught the works covered in this study. Bouncing ideas around with my students in class remains my main source of inspiration.

Chapter 3 on *Their Eyes Were Watching God* has been adapted (with the permission of the College Language Association) from an article that appeared as "The Sterile New South: An Intertextual Reading of *Their Eyes Were Watching God* and *Absalom, Absalom!*" in *College Language Association Journal* 36 (1993), and an earlier, slightly different version of chapter 5 was published under the same title in *Pembroke Magazine* 33 (2001).

Acknowledgment is made to the publishers and other copyright holders listed below for permission to quote extensively and/or to quote passages used as epigraphs:

From *Absalom, Absalom!* by William Faulkner, copyright 1936 by William Faulkner and renewed 1964 by Estelle Faulkner and Jill Faulkner Summers. Used by permission of Random House, Inc. and Curtis Brown Group Ltd., London on behalf of the Estate of William Faulkner.

From *As I Lay Dying* by William Faulkner, copyright 1930 and renewed 1958 by William Faulkner; from *Go Down, Moses* by William Faulkner, copyright 1940 by William Faulkner and renewed 1968 by Estelle Faulkner and Jill Faulkner Summers. Used by permission of Random House, Inc.

From *Lonesome Dove* by Larry McMurtry, copyright 1985 by Larry McMurtry. Reprinted with permission of Simon and Schuster Adult Publishing Group and The Wylie Agency, Inc.

From *A Gathering of Old Men* by Ernest J. Gaines, copyright 1983 by Ernest J. Gaines. Used by permission of Alfred A. Knopf, a division of Random House, Inc.

From *Their Eyes Were Watching God* by Zora Neale Hurston, copyright 1937 by Zora Neale Hurston, renewed 1965 by John C. Hurston and Joel Hurston; from *Jonah's Gourd Vine* by Zora Neale Hurston, copyright 1934 by Zora Neale Hurston, renewed 1962 by John C. Hurston. Used by permission of HarperCollins Publishers.

From *Song of Solomon* by Toni Morrison, copyright 1977 by Toni Morrison. Used by permission of International Creative Management, Inc.

From *Oral History* by Lee Smith, copyright 1983 by Lee Smith. Used by permission of G. P. Putnam's Sons, a division of Penguin Group (USA) Inc. and the Darhansoff, Verrill, Feldman Literary Agents of New York.

From *Many Things Have Happened since He Died, and Here Are the Highlights* by Elizabeth Dewberry, copyright 1990. Used by permission of Elizabeth Dewberry and Harold Ober Associates.

From *The Sheltered Life* by Ellen Glasgow, copyright 1932 by Ellen Glasgow. Used by permission of the Richmond SPCA and the University of Virginia Press.

From *Kite-Flying and Other Irrational Acts: Conversations with Twelve Southern Writers* by John Carr, copyright 1972 by Louisiana State University Press; from *Porch Talk with Ernest Gaines: Conversations on the Writer's Craft*

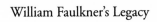

William Faulkner's Legacy

Crossing the Tracks of the Dixie Limited

Overcoming Anxiety
of Influence and
Filling in the Blanks

Suddenly he was conscious of a great rumbling at hand and the train schickalacked up to the station and stopped.

John stared at the panting monster for a terrified moment, then prepared to bolt. But as he wheeled about he saw everybody's eyes upon him and there was laughter on every face. He stopped and faced about. Tried to look unconcerned, but that great eye beneath the cloud-breathing smoke-stack glared and threatened.

Hurston, *Jonah's Gourd Vine*

INTERVIEWER: Do you think there will continue to be a Southern novel . . . ?

[SHELBY] FOOTE: It appears so, and it's somewhat regrettable, because I think the Southern novel has run its string. Maybe Faulkner used it up.

Carr, *Kite-Flying and Other Irrational Acts*

Flannery O'Connor's famous statement that "[t]he presence alone of Faulkner in our midst makes a great difference in what the writer can and cannot permit himself to do. Nobody wants his mule and wagon stalled on the same track the Dixie Limited is roaring down" (45) reflects the resistance writers felt—particularly southern writers of the generation that followed Faulkner—to being compared with Faulkner; it reflects, as Harold Bloom terms it, their anxiety of influence. More contemporary writers, however, are not so intimidated by the legacy of this giant of southern, American, and modern literature. For example, three of the writers covered in this study—Donald Barthelme, Larry McMurtry, and Pat Conroy—echo Faulkner without reservation. They recast his plots and themes but continue to pursue the issues and examine the characters that intrigued this apparent mentor.

One might argue that one reason Barthelme and McMurtry are not self-conscious about echoing Faulkner is that they feel less likely to be compared to Faulkner than would writers from (or at least writing from) the Deep South. Barthelme was not born in the South, and his literature is hardly "southern"; however, he did grow up and live the majority of his life in Houston, a very "southern" city. McMurtry, though, is from *West* Texas, which is not so often considered part of the South as East Texas is. Still, these two writers are included in this study because of the provocative distinction between how they *employ* Faulkner in their fiction and how the other contemporary writers covered in this study (except Conroy) *revise* Faulkner in theirs. Ernest Gaines, Toni Morrison, Lee Smith, Elizabeth Dewberry, and Tim Gautreaux[1] reveal themselves to be unintimidated by their literary precursor by boldly and unapologetically recasting, revising, even correcting Faulkner's perception of the people he wrote about.

To some extent not so surprising—and yet more surprising for different reasons—the two other writers to be discussed in chapters to follow, Zora Neale Hurston and Ellen Glasgow, echoed Faulkner, seemingly without trepidation. Since they were contemporaries of Faulkner, perhaps their lack of anxiety about being on the same track as the Dixie Limited was due to Faulkner's reputation not yet having been so firmly established, his work not yet being considered a defining agent of the South. Glasgow, of course, had been publishing novels long before Faulkner (and critics have been more inclined to show echoes of her work in his than vice versa). Certainly there was not enough time between the publication of Faulkner's *Absalom, Absalom!* (1936) and the publication of Hurston's *Their Eyes Were Watching God* (1937) to argue a case for influence. Indeed, neither Glasgow nor Hurston would have had the time to become as familiar with Faulkner's works as writers two generations later would—which makes the parallels I examine between their works and Faulkner's all the more provocative: Hurston simultaneously exploring the same issue of the sterile New South, Glasgow expressing impatience with Faulkner's prototypical character so soon after its inception. Whatever the motivations of these two women writers, they unabashedly explored concerns about the New South similar to Faulkner's but from perspectives quite different.

Patricia Yaeger asks, "How do we reinscribe a literature that keeps repeating stories about race-thinking that everyone knows but no one wants to hear?" (11). She explains "that white southern literature is obsessed with . . . stories that will not go away, that keep repeating themselves endlessly," and she suggests that "black literature about the South contributes to the exorcism of this repetition by ringing these stories backwards" (12).[2] I would suggest that not only black writers but also women writers, white and black, as well as blue-collar southern writers, male and female, are, by repeating familiar plots and recasting familiar characters, retelling the same stories "backwards" and thereby providing new perspectives on southern history.

Examining echoes of Faulkner in works by his contemporaries and by ours draws readers' attention to themes and characterizations in Faulkner's works that had been previously neglected by critics. In his paper for the 1986 Faulkner and Yoknapatawpha conference (in an argument that anticipated Toni Morrison's concern about the role of blackness in works by white writers, which she would develop in *Playing in the Dark* [1993]), Noel Polk expressed his perception of the criticism on "Faulkner's general treatment of blacks" as "stuck at considering them simply tragic victims of white oppression, and so symbols, rather than human beings" (149). One might make a similar argument about the criticism on Faulkner's female characters at least until the late twentieth century. My study exposes the Faulknerian *perspective* that, intentionally or not, marginalizes and/or objectifies African-Americans and women, thereby explaining why critics may have difficulty perceiving these characters as subjects in and of themselves rather than as objects of another's perspective.

Chapter 1 of this book first discusses the correspondence between the plots of Faulkner's *As I Lay Dying* (1930) and Donald Barthelme's *The Dead Father* (1975), which is established in the first chapter of Barthelme's novel when we learn that the title character is being hauled *cross-country* for burial by his sons. Undeniably, this plot echoes the main action of Faulkner's novel, though the parent to be buried in the more recent novel is, in contrast, the father, and the landscape is not distinctly southern (indeed, it is not identifiable as any particular place). These and other differences from the Faulkner work that Barthelme's novel echoes do not seem to be deliberate. Barthelme is not revising Faulkner; in both novels, the central conflict involves the continued influence of the dead parent upon her/his children. Barthelme employs Faulkner's novel as an objective correlative for the reader, prompting the reader to fill in the postmodern spaces and silences in *The Dead Father*—significantly, in the tradition of early Faulknerian criticism.[3]

The second section of chapter 1 then examines the significance of another *cross-country corpse*, this one in Larry McMurtry's *Lonesome Dove* (1985). At the end of this novel, Woodrow Call brings the body of Augustus McCrae back to Texas (from Montana) for burial, thereby also keeping a promise he made to the dying. Much like Faulkner's Addie Bundren, Augustus McCrae solicits this deathbed promise in an attempt to force recognition of himself (Gus)—but also others (particularly Call's son, Newt, and Newt's deceased mother)—upon his partner and friend. Examining these two works together, then, one can also draw a comparison between the Woodrow Call/Newt Dobbs relationship and the Thomas Sutpen/Charles Bon relationship in Faulkner's *Absalom, Absalom!*, which leads to an analysis of the connection between McMurtry's development of the journey—north, ironically—as an attempt to find paradise and Faulkner's development of the view of the South as a false Eden. While McMurtry has set his novel in the West rather than the South, as with the gender switch that Barthelme effects upon his dead parent, this recasting does not lead to a "re-vision" of Faulkner. Rather, the Faulknerian echo provides an intertext that may be used as a tool toward a fuller understanding of Gus's motivation for soliciting the promise from Call and of the flaws McMurtry ultimately finds in the western idyll.

Chapter 2 is the longest chapter of this study, reflecting the complexity and provocative nature of Ernest Gaines's relationship with Faulkner. In one of the earliest critical studies of Gaines, a 1976 article first published in French (an interesting coincidence, since Faulkner's genius was first recognized by French critics), Michel Fabre recognizes the risk Gaines takes in writing about the South. Somewhat echoing Flannery O'Connor, Fabre writes, "The excellence of the Faulknerian style makes anyone who takes up his challenge look like an imitator." At the outset of his article on Gaines, Fabre considers how "Faulkner's shadow . . . hovers over every American novelist who writes about the South" and then suggests, "This is perhaps more true for the black novelist because Faulkner spoke of his people with so much depth at times and often with so much compassion that his racial myths are the most indestructible. They remain an inevitable reference, the insidious point of convergence of new myths raised in response and in criticism" (110).

The chapter on Gaines begins with points of comparison and contrast between the title character of Gaines's *The Autobiography of Miss Jane Pittman* (1971) and Faulkner's black women characters, particularly Dilsey and Clytie, but also his white women characters like Caddy Compson. Gaines has frequently commented upon writing about Jane in her own kitchen (as opposed to, as Gaines puts it, Faulkner writing about Dilsey in *his* kitchen). Jane's role in the novel is certainly more than that of a family servant, but she is still not an *actor* in the novel so much as she is the chronicler, the one who tells the stories of the novel's primary actors. Unlike the novel's heroes, she survives, not so unlike Dilsey and Clytie, in large part for the purpose of telling the heroes' stories. (Of course, Faulkner's women do not have even this much voice.) What this comparison signifies is that while Gaines is concerned in his fiction with removing his African-American male characters from the margins where he perceives Faulkner's African-American characters to be confined, he does still marginalize the women of his novels and short stories. This marginalizing of women is particularly evident, surprisingly, in this novel in which a woman, Jane Pittman, is seemingly central, as well as in other Gaines works discussed in chapter 2, including *A Gathering of Old Men* (1983), which is examined in connection with, in particular, the stories of Faulkner's *Go Down, Moses* (1942).

The marginalized roles that the women play in Gaines's work should not necessarily be seen as a flaw, for Gaines is telling the African-American man's story in his fiction. Similarly, then, one might recognize that the marginalized position of African-American men and white and black women in Faulkner's fiction is due to his dominant interest in telling the story of the southern white man. Craig Werner points out that "Faulkner fails to excavate Afro-American history as thoroughly as he excavates Euro-American male history"; therefore, according to Werner, "a new stage of Afro-American response to Faulkner appears to have begun opening. . . . In this stage, Afro-American writers both draw on Faulkner for insight into their own cultural situation and contribute important insights to the excavation which he began" (37). Werner suggests, however, that "[r]ereading Faulkner through the Afro-American responses to his work highlights the fact that his work *is* grounded in social, specifically racial, *realities*" (53; emphasis added). That Faulkner did not, in his fiction, set out to tell the story of the whole South, for which he has been credited by early literary critics and for which (*presumed*) intention he has been criticized in more recent studies, does not lessen the validity and the value of the story he does tell.[4] More specifically, it seems that Faulkner's primary focus is upon the reactions of the romantic and educated, liberal-minded southern white man to the Old and New South, just as Gaines's primary focus is upon the heroic African-American man's struggle to assert his manhood.

Before moving on to how Faulkner is re-visioned by contemporary women writers and to these writers' less sympathetic treatment of the Faulkner prototype just described, I back up in chapter 3 to examine the connections between *Absalom, Absalom!* and *Their Eyes Were Watching God,* published the year after this Faulkner novel by Faulkner's own contemporary Zora Neale Hurston. Then, in chapter 4, similar connections are explored between *Absalom, Absalom!* and Toni Morrison's *Song of Solomon* (1977), published forty years after Hurston's novel. It is interesting to note how both of these African-American women writers have created characters very similar to Faulkner's Thomas Sutpen. With Joe Starks and Macon Dead II, respectively, Hurston and Morrison expose the black man's self-interested concern with his own oppression and his attempt to gain the power and position of the white man—at the expense of the black woman, whose oppression and suffering he either neglects to notice or contributes to (or both). While Faulkner explores the tragic irony of Sutpen, with his poor white roots, modeling his design after the white plantation system under which his own family has been oppressed, Hurston and Morrison examine the deeper irony of a black man striving to achieve the white man's success.

As Faulkner does in *Absalom, Absalom!,* in *Their Eyes Were Watching God* Hurston reveals the sterilizing nature of the plantation system: Starks rebuilds Eatonville in the fashion of a plantation, with his own home as the big house, his store as the plantation commissary, and the rest of the community positioned—and treated—like the "quarters." Significantly, children appear only three times in these "quarters." Furthermore, Hurston's main character, Starks's wife, Janie, remains inexplicably childless and may even, like Thomas Sutpen's son Henry, come home to die (still childless and thus leaving no Starks heir) at the novel's end. In Hurston's novel, however, Joe Starks does not share Thomas Sutpen's concern about having heirs, Starks's God complex having reached the point where he perceives himself invincible. And rather than ending her novel with the bellowing of a retarded, mixed-race representative of "what the New [South] hath wrought,"[5] Hurston ends with an ambiguous but uplifting image of her female protagonist, whether preparing to die or starting a new life, free from the Old Southern (flawed) ideals of her husband and embracing, instead, love and compassion, which neither Joe Starks nor Thomas Sutpen knew anything about, since their worldviews were formed by a social construct that practiced quite the opposite.

In contrast to Hurston's novel, which is Janie's (not Joe's) story, Morrison casts a man as the central character of *her* exploration of these issues, suggesting, perhaps, that her novel is a *conscious* re-vision of *Absalom, Absalom!* Not surprisingly, even in this novel in which the central character is a man, Morrison (like Hurston) is much more complimentary and/or sympathetic in her depiction of women than is Faulkner (or Gaines). Pilate Dead is perhaps the most heroic character in this Morrison novel; certainly, she is a more reliable narrator than Faulkner's Rosa Coldfield. And Ruth Dead, while questionably reliable, is more sympathetically developed than Rosa. This difference leads to an analysis of the influence of the authors' different sexes, rather than races, upon their creations.

In comparison, all three of these authors (Faulkner, Hurston, and Morrison) are distanced from the Old South that they critique as they send their central characters back into it to discover the significance of their families' pasts to their own lives. Faulkner began writing after returning to the South from his World War I tenure away from it, and the traditional opinion of his genius holds that that time away contributed to his objectivity about the South (in contrast to the earlier generations of southern plantation fiction writers).[6] Of course his point of view is still that of a white man. In contrast, as an African-American woman, the "mule [of the] world" (significantly, a sterile animal), as Janie's grandmother calls the black woman in *Their Eyes Were Watching God* (14), Hurston understood the oppression of the Old South as well as its continued influence upon the New reflected in the African-American man finding more role models among the empowered race (and gender) than among his peers and thus sometimes participating in the oppression of the African-American woman.

Morrison is even more distanced from the Old South than Hurston—not only in time but also in place since she is from the Midwest; however, her perspective on the Old South as an African-American would not likely be romantic even if she were southern herself. Carolyn Denard notes, in her introduction to the 1998 special issue of *Studies in the Literary Imagination* devoted to Morrison and the South, how "Morrison's distanced perspective [on] what the South meant to those who left the region . . . has made her treatment [of the South] so valuable" (ii). Morrison therefore sends her characters (like Milkman Dead) south to look around and discover what it and its history means to them. This chapter examines such epistemological issues in *Song of Solomon* and *Absalom, Absalom!*, which are developed as Milkman Dead and Quentin Compson each put together from various narratives the story of a southern family whose troubles began during the South's slave period. Within this discussion, the chapter explores the roles that Shreve and Guitar play in motivating their respective friends to seek the truth about the central family of his novel.

The analysis of Lee Smith's Appalachian-set novel *Oral History* (1983) in chapter 5 reveals numerous echoes of techniques, issues, and character types found in several Faulkner novels, including multiple narrators to tell the history of a "cursed" family; romantic (anti)heroes and the (female) manifestations of these men's romantic heroic ideals; and Old versus New South conflicts. The points of contrast between Smith and Faulkner remind the reader, first of all, that the South is not monolithic. Her novel introduces many readers to Appalachia, a region of the South very different from Faulkner's mythological, but long perceived as prototypical, Yoknapatawpha County, Mississippi. Other distinctions between the two writers' works ultimately illuminate what reading *Oral History* intertextually with novels by Faulkner reveals about each author: first, the focus on sexual rather than racial oppression in Smith's South, in which there are few African-Americans, but also that Faulkner's fiction does deal with the issue of sexual oppression, though only fairly recently have critics turned their attention to this issue, having for decades concerned themselves almost exclusively with his interest in race relations. Most provocative, Smith's reincarnation of Faulkner's Quentin prototype in the character of Richard Burlage illuminates how great a role these would-be knights actually play in the oppression of rather than rescuing of southern ladies. And the parallels one can see between Richard Burlage and Almarine Cantrell—and between Almarine and Thomas Sutpen—reveal the connection between this Faulknerian villain and Faulkner's prototypical romantic, a man seemingly too weak to be a villain, but villainous in his weakness.

If the period referred to as the Southern Renascence ended in the 1950s or early 1960s, as J. A. Bryant Jr. suggests in his study of *Twentieth-Century*

Southern Literature (6), then southern American literature is currently enjoying a second flowering, one possible reason for which is the willingness of
contemporary southern writers like Smith to take other skeletons out of closets and thus tell stories previously untold.[7] Bryant defines "the true legacy of
the renaissance" as being "southern writing," which is, Bryant reports, "alive,
if numbers tell us anything, and well, to judge by the vigor and quality of
some of the recent work" (7).[8] He points out that the newer writers have
"little real knowledge of the older South, the living traces of which were still
available to nourish people such as Faulkner" (6), but later in his study, he
notes how "in probing the roots of the southern experience [Faulkner] had
provided a definition of the South that would enable a new generation of
writers to avoid the path of stultifying romanticism and exploitations of local
color and begin to create a literature fully representative of the region's diver-
sity and complexity" (86).

The progression of my study of Faulkner with other southern writers reveals how this legacy of William Faulkner—not serving as *the* voice of the
South authorized to define the region but as *a* voice telling about the actual
South rather than some romanticized version of it—may be detected in the
works of contemporary writers who still deal with the issue of the continued
oppression of African-Americans in the South and have begun to deal with
the oppression of women as well. Upon collecting the essays for their 1997
volume, *Haunted Bodies: Gender and Southern Texts*, Susan V. Donaldson and
Anne Goodwyn Jones determined "that gender in the end may be as important an analytic category for making sense of the South as race itself traditionally has been acknowledged to be." They point out that the essays in
their edited collection repeatedly show that "one can hardly tell . . . where the
region's age-old worries about race and class end and its anxieties about gender begin" (Donaldson and Jones 16).

My study notes a distinction between, for example, Faulkner's treatment
of oppression in his work and its treatment in southern literature by women:
that these women writers examine the issue not from the perspective of the
sensitive white male aristocrat out of place in and trying to change the social
system that would support such oppression but rather from the perspective
of the victims of the oppression. In other words, exploration of the violence
enacted against these groups is no longer so often an avenue through which
to understand the development of a more liberal-minded southern white
male—except in the work of writers who follow more directly in Faulkner's

footsteps. The sixth chapter of this study traces how rape, being such a significant manifestation of women's oppression, has been treated in southern literature, from plantation fiction to several contemporary southern novels in which a rape plays a central role. Chapter 6 examines most thoroughly the novel *Many Things Have Happened since He Died, and Here Are the Highlights* (1990), by Elizabeth Dewberry,[9] as exemplary of contemporary southern women writers' treatment of this violent crime of oppression and then contrasts Dewberry's treatment with Pat Conroy's treatment of rape in *The Prince of Tides* (1986). Conroy's focus on the effect of rape upon his sensitive male character, who not only cannot defend his mother and sister against their rapists but is also raped himself, is reminiscent of Faulkner's concern as he dealt with the rape of Temple Drake in *Sanctuary* (1931)—that is, with his male characters' inability to defend her rather than with her own suffering.

Also significantly distinct from Pat Conroy's continuation of Faulkner's tendency to focus on a sensitive but impotent white male is the manifestation of this character found in the fiction examined in chapter 7 of, first, Faulkner's contemporary Ellen Glasgow, who as a female member of the aristocracy seems impatient with this perception of the white man as a victim, and then, in an interesting juxtaposition established by a similar Faulkner echo, our contemporary Tim Gautreaux, who writes of the not-so-empowered blue-collar men of Louisiana. Like Faulkner (and Conroy), Gautreaux tends to put his male protagonists in a position of having to go to the aid of some damsel in distress—but Gautreaux's men tend to *act* rather than worry; certainly they do not overthink the situation to the point of talking themselves out of helping or into believing there is nothing they can do. Ironically, these male protagonists come from much less privileged social positions than Quentin Compson, Horace Benbow, Isaac McCaslin, or Gavin Stevens.

After backing up historically once again to trace the frustration with the empowered but impotent prototype of Faulkner's fiction, which can be detected in Glasgow's development of General Archbald in *The Sheltered Life* (1932),[10] the concluding chapter of this study then examines Gautreaux's unlikely (sometimes seemingly anti)heroes who emerge out of the perhaps most marginalized, certainly most denigrated social group in Faulkner's fiction, "poor white trash." Faulkner may have shown how some members of this group—like Flem Snopes—escaped their economic oppression, but still he portrayed not only Flem Snopes but also the Bundrens, and even such more likeable but not much more positively developed characters as Lena Grove, as "trash" whose rising influence would result in the manifestation of H. L. Mencken's worst predictions for the New South in his infamous essay "The Sahara of the Bozart."[11] "Poor white *trash*" can certainly be found in Gautreaux's work, but so can decent men who hold down blue-collar jobs and earn the respect of their fellow citizens, rich and poor. And these men *act* upon situations about which the Quentin Compsons and David Archbalds only fret. The contrast illustrates Matthew Guinn's thesis about contemporary writers of "poor white" rather than genteel ancestry: "Writing from the almost unprecedented perspective of southern poor whites speaking for themselves, these authors expose the dark underside of an ostensibly genteel culture" (xiii).[12]

Flannery O'Connor prefaced her Faulkner/Dixie Limited analogy with the warning, "When there are many writers all employing the same idiom, all looking out on more or less the same social scene, the individual writer will have to be more than ever careful that he isn't just doing badly what has already been done to completion" (45). Although O'Connor seems here to be suggesting that the South "has already been [written] to completion" by Faulkner, Michael Kreyling points out the significance in the diction chosen for her metaphor for him—the Dixie *Limited* (not the Dixie Special, as she is sometimes misquoted, according to Kreyling): "She chose 'limited' to shoulder some room in the southern literary space dominated by 'Faulkner' and by critics who had named him the Major figure, legitimizing a cultural sovereignty, southern literature, over which they (the critics) claimed ministerial status" (128). As most of the writers of my study do in their fiction, I challenge in my examination of their work the view of Faulkner as representing the whole South in his writings. These writers are not intimidated by the "shadow . . . stain . . . mark" (one's choice of descriptor depending on one's perspective) of the writings of William Faulkner (Faulkner, *Go Down, Moses* 111–12). They recognize that his legacy is largely in his telling southern stories that either had not yet been told at all or had not yet been told from the perspective he provided. Furthermore, they recognize that *the* southern story remains incomplete as long as there are perspectives not yet given voice or attention. My study recognizes and explores the significant contributions to telling more of southern his- and her-story of Glasgow, Hurston, Gaines, Morrison, Smith, and others like them, including Dewberry and Gautreaux.[13] In spite of Flannery O'Connor's warning against doing so, the writers in this list have courageously driven their mules and wagons onto the track with the Dixie Limited, and they are catching up to him. Of the writers covered in this study, only Glasgow and McMurtry have produced the volume of work that Faulkner did in his lifetime, but what the other writers have produced is certainly measuring up to, even in some areas (particularly in their perspective on the central concerns of women and African-Americans) surpassing, Faulkner's achievements.

chapter 1

Cross-Country Corpses in Faulkner, Barthelme, and McMurtry

A Faulknerian Objective Correlative in Donald Barthelme's *The Dead Father*

Maybe we are both Father. Maybe nothing ever happens once and is finished.

Faulkner, *Absalom, Absalom!*

"Dead, but still with us, still with us, but dead" (3), a line from the prologue to Donald Barthelme's *The Dead Father,* sums up the plight of this novel's characters, as well as the situation through most of William Faulkner's *As I Lay Dying.* The *Dead Father/As I Lay Dying* parallel was, in fact, noted by Frederick R. Karl, author of a 1989 critical biography of Faulkner, in his 1983 book *American Fictions* (385). In both novels, the central character is, surprisingly, dead—and yet not so; for death does not terminate the influence of either the Dead Father or Addie Bundren over the thoughts and actions of their survivors. André Bleikasten's summary of "the trouble with" fathers in Faulkner could be applied to Barthelme's Dead Father, as well as to this Faulkner mother, Addie Bundren: "The trouble with them is that they are dead, but not dead enough to allow their descendants to live" ("Fathers" 143).

Addie's continued influence upon her children even after her death was summed up in 1975 by Irving Howe: "As the children try, each in his [or her] own fumbling way, to learn the meaning of living as son or brother [or daughter], Addie's authority persists and grows; indeed, her power is never greater than during the moment after death, when the Bundrens realize how thoroughly the dead live on, tyrants from the past" (180). Also in 1975, Donald Barthelme published *The Dead Father*, within which a passage from *A Manual for Sons* (a book included within the novel) sums up similarly the enduring influence of the father: "Fatherless now, you must deal with the memory of a father. Often that memory is more potent than the living presence of a father, is an inner voice commanding, haranguing, . . . governing your every, your slightest movement, mental or physical" (144). The apparently invincible parental control and the child's consequential desperate search for an independent identity are subjects that both of these novels explore. Upon noting this parallel, the reader might fill in the postmodern spaces and silences in *The Dead Father* by employing *As I Lay Dying* as an intertext.

These two novels are, of course, very different—and not only regarding the gender of the parent being transported. Certainly the novels' narrative styles are hardly comparable. Yet, even if the products of Barthelme's postmodern, experimental style seem to descend more from such modernists as James Joyce and William Butler Yeats, as Carl D. Malmgrem has pointed out (36),[1] still the tendency to experiment with style might also be traced to Faulkner. In the introduction to *The Future of Southern Letters*, John Lowe suggests that "[a]n often-overlooked component of Faulkner's continuing influence on southern letters has been evident in the experimental nature of much of southern fiction of the last few decades" (8). Barthelme's *The Dead Father* might be added to Lowe's list of experimental novels. This novel, which attracted critical attention upon its publication but only a few in-depth critical examinations, evolves around the title character's surreal funeral procession. Nineteen of his sons serve as pallbearers, but instead of carrying their father's inanimate corpse in a coffin, they are dragging his 3,200 cubits long, still quite vibrant body to its grave. How can one read about the journey to bury a parent without conjuring up Faulkner's burial odyssey? The giant, strangely vital corpse of *The Dead Father* is Barthelme's version of Addie Bundren's monologue in Faulkner's novel, since she has been dead for several days by the time her voice participates in the narrative.

Before the Dead Father can be buried, his powers must be stripped from him and passed on to someone else. His oldest son, Thomas, who, in spite of his insistence otherwise, seems to aspire to receive the legacy of power, leads the funeral procession; also distinguishable among the mourners are Thomas's alcoholic brother, Edmund, and two women, Julie and Emma. Although the Dead Father goes along quite willingly on the journey, he contests the usurpation of his power by Thomas, who confiscates first his father's belt buckle (since *he* now "wears the pants in the family"), later his father's sword (an obvious phallic symbol), and finally his father's keys (which Thomas may hope will unlock the secrets of being a father), symbols of the Dead Father's sexual virility and of his patriarchal power. The Dead Father tries to counter his son's expropriation of his possessions with the seduction of Julie, who is Thomas's lover, and later Emma, but he fails with both women and is thereby further humiliated by this more devastating evidence of his impotence. His consolation, however, is his belief that "[a] son can never, in the fullest sense, become a father. Some amount of amateur effort is possible. A son may after honest endeavor produce what some people might call, technically, children. But he remains a son. In the fullest sense" (33). It is such insensitive, oppressive boasting as this that incites the desperate cry in the prologue of the novel (apparently voiced by the members of the procession): "*We* want *the Dead Father to be dead. We sit with tears in our eyes wanting the Dead Father to be dead*" (5; Barthelme's italics and emphasis).

After this candid, if seemingly callous, expression of desire for the death of the novel's central figure, which echoes the *unexpressed,* though easily discerned, wish of several of Addie Bundren's family members that their mother's imminent death would hurry along, the correspondence between Barthelme's novel's plot and that of Faulkner's *As I Lay Dying* is further established in chapter 1 of Barthelme's novel with the reference to the Dead Father being hauled by "a little band of brothers" (6). Undeniably, this detail is reminiscent of the notorious journey of the "band of brothers" in Faulkner's novel, and the central issues of both books involve the relationships between the sons and the dying parent, again suggesting Faulknerian influence. In an interview with Barthelme, Jo Brans mentions the comparable plots of the two novels, noting, "except with you it's the father that has to be buried, in Faulkner it's the mother" (123).[2]

Surprisingly, in the difference between the deceased parents' genders, Barthelme's can be viewed as the more traditional novel in its exploration of anxiety of *patriarchal* influence. In contrast, *As I Lay Dying* is, as noted by Diana York Blaine, the "mutant modern version of the traditional patriarchal tragedy," which leaves Blaine "wonder[ing] why [Faulkner's] average, impoverished and unhappy farmer's wife" is "promoted" to "center stage" in this way (419). Blaine determines, however, that even though Faulkner apparently felt it was appropriate to grant the mother such power, to portray her in a traditionally masculine position, he also felt it necessary to kill her off without leaving behind an intact matriarchy to carry on her reign, to reify her authority. Instead we see woman as symbol of power eclipsed as she ascends, her putative centrality undermined by the symbolic system that subsumes her abject corpse into the ground at the end. (420)

Once buried, Addie is quickly replaced (with an apparently less defiant new Mrs. Bundren), and patriarchal status quo is thereby reestablished. Similarly, the reader will find that, although the tyranny of the Dead Father's reign is interrogated and rebelled against throughout the journey to bury him, by the time of his burial, Thomas is prepared to take his father's place as dominating, oppressive patriarch.

Backing up to the onset of each journey to bury the deceased parent, one realizes early on that, in spite of the deceased parents' different genders, at issue with their deaths is whether the next generation will continue to support patriarchal domination. Much of the criticism of *As I Lay Dying* focuses on the different relationships between Addie and her four sons: Cash, Darl, Jewel, and Vardaman. Faulknerian critics of the same period in which Barthelme wrote his novel about an influential deceased parent focused on the Bundren sons' reactions to their mother. Irving Howe, for example, summarizes the conflict of the novel as: "Addie's sons, in their struggle toward self-definition, discover that to answer the question, Who am I?, they must first consider, What was my mother and how did she shape me?" (180). And just over a decade before Barthelme published his novel, Olga Vickery wrote:

> Thus, it is Addie not as a mother, corpse, or promise but as an element in the blood of her children who dominates and shapes their complex psychological reactions. Their motivation lies within her life, for she is the source of the tension and latent violence which each of them feels within himself and expresses in his contacts with the rest of the family. Obsessed by their own relationships to Addie, they can resolve that tension only when they have come to terms with her as a person and with what she signifies in their own consciousness. (52)

Like the Bundren sons, Thomas of *The Dead Father* spends much of his time contemplating and struggling with his recently deceased parent's influence upon him, an influence that, like Addie's, has not been positive, and that does not expire with his father. As Michael Zeitlin explains, "The father has taken up permanent residence in his son's soul, intertwining himself with the son's own most intimate definition of self" (200). By the time of the burial, then, Thomas has *become* his Father, has joined the patriarchy. Similarly, as the journey to bury Addie draws to its end, Cash finds his voice and Jewel his place within the family unit. These men will go home with Anse (whom Addie referred to as "dead") and the new Mrs. Bundren, while Darl, who was more concerned about Addie herself than about burying her, is institutionalized and thus will have no further influence upon the still malleable youngest brother, Vardaman.

The Bundren daughter/sister and the women who go along with Barthelme's sons to bury their father are not being overlooked here, but Dewey Dell's presence and conflicts are merely a subplot of the novel, not unlike the presence and conflicts of Julie and Emma in *The Dead Father*. Indeed, these young women's common role in their novels seems to be merely to illustrate the perpetuation of the oppression of women by the patriarchy of both novels. Consider Jill Bergman's interpretation of Addie's monologue, in which she explains that Addie married Anse in an "attempt to escape the drudgery of the school children and to express her sexuality freely" only to realize the consequences of sexual expression—pregnancy (and thus the drudgery of housework); from this realization, according to Bergman, Addie determines "that life is terrible" (397). With this understanding of the compromised appeal of a woman's sexuality, which seems to promise passion but results in more oppression, one might compare Dewey Dell's sexual tryst with the drugstore clerk and the episodes of sexual titillation between Julie and Thomas, although the latter pair never has actual intercourse. (The former pair, for that matter, engages in no foreplay; they merely copulate and then separate.) The comparison's significance lies in the absence of sexual pleasure on the women's part; both are merely servicing the men—a not-so-subtle reflection of their roles in their respective novels—and of women's role in a patriarchal society.

Returning to disparities between the two novels, another can be found in the Dead Father's apparent misconception of the true goal of their pilgrimage—that is, to bury him—as opposed to Addie's knowledge, even instigation, of her family's expedition. Addie specifically requests that her husband take her corpse to her chosen burial site. This request was early interpreted by critics as a desperate last attempt to force her family into some *action* that would *demonstrate* their acknowledgment of her significance. "Her purpose in living," according to James L. Roberts in 1960, "had been to force an awareness of herself on other people" (27).[3] Recalling Addie's treatment of her students, Roberts explains that she felt "she could attain reality only when she imposed herself upon the consciousness of others" (28). I would add, to further support and develop this explanation of the motivation for her request, Addie's initial distress upon learning that she was pregnant with Darl. Significantly, the promise is solicited from her husband after she gives birth to Darl and realizes that her identity is now split in three. Anse thinks Addie believes she is dying right then, and therefore he responds to her burial request, "Nonsense, . . . you and me aint nigh done chapping yet, with just two" (173). Though he means it as a comfort, this statement only confirms what Addie has begun to fear: that as long as she lives she will have to focus on her children rather than herself.[4] Her own identity, consequently, will be lost in the crowd. Thus, she wants to be buried far from this family where she is the mother, indeed, in a place where she is the daughter. Paradoxically then, Addie hoped to receive new life from her burial: not only recognition of her value from her survivors but also a return to the position of child with her ancestors. Interesting for its echo in Barthelme's novel, after telling of Anse's response to her burial request, Addie remarks, "He did not know that he was dead, then" (173). To Addie, Anse is a "dead father," a character who is "dead but still with [her]" (Barthelme 3). She repeats this sentiment following her narration of Cora's response to her regarding her duties as a wife and mother: "And then he died. He did not know he was dead" (174). Accepting the *duties* of wife and mother but rejecting the identity of being *merely* wife and mother, Addie pursues an affair with Reverend Whitfield. With Whitfield, she had sought sex that was not about her duties as a wife, an identity that is more than a word (like "wife" or "mother"), a living lover rather than a "dead" husband.[5]

The Bundren family members are determined to fulfill their wife's/mother's burial request despite the obstacles they must overcome in the process, and they do ultimately *bury* her. Hence, subconsciously, at least for the three older sons, the purpose of their trip is to *dispose of* their mother so that they can get on with their lives. It is therefore understandable that Addie's sons, who reveal the destructive nature of their mother's influence in their jealousy, selfishness, and overall confusion, would recognize on some level the necessity of laying their mother to rest in order to get out from under her control. Support for this notion can be found in their immediate acceptance of Anse's new wife, which Peter Swiggart calls "a further betrayal of Addie and the public motive behind their trip" (116). This betrayal, together with the selfish, true motives behind her children's participation in the fulfillment of her request—Cash's intention to buy a gramophone, the hopes of Darl and Jewel to outshine each other during their journey, Dewey Dell's plans for an abortion, and Vardaman's wish to see the toy train in a store window—provoke some critics to condemn Addie's family and, consequently, to pity Addie for her family's treatment of her while she was alive and of her corpse after her death. These critics tend to see Addie in a positive, somewhat romantic light, as described by Hyatt H. Waggoner: "Some critics have interpreted Addie as a wholly sympathetic character, the 'heroine' of the work even in death. . . . The 'traditionalist' interpretation . . . emphasizes her effort to achieve a relation of love with others. . . . She is a redemptive character [to others] . . . because she recognizes both the difficulty and the necessity of love" (81). Waggoner himself, however, much as I will in this chapter, questions such a one-sided view of Addie, a view that, for example, ignores her negative influence upon her children, which, I would argue, causes the failure of the intended spirit of her quest.

As Amado Chan points out, Addie's family's "cold and impersonal attitudes" toward her death "indicate that she is incapable of raising a family with love, caring, and concern in the very least" (Chan). Addie's children do not spend the journey sharing memories of their mother or contemplating how much they have lost with her passing. Rather, they are focused on each other and themselves, and it is Addie's previous treatment of them that causes the eruption of conflicts between and within them. It is, for example, her denial of love to Darl that apparently causes him first to torment Jewel, whom she favored, and later to set the barn on fire in an attempt to destroy the rotting corpse and thus stop the humiliation of his mother, for it is often the neglected child who goes to the greatest lengths to prove his love and thus his worthiness for the parent's returned affection.[6]

As mentioned, unlike Addie, the Dead Father does not understand that the purpose of the journey is to bury him. In her analysis of *The Dead Father*, Barbara Malory defines the novel's central conflict as "the tension [that] develop[s] between the Dead Father and Thomas, both participating in the journey but having different goals. Thomas intends to bury the Dead Father, while he (the Dead Father) seeks rejuvenation and continued life" (86). The

disparate goals of father and son may remind the reader of Addie's motivation for requesting a Jefferson burial versus her family's reasons for carrying it
out. Comparable, too, the Dead Father reveals that he has completely misinterpreted his children's motives when he says, "That they should so love me
as to haul and haul and haul and haul, through the long days and nights and
less than optimal weather conditions" (6). It is not love that prompts this
procession; rather, it is the same emotions as those motivating the Bundren
brothers (who also travel in "less than optimal weather conditions"): jealousy, selfishness, confusion, desperation. The reader will witness these same
emotions surfacing and clashing during the search for a separate identity of
each of the Dead Father's sons, who have thus far been grouped together to
such an extent that only Thomas and to some extent Edmund emerge as individuals, though the reader understands that the conflicts these two have
with the Dead Father are representative of the conflicts that every member of
the group has with him.

The Dead Father believes—or deceives himself into believing—that he is
being taken to the golden fleece, which will rejuvenate him: "I will be young
again. . . . I shall once more be wiry." All the trials of the journey, he says,
"will [then] be worthwhile" (9). The golden fleece, the reader learns in the
final chapter, turns out to be Julie's pubic hair (or, more precisely, that which
lies beneath her pubic hair), which has of course been with them all the time
and which he has not been allowed to touch and is still not allowed to touch,
even after recognizing it as that which he seeks, a passage to new life in the
physical world. It is actually Thomas who will receive the golden fleece at the
end of the journey. Although he has had access to it throughout the journey,
he has only fondled it thus far, having been, for some reason, kept from fully
claiming it by his father's presence—hence another reason to bury his father.
One can conclude, then, that the only way the golden fleece will mean rejuvenation to the Dead Father is through his son, Julie's lover, who will soon
take up his father's role by fathering sons of his own.

Similarly, *As I Lay Dying* ends with Dewey Dell still pregnant, and it is
difficult to consider this pregnancy in positive terms (as a promise of new
life). Rather, the reader wonders if this first pregnancy sets Dewey Dell to
following in her mother's footsteps to an early grave and whether her experiences with men will result in bitterness as strong as her mother's; already she
has been deserted by the father of her child, refused and chastised by one
man from whom she seeks help (the druggist), taken advantage of by one

who offers help (the druggist's clerk), and then robbed by her father, thereby ensuring that she will not be able to buy abortion-inducing chemicals from anyone in any town they might pass through on their journey home. The novel offers no promise of better lives for any of the other members of the next generation of Bundrens either: not for Darl, who is institutionalized; or for Cash or Jewel, who will both probably continue to help support Anse for the rest of their lives; or for Vardaman, to whom only Darl has tried to explain what is going on, and whose odd monologues, consequently, leave the reader worried that he may follow his brother to Jackson (although, as I suggested earlier, with Darl gone, he will grow up under the influence of these other men, which still does not bode well for him).[7] However, a closer look at Addie's section—her explanation for wanting to be buried in Jefferson and the part of her story that follows—provides a surprisingly more positive perception of her fate if not of her children's. Significantly, for example, while Addie is longing to regress to her position as daughter, before she took on the burdens of motherhood (as reflected in her wish to be buried in her hometown), her death, as Amy Louise Wood points out, "coincides with [her daughter's] emergence into womanhood, disconnecting [Dewey Dell] from her child-self and forcing her to negotiate her way in the world" (109).

Addie's request to be buried where she will forever be a daughter suggests a desire to spend eternity as a child—that is, being taken care of rather than doing the caring for. Following the birth of Darl, having recognized how hard her life was going to be in this world, she sought assurance that there was another world to follow—which I would argue is another and perhaps the most significant reason behind her affair with Whitfield, a preacher: she wanted to test the wrath—and thus the existence—of God. Since God did not strike her dead for corrupting this holy man, it either meant that there is no God or that He is merciful. The conception of a child from this affair seems to be evidence to her of God's mercy, given her choice of names for this product of her affair (and her subsequent favoring of this son): God had not punished her for her sin; rather, He had blessed her with this "jewel," which suggested to her not only His mercy but also His compassion.[8] This interpretation of Addie's narrative would explain her sudden need to make everything right with Anse: "And so I have cleaned my house" (176)—that is, paid for her sins by giving Anse children to replace those she kept from him. If "the reason for living is getting ready to stay dead" (176), one of her father's aphorisms, which she recalls just after she finds out she is pregnant with

Jewel, then she must make up for her sins so that she can spend eternity with this merciful, compassionate God. As Patricia McKee points out regarding this passage, "To say that the reason for living is getting ready to stay dead is to insist on thinking and acting with reference to something beyond the present, beyond life even. It is an insistence on the consequential character of both life and action" ("*As*" 603).[9] Indeed, Addie concludes her section implying her belief in life after death: "[P]eople to whom sin is just a matter of words, to them salvation is just words too" (176). But to people like herself, who know the meaning of their sins, as her narrative has shown, the promise of salvation is very real.

This more positive reading of *As I Lay Dying* leads the intertextual reader of the two novels to examine how or if the optimism translates into the postmodern novel at hand. Whereas the modern novelist often sought reassurance that God, though seemingly silent, was not as dead/nonexistent as the First World War suggested, postmodern novelists often begin on the assumption that if God is not dead it is because He never existed to begin with. Yet Barthelme's novel may be read as a postmodern retelling of the transition from the Old Testament to the New Testament God. The Dead Father represents the wrathful Old Testament God who was quick to avenge those who displeased Him. Thomas may seem an unlikely Christ figure—as unlikely as Benjy Compson, one might say, though the latter has often been viewed in such terms—but Barthelme's description of Thomas suggests that he is to be perceived as such. As Faulkner gave Benjy the blue eyes and blond hair of the Western image of Jesus and then had him celebrate his thirty-third birthday to make sure the reader thought of Jesus in connection with his character, Barthelme includes a scene in which Julie washes Thomas's feet and another in which Thomas lies in a cruciform position (while Julie fondles him). Surprisingly, too, given how much sexual titillation can be found in the novel, Thomas remains a virgin, as far as the reader knows. A less obvious association between Thomas and Christ are Thomas's tights and boots, which are orange, like the sun, suggesting Son.

Like my reading of Addie's monologue's testament to her belief in the possibility of salvation after death, reading Barthelme's novel in a Christian context provides the *possibility* of a more hopeful vision of the future, after the burial of the Dead Father. Although Thomas seems to have become like his father during their journey, he may, like Christ, be a more merciful version, as suggested by his recognition of the harshness of his father's rule. Indeed, *A*

Manual for Sons, which Thomas and Julie read, allows for the *probability* that the next generation of the patriarchy will be less dominating when it explains that the son will "become [his] father, but a paler, weaker version of him . . . *thus moving toward a golden age of decency, quiet, and calmed fevers*" (145; emphasis added). On the other hand, Barthelme has shown with his development of Thomas how power so easily corrupts. If Thomas is a Christ-figure, he is one who gave in to the temptations in the desert. Like his human forefather Adam, this Christ has fallen to the temptation to be God-like. A significant contrast between this novel and *As I Lay Dying*, then, is that this novel provides no hope of salvation because it sees no difference between the Dead Father and the next generation's patriarch.

And yet, *The Dead Father* ends as peacefully—though perhaps orderly is the more appropriate adverb—as does *As I Lay Dying*, and both families ultimately resume status quo. In Faulkner's novel, after the chaos of the struggle involved in the arrest of Darl and of the madness of Darl's last section, the reader is given a final word from Dewey Dell, in which she tells of her father taking her abortion money to buy his teeth, thereby making it more likely that she will have the baby. This potential birth suggests that regardless of what ethereal plane the deceased Addie's voice might be coming from, the earthly cycle of oppression will probably continue undisturbed. Dewey Dell's section is followed by the novel's final monologue, from the perspective of Cash, perhaps the calmest voice in the novel, in which he tells of Anse's new wife, suggesting that the "order" of their lives, ironic an order as it may be, has been restored. Surprisingly, the burial of the Dead Father goes as smoothly. Although he questions why and whether he must indeed be buried, the Dead Father eventually accepts his fate and lies down in his grave of his own accord. Thomas's corruption having been established by this point, the reader, along with Julie and Emma, is more sympathetic toward the despair of the Dead Father. His disappointment that the end of the journey did not result in rejuvenation is all the more poignant because of his desperate hold on the false hope to the very end.

Upon his realization of the futility of his quest for new life, the Dead Father resigns himself to his true fate—death—and lies down in his grave, finally a more human—and thus more sympathetic—character in his acknowledgment of his mortality than he had appeared previously in the novel. As one reviewer remarks, "The 'end' of *The Dead Father* is curiously moving. We expect the journey to continue—there have been many false starts and conclusions—and when 'bulldozers' . . . bur[y] the pleading father . . . we are unhappy" (Malin 380).[10] In fact, there are several places in the novel where the reader is moved to sympathize with the Dead Father, particularly as Thomas takes advantage of his own youthful strength at the expense of his weakening mentor. And yet, still one cannot overlook the abundant evidence in the novel that Thomas inherited from his father this manner of establishing authority through the debasement of others. As Lois Gordon notes, even "while he is humiliated by his children, [the Dead Father] is the equally unsympathetic sensualist—self-righteous and tyrannical, refusing to relinquish the slightest power" (166).

Indeed, the narrative reference in the novel's prologue to the Dead Father's left leg "*working ceaselessly night and day through all the hours for the good of all*" (4; Barthelme's italics) is quickly forgotten in light of the Dead Father's otherwise completely self-centered nature. Similarly, although several of the outside narrators of Faulkner's novel—Dr. Peabody, Vernon Tull, Samson, and Armstid—remark on the hard life of endless work that a woman like Addie has, and in spite of early critics' tendency to romanticize and some of the more recent criticism that heroicizes Addie, even regardless of my own reading of Addie's actions, which suggests that she has ultimately recognized and redeemed her sins, the reader's sympathy for Addie is undermined by her own and her children's monologues, which provide an image of an egocentric, bitter woman who first physically brutalized her students to impose awareness of herself on them and/or out of her frustration with having a woman's limited options for employment, then punished her own children by withholding affection when her husband disappointed her. Although the reader may understand, as Amado Chan shows, that her behavior can be traced back to her being "a victim of the patriarchy" (Chan), her effect upon innocent bystanders, children, is still troubling. (In other words, the reader may not be as forgiving as Addie seems to believe God will be.) The reader's sympathies turn, then, in both novels, from the dying/dead parents to the plights of their selfish, but less destructive children.

Peter Swiggart comments that the "technique of dehumanization [of the characters of *As I Lay Dying*] enables Faulkner to heap misfortune after misfortune upon [them] without making them the objects of the reader's pity or empathy" (111). I would limit this argument to "empathy," for I do find the children's inner conflicts "pitiable." Since the book's publication, readers have had trouble *identifying* with the Bundren family, regardless of the universal themes of parental influence and the quest for identity. The reasons are obvious, given Faulkner's characterization of them as ignorant, foolish, brutish—essentially, "poor white trash"; however, Panthea Reid Broughton may be going somewhat too far in saying that the reader is "so distance[d] . . . from them that [he/she] read[s] it almost without emotional reactions at all" (92). Since Broughton does note that Faulkner "gives . . . not simple natural catastrophes, but the most bizarre, perverse circumstances imaginable" and lists several events from the novel to illustrate her point—"a boy bores holes through the face of his dead mother, . . . a broken leg is set in concrete, and a stinking corpse is carted across the country for nearly a week" (91–92)—it is surprising that she denies reader response. It is more likely that while reading *As I Lay Dying*, the reader experiences diverse emotions, from humor to horror.[11] Still, as already suggested, empathy may not be among one's initial reactions. Again, this lack can be attributed to the reader's difficulty in finding a single character with whom he/she can or at least would want to identify.

Surprisingly though, despite the fantastic nature of the characters and their incredible behavior in *The Dead Father,* the reader *is* able to identify with the plights of one or more of them: the one son (Thomas) who strives to assert his own unique identity but finds himself becoming just like the father whose ideology he has always despised; the other son (Edmund) who will rebel against his father's way of life at any cost to himself and thus finds himself wasting his own life; the women—the wife of the Dead Father/mother of his sons and the lovers of his sons—who find themselves in the middle of these conflicts and consequently realize that their own inner conflicts are ignored. However, such identification does not occur easily, for it is a novel of absences: its structure is fragmented, and the language is often—borrowing from postmodern terminology—the language of silence. Therefore, in order to grasp its meaning, the reader must participate in this novel rather than just passively read it. To flesh out these characters toward the point of their being more human than abstraction, the reader may bring with him/her to the work his/her own experiences, including the experience of reading other works, such as *As I Lay Dying*. Once the reader makes the connection between *The Dead Father* and *As I Lay Dying* and thus perceives the earlier work as an intertext of the more recent one, he/she can fill in much of what is absent, draw correspondences between the fragments, and find meaning rather than silence.

Perhaps, too, this assistance will be reciprocal. Paradoxically, once the reader sees the Bundren characters as prototypes for these later characters, their humanity surfaces from beneath their grotesque characterizations and absurd actions. In particular, the reader may then worry about the two youngest members of this family. Has Dewey Dell, whose pregnancy has not been terminated, thus begun her journey to an early grave? On the way, will she adopt her mother's bitterness? Will Vardaman eventually follow Darl to the mental institution? Regarding those sons who seem to have been released by the burial of their mother—Cash, who has found his voice at last, and Jewel, who has found his place in the family—will they now go on with their lives or merely go home with the new Mrs. Bundren and continue life just as they have lived it thus far? Considering what one has learned from *The Dead Father* of the circular nature of life, the reader may decide it is as unlikely that anything will change for the children as it is that Anse will treat the new Mrs. Bundren any differently from the way he treated Addie.

Consciously employed by Barthelme or not, *As I Lay Dying* can be used by the reader as an objective correlative of *The Dead Father*. The image of a corpse being hauled to its burial allows the reader to grasp, from the start of Barthelme's novel, the powerful, undying influence that the supposedly dead central figure maintains upon his survivors. He makes significant changes in the story he tells about a dead-but-not-dead parent; most significant, he changes the parent's sex. His novel then becomes an indictment of patriarchal society (a more secular reading than offered earlier; the novel lends itself to both). The Law of the Father (borrowing Lacan's terminology) corrupts even the most sensitive son, who will follow in his father's footsteps, assuring that the patriarchy continues within the next generation. On the one hand, recognizing the comparisons between the two novels may lead one to consider the antipatriarchal elements in Faulkner's book—for example, its criticism of Anse, the one person in the novel whose negative characterization is not softened by any understanding of how he became the selfish, lazy man he is (as Addie's negative characterization is softened by an understanding of what living with such a man must be like). However, one might at the same time notice that the aforementioned recognition of the hard life of the woman in such an agricultural society is softened by the negative characterization of Cora Tull, the wife of the man insightful enough to recognize this fact about lives of farm women. Thus, even as he expresses his support of women, Vernon Tull emerges as a more positive character than his wife. And the other men in the novel (those who are not Bundrens, that is) are more comparable to Tull than they are to Anse. Samson and Armstid, for example, may not understand, but at least they perceive their wives' despair as the Bundrens stop at their homes with the rotting corpse. Furthermore, like *The Sound and the Fury, As I Lay Dying* focuses much more on the concerns and conflicts of the male characters, even as it pretends to have a female character at its center.[12]

In direct contrast to Barthelme's novel, then, *As I Lay Dying* is actually an antimatriarchy novel: it indicts the power of the rebellious mother in the lives of her children just as strongly as Barthelme's novel indicts the power of the father. Therefore, it is interesting to note that whereas, unlike several of the writers to be discussed in this study, Barthelme does not set out to "correct" or "revise" Faulkner's novel, a comparison of his novel with Faulkner's does focus our attention on the earlier work in such a way that the reader recognizes its somewhat misogynistic tone. Even when Faulkner tried to write a novel with a pivotal woman character, a woman whose life deserves sympathy, the female character often ultimately emerges as the novel's villain: besides Addie, one can name Temple Drake, Narcissa Benbow Sartoris, Rosa Coldfield, even Caddy Compson in the fact that she deserted the unfortunate Benjy, who loved only her, and her own daughter and drove her other devoted brother, whose conflict is more central to the novel and thus who gains the reader's sympathy (whether he deserves it or not), to suicide. One might apply Diana York Blaine's assessment of Faulkner's depiction of Addie's ultimate destructiveness to all of these women: "rather than being allowed symbolic status, as nominal head of the family, or at least as an irreplaceable individual in the lives of her children, *she functions, a direct descendent of Eve, as the agent of chaos and representative of death*" (420; emphasis added).

It is not that Faulkner meant to condemn women, but rather that his central interest was primarily in the conflicts and concerns of the men in his novels, particularly, as will be shown in the chapters to come, the sensitive white men—like Darl in *As I Lay Dying*—who "suffer" from their inability to help the victims of oppression. Donald Barthelme did not only borrow an image from Faulkner's novel, he also borrowed Faulkner's technique. In *The Dead Father*, even as Barthelme condemns patriarchal rule, he marginalizes women. His novel may not be antimatriarchy, but he offers no more positive depictions of women than does Faulkner, and his sympathy in the novel, like Faulkner's, is with the conflicted son's dilemma as he faces the seemingly un- changeable "fact" of his life: that he will become like the father he despises.

The present intertextual reading of Faulkner and Barthelme, revealing if not correcting the negative depiction of women in *As I Lay Dying,* prepares the reader for the forthcoming analyses of Faulkner's novels with works by Toni Morrison and Lee Smith, who offer revisions of Faulkner's vision in their writings. But prior to considering the various revisions of Faulknerian works, I will turn to another "cross-country corpse" in contemporary Ameri- can literature: the body of Augustus McCrae being dragged back to Texas by his partner, Woodrow Call, in Larry McMurtry's *Lonesome Dove.*

Pigs and Paternity: Faulknerian Intertexts in Larry McMurtry's *Lonesome Dove*

Now you are aware of me! Now I am something in your secret and selfish life.

Faulkner, *As I Lay Dying*

In turn, both early American literature in general and then early southern literature in particular, depicted the respective regions as New Edens. In the mid-nineteenth century, however, New England's Nathaniel Hawthorne de- constructed the Puritan view of themselves as God's Elect living in the "New English Canaan," and James Fenimore Cooper sent his characters west in search of still another paradise, as yet uncorrupted by civilization—or women. It was not until the early twentieth century that writers of the South- ern Renascence began to depict the Old South as a more appropriate micro- cosm of the *fallen* world, due in particular to its original sin, the institution of slavery. Whereas this new generation of southern *writers* may have changed their view of the Old South, their *characters* continued to hold on to their false vision of the past. Consider Quentin Compson of *The Sound and the Fury,* who, perceiving the inherent flaws in his idealistic perception of the Old South, would rather die than give up his vision. Faulkner used Quentin again in *Absalom, Absalom!,* recognizing that this romantic idealist was the person through whom he could best filter his message regarding the falseness of the view that there was anything romantic about the Old South. In par- ticular, Quentin learns how the dreamer (Thomas Sutpen) brings about the destruction of his own dream (creating a plantation that would open its doors to all rather than just the aristocratic "elect") due to the corruption of the model on which the dream is based (the falsely Edenic Old South). Quentin learns that Sutpen not only deserted his own first-born son—the very kind of child for whom Sutpen said his design originated—but then later denied him again, even though by that time the intended haven had been built.

In his 1985 best seller *Lonesome Dove,* Larry McMurtry echoes the Thomas Sutpen/Charles Bon plotline of *Absalom, Absalom!,* thereby calling the reader's attention to his novel's deconstruction of romantic visions, in this case of the West rather than the Old South. In McMurtry's novel, the issue between father and son is not the denied son's race, though noting the parallel between the two novels' father/son relationships may lead one to recognize that McMurtry does pursue, in another of his novel's plotlines, issues of race similar to those explored by Faulkner in his novel. Writing about the West instead of the South, McMurtry appropriately replaces the sin of slavery, the cause of the fall of the South, with the sin of the usurpation of the land from the Native Americans.[13] The conflict between the band of cowboys and the Native Americans they confront as they journey to Montana, along with the conflict between the leader of the cowboys, Captain Woodrow Call, and his unacknowledged son, Newt Dobbs, particularly as these conflicts echo those found in Faulkner's novel, prepare the reader for the inevitable failure of Call's western dream: to escape the influences of civilization by starting a ranch in the as-yet unsettled Montana. Thomas Sutpen could not escape corruption by the Old Southern prototype upon which he modeled his plantation; and once Woodrow Call begins to settle Montana with his ranch, civilization will inevitably follow.

In his study of contemporary southern writers who set works in the West, Robert H. Brinkmeyer Jr. notes, "In their interrogation of the American legend of the West, contemporary Southern writers focus primarily on the dark undercurrents typically masked in the optimistic versions of American expansionism, particularly the violent dispersal of Native Americans and the raw capitalistic enterprise that pillaged land and people for profit" (31). Brinkmeyer does not, however, list McMurtry among the writers to whom his study might apply—not surprising given McMurtry's *West* Texas settings (East Texas being the section of the state considered part of the South). In contrast to contemporary southern writers who write about the West and who in doing so, according to Brinkmeyer, ultimately "embrace something very close to" southern ideals regarding "place and continuity," McMurtry's surviving protagonist—Woodrow Call—will ultimately reject "place and continuity," leaving the Montana ranch he has finally established and the son that he could bequeath it to.

Lonesome Dove begins with a description of two pigs eating a rattlesnake. This snake may be dead, but only a few moments later Augustus McCrae faces a live rattlesnake when he goes to get his jug of whiskey out of the springhouse. This confrontation provides the first opportunity for Gus to ruminate about a difference between himself and Woodrow Call, his partner since their days as Texas Rangers almost twenty years before: "Call had no respect whatsoever for snakes, or for anyone who stood aside for snakes" and "treated rattlers like gnats, disposing of them with one stroke of whatever tool he had in hand," while remarking on the subject, "A man that slows down for snakes might as well walk." Gus, in contrast, "held to a more leisurely philosophy. He believed in giving creatures a little time to think" and did not understand the logic in Call's maxim (14). Since it is Gus who comes upon this particular rattlesnake, the snake is allowed time to calm down, and it slithers away neither harmed nor harming.

However, since serpents in literature rarely go unnoticed, even by the most casual reader, who recognizes that they traditionally represent forces of evil or temptation, one may be disturbed by already meeting up with two snakes only two pages into the novel, especially since one of these notorious enemies of man is allowed to live.[14] Of course, paraphrasing Freud, "sometimes a [snake] is just a [snake]"; after all, the setting *is* West Texas. Still, the symbolic significance of serpents might lead one to examine the difference between the two men's reactions to snakes. Call's lack of respect "for snakes, or . . . anyone who stood aside for snakes" reflects his major character flaws: his superior attitude toward others and his intolerance of any kind of weakness in anyone, including himself. Gus, in contrast, is not so quick to judge either people or snakes. In this case, he does not condemn the snake to death just because it threatened him, recognizing that it is only protecting itself; later in the novel, he will be the one to express understanding toward the very Native Americans from whom he receives a fatal wound: "We won more than our share with the natives. They didn't invite us here. . . . We got no call to be vengeful" (785).

Gus makes these conciliatory remarks about Native Americans on his deathbed, and it is just this kind of understanding and insight that seems to motivate Gus's last request of Call. As Call fulfills Gus's dying wish to be buried back in Texas, the opening image of the pigs is given further significance. During his journey to bury Gus—his life-partner, his closest friend, his nemesis—Call appears as foolish to those he meets as these two pigs do to Gus in the novel's opening. The reader then wonders if it is part of Gus's plan, in soliciting Call's promise to bury him in Texas, to force his friend to realize that people are not much more developed than swine and therefore should not have the unreasonably high expectations of themselves and others that Call holds, for it is just this false pride, Gus recognizes, that causes Call to keep himself distant from others, including his own son as well as, in earlier years, his son's mother.

It is too late for Call to make up to the now long-deceased Maggie for his earlier rejection of her. He excuses his past behavior to himself and to Gus (as he earlier did to Maggie) with the feigned uncertainty that he is indeed Newt's father—since Maggie was a whore by occupation. In truth, the reader realizes, as has Gus, that Call's developing love for Maggie probably scared him, as it may have threatened to tie him to the tedium of Lonesome Dove. Ironically, though, Call does not leave Lonesome Dove until several years after Maggie's death. Thus, he gave up the chance for this woman's love for nothing, since it would ultimately not have caused him to miss any other opportunities. Gus wants Call to make up for that wrong, as well as that missed opportunity for love. He does not want his friend to miss a second chance at love, this time the love of his son, but Call maintains his claim that no one knows for certain that Newt *is* his son—though apparently it is quite obvious in Newt's countenance. When Clara first sees Newt, for example, she notes to herself, "he was the spitting image of Captain Call, built the same way, and with the same movements. So why is your name Dobbs? she wondered" (685). When Gus later explains to her that "Newt don't know Call's his father," she responds, "And Call don't claim him *when anybody can see it?*" (690; emphasis added).

Although he won't even admit to himself that Newt is his son until the end of the novel, Call's words and actions do suggest that he does recognize it at some level. For example, when Gus questions Call's desire to develop a ranch in Montana—"You ain't a cattleman. . . . No more than I am. If we was to get a ranch I don't know who would run it"—Call responds illogically, "the boy could run it" (84). If Call and Gus are not cattlemen, then certainly Newt is not, having been raised by them since his mother's death. The most poignant scene supporting Call's subconscious awareness of Newt's relation to him is in Ogallala when a soldier takes a whip to Newt, who had refused to hand over one of the horses to the army. Call sees the man whip Newt, goes into a blind rage, and must be pulled off of the man by Gus. One wonders, what would it have hurt to claim this boy, give him a father, even if Call truly doubted that he was the man who actually fathered him? The answer is that it would hurt Call: were he to acknowledge Newt now, even to himself, he would have to acknowledge, at least to himself, the lost opportunity for a love that might have brought an end to his loneliness.[15]

Yes, Call seems to desire solitude; he seeks it out nightly during his years at Lonesome Dove, going out in the evening, supposedly to check the security of the area when "[t]here was really little in the way of a threat to be looked for. . . . Lonesome Dove had long since ceased to need guarding" (27). At the same time, one senses that Call welcomes Gus's occasional intrusion upon his seclusion, even though he expresses annoyance at the imposition and is unquestionably aggravated by the subjects Gus chooses to chatter on about, particularly women and Newt. In truth, the reader suspects, Call seeks to maintain his privacy in order to avoid experiencing in any form that which he has missed, the pleasures of a life joined with another. And yet, ironically, Call has created a Cooperesque (that is, womanless) mock family with the men with whom he has lived in Lonesome Dove: he is the father, and Newt is the son, Gus is the wife-figure for him (stereotypically nagging but also expressing emotions that Call cannot express), Deets the mother-figure for Newt, Bolivar their cook, and Pea Eye the yard-hand. The fact that Call has tolerated this domestic arrangement for so many years suggests that he is not so loathe after all to have the very company and comfort of the home that Maggie had offered him.

Gus, too, had once been made an offer of a more traditional domestic life, and the memory of his own loss may also inspire him to solicit the promise from Call to take his corpse back to Texas. Perhaps he hopes that burying him in the place he calls Clara's Orchard will remind Call that Gus once knew the kind of love that Call had refused (Gus had shown Call the orchard on their way out of Texas and told him why it reminded him of his lost love, Clara). Gus may be hoping that Call will realize in that setting that, although it is too late for Gus to go back to Nebraska (where they had visited Clara's ranch on their way to Montana) and make a home with Clara, it is not too late for Call to have a home with his son. Gus's insistence that Call acknowledge Newt, which he repeats during their last argument on the subject during their final meeting, suggests that he understands that Call will never have any kind of love until he swallows his pride, admits he made a mistake, and sacrifices at least that much of his independence.

Ironically, at the time of his death, Gus himself has only recently had similar trouble admitting his past mistakes and taking the second chance at love offered to him by Clara, who wanted him to stay with her rather than continue his journey with Call. Gus may be so insightful about Call, then, because he (Gus), too, chose his independence over love, or rather, chose what he and Call believe is an independent life on the range in contrast to a life tied to a particular place. Of course, they are planning to develop a ranch in Montana, so they are presumably preparing to tie themselves to another place. And they have only recently left their home of fifteen years in Lonesome Dove. Thus, the reader realizes that what they both fear after all is life tied to a woman. Given a second chance with Clara, Gus chooses Call instead. Consequently, he understands Call's rejection of Maggie, even while he berates Call for not at least admitting that he loved her. Gus admits freely that he loves Clara; his false excuses are for why they couldn't be together. Understanding Call as he does, then, he has found a way that his partner can have something of what they both missed out on, even while maintaining his independence of women: by acknowledging his son, Call can have a family without having to have a wife.

At the same time, Gus's explanation of how "[t]he favor I want from you will be my favor to you" reveals, too, that Gus knows that a ranch in Montana will not be enough for Call, even were Call to acknowledge his son. Gus has recognized that the thrill for Call is in the struggle, so he provides Call with another difficult chore—perhaps the most generous motivation behind his dying wish. He explains to Call: "It's the kind of job you was made for, that nobody else could do or even try. Now that the country is about settled, I don't know how you'll keep busy, Woodrow. But if you'll do this for me you'll be all right for another year" (783). Again, Gus seems to be mocking Call even as he shows his understanding of Call's nature and his concern for Call's well being. Underneath his joking, Gus worries that even if Montana were "Paradise Regained"—or rather, *especially* if it were—Call would become bored there, for it is the journey, the struggle to live, that Call thrives on.[16] Gus's favor to Call reveals that he knows that Call's western Eden is ultimately unattainable, not only because civilization will inevitably follow them to Montana but also because Call's wanderlust will continue to drive him to seek adventure.[17] As Janis P. Stout points out, "when the herd finally crosses what ought to be the last river and everyone has arrived in the Promised Land, the leader, Captain Call, cannot bear to stop. He pushes on, day after day, nearly to the Canadian border, and wishes vaguely that he could cross that too and just keep going" (247).

Beneath all of this understanding of, concern for, and good will toward his friend and partner, one might also find some anger and resentment motivating Gus's last request of Call and a desire to punish Call for his (Gus's) own missed opportunities (even though, as already suggested, he has actually used Call as an excuse to pass up these opportunities). Such less generous motivations for soliciting the promise from Call to bury him in Texas can be culled from this lengthy novel with the help of recognizing the echo of Faulkner's *As I Lay Dying* in this last request and then recalling one of the reasons for Addie Bundren's similar last request—that her husband bury her in Jefferson—which required a similarly arduous and humiliating journey. To start, like Addie, who seems to have wanted to force her family's recognition of her past presence by disrupting their lives during the time it takes and through the effort they must make to bury her away from home, Gus may want to disrupt the life of the man who has not fully appreciated him during their long partnership, thereby forcing Call's awareness of Gus's past presence at least during the period of the journey. The possibility that Gus resents Call's lack of appreciation for Gus's contribution to their "home," particularly when compared to Addie's resentment of her family, especially her husband, reminds the reader of Gus's role as wife in their mock "family." The reader may smile when recalling Gus's pride in his communal reputation as a ladies' man (in Lonesome Dove that would be lady's [singular] man, as there has only been one woman in residence there at a time) to hear me placing him in the feminine role, first within their home in Lonesome Dove and then on the range during their travels. But Gus has served Call in this capacity by his expressive nature, as it complements Call's stoicism. Furthermore, he has remained loyal to Call; he has committed himself to a partnership with Call in which it is Call's (the husband's) dreams that are followed. And finally, he has subtly offered Call understanding as evidenced in the way he explains his partner's behavior to those who find Call enigmatic. For example, he tries to explain Call, as well as his devotion to Call, to Clara when she berates him for having, essentially, chosen Call over her. It is interesting to note that within her chastisement, Clara remarks, "I wish I knew of some way to *divorce* you from that man" (699; emphasis added).

The reader, who is privy to some of Call's thoughts, feels certain that Call will miss Gus and, with his partner's absence, also miss the loyalty, another's commitment to his own dreams, and Gus's understanding of his behavior. But Gus may want Call to have time to think about these losses and recognize their connection to his partner's death—hence the solicited journey, which will be taken in solitude. In connection, just as, at the time Addie Bundren solicits the promise from Anse, she may want to punish her husband for her miserable life, Gus may want to punish Call for the hardships he seems to at least partially blame Call for—culminating in Gus's imminent death. Looking back to the start of their journey, one will find Gus's declaration "I'll be a little riled if I end up being the one to die in the line of duty, because this ain't my duty" (223). Such a statement supports the possibility of an element of revenge behind his last request: Gus does "end up being the one to die" (the one of the two leaders, that is, for there are several deaths along the way), and he would probably not have died at this time or in the same way (from the poison of an arrow wound) had it not been for Call's Montana dream. If it weren't for Call, Gus could easily reason, he would have stayed on Clara's ranch where he would have lived comfortably until his death of old age. However, it is important to recognize once again Gus's own complicity in his violent death. He is not, in fact, Call's "wife"; he has taken no vow of obedience (standard in the wedding ceremony of the time). In other words, he has repeatedly *chosen* to follow Call, long after his "duty" as a Texas Ranger had expired. Consequently, recognizing the possible negative motivations behind Gus's request serves to illuminate that which the two men have in common: their tendency to excuse their own behavior. Not surprising, the insightful Gus (insightful when it comes to analyzing Call's flaws, that is) does not recognize his similarity to Call. Indeed, just prior to telling Call he will be angry "if [he] ends up being the one to die," Gus had remarked, "If we was to meet now instead of when we did, I doubt we'd have two words to say to one another" (222).

The reader should recognize, then, that Gus's earlier assertion to Call that their journey to Montana is not part of his "duty" is further evidence of his own lack of self-knowledge. He doesn't realize that by going along with Call he is volunteering for this "duty." Further evidence of Gus's blindness about himself can be discerned from his explanation to Newt about Call's supposedly unique devotion to duty: "He likes to think that everybody does their duty, especially him. He likes to think people live for duty. . . . He knows perfectly well people don't live for duty. But he won't admit it about anybody if he can help it, and he especially won't admit it about himself" (746). Ironically, despite this logical insight regarding the average person's lack of obsessive devotion to duty, it is Call's partner, Gus, who provides Call with support that duty is important to everyone: if Gus will go along with Call even while expressing his disgruntlement with the "duty" at hand, then he must be participating out of a sense of "duty."

Returning to the positive motivations behind Gus's deathbed request, one can still use *As I Lay Dying* as an intertext to illuminate its significance. Just as Addie's request may have been motivated in part by the desire to force her family to acknowledge her existence, Gus seems to hope that this promise, which will require Call to leave his men in Montana for quite some time while he journeys to and from Texas, will motivate Call to wait no longer to acknowledge Newt as his son. Gus knows that, unlike the other deaths on the range, his partner's death would remind Call of his own mortality. Gus seems to hope, then, that Call, realizing he might be killed on his way back to Texas, would be compelled to recognize Newt before leaving. Interestingly, in both novels, these hopes are not exactly fulfilled: Addie's husband and children may ponder her role in their lives as they journey, but they do not do so generously—that is, they do not come to a recognition of how much she will be missed. Quite the contrary: they spend the journey to bury her trying to bury, too, the memory of her negative influence. And though Call does heartily regret the loss of Gus and seems to acknowledge Gus's value to him; though he ultimately questions the value of his own dreams and accomplishments in light of the losses he and his men have suffered; and though he leaves his son, Newt, in charge in Montana during his absence and gives Newt his horse, his gun, and his own father's watch, he still does not give him his name or proclaim their relationship.[18]

In truth, then, Gus's interference in Call and Newt's relationship has backfired, not unlike the way that Addie's plan does. At the end of *As I Lay Dying,* shortly after burying Addie, Anse introduces a new Mrs. Bundren to his children. Ironically, he met her when he knocked on her door to borrow a shovel to dig Addie's grave. Thus, Addie's last wish ultimately leads to the means by which her family will more quickly overcome their loss. They may not have been able to forget about her during the journey, but with a new wife and mother, they will not have the chance to experience the absence of all that she did for them. Similarly, Gus is the cause of the magnitude of Newt's disappointment, for he is the one to give a face to the father fantasy image in Newt's imagination. Following Gus's revelation to Newt, the chapter ends with Newt's pondering of this new information: "Newt knew Mr. Gus was trying to be kind, but he wasn't listening. Much of his life he had wondered who his father was and where he might be. He felt it would be a relief to know. But now he knew, and it wasn't a relief. There was something in it that thrilled him—he was Captain Call's son—but more that felt sad" (747). Had Gus never told Newt that Call was his father (which he does shortly before he is wounded), Newt would not have known that he was being denied. Once again, then, Gus shares his partner's responsibility for causing pain to others.

Paradoxically, what stops Call from speaking as he faces Newt before departing for Texas is an overwhelming sense of shame and failure, even though he is looking at the one thing in his life that should make him proud. But he sees Newt as evidence of his failure to live up to his own code of honor: "All his life he had preached honesty to his men and had summarily discharged those who were not capable of it, though they had mostly only lied about duties neglected or orders sloppily executed. He himself was far worse, for he had been dishonest about his own son" (822). Even now, it is pride that keeps Call from speaking to Newt, the pride of Hawthorne's Ethan Brand, who seeks the unpardonable sin, not realizing that it is just such a quest that is the sin, for in seeking the sin that even God will not forgive, one is being prideful. By viewing himself as the greatest of sinners, Call is continuing to set himself apart from—and ironically above—his men. Thus again, returning to the first reason suggested for Gus's last request—to show Call that it is okay to be the fool occasionally, that it is human to make mistakes, and therefore, that one should forgive himself for doing so—one can see the need for Call to go on a humbling quest.

At the end of his last journey with Gus (or rather, Gus's corpse), Call faces the truth about his "vision" of a New Eden in Montana. That dream, too, was prideful. The pair of pigs (a shoat and a sow) with the snake at the novel's start is here given even further significance. Before their fall, Adam and Eve had not been so far removed from the animals of Eden, but they were tempted to strive for God-knowledge, which would ultimately set them apart from the animals. Like Adam and Eve, Call had sought to be God-like, in his case to re-create Paradise. During his journey, however, he has repeatedly been faced with his men's mortality, and recently he has confronted his own human frailty. When someone remarks to him toward the end of his return with Gus's body, "They say you're a man of vision," Call replies, "Yes, a *hell* of a vision" (838; emphasis added).[19] Apparently he has come to realize that he has founded no New Eden, for even if civilization has not yet reached Montana, his own sinful nature has already corrupted the new land. Many people have died because of his proud refusal to give up his prideful dream, and now his son has adopted his philosophy of life to protect himself from the pain of his father's apparent rejection: after Call's departure, when Pea Eye remarks, "He gave you his horse and his gun and that watch. He acts like you're his kin," Newt responds, "No, I ain't kin to nobody in this world. . . . I don't want to be. I won't be." Call has damned his son to relive his own lonely life. Indeed, during their parting Call notices how "lonesome" the boy looks, and after Newt expresses to Pea Eye his rejection of any relation to anyone "in this world," he "mounted [Call's horse] as if he had ridden her for years" (823). Thus, Gus's last request may ultimately lead to Call achieving insight into the nature of himself and his vision, but it also starts Newt down the same lonely path that his father has traveled.[20]

It is not surprising, then, to find that the Newt/Call conflict in *Lonesome Dove* is reminiscent of the Charles Bon/Thomas Sutpen conflict of *Absalom, Absalom!*, another Faulknerian intertext that might be used to illuminate the conflicts within this novel. Charles Bon, too, longs for his father's recognition, and in spite of (and resulting from) his disappointment over not receiving it, he becomes very much like his father. As Sutpen does whatever it takes to achieve his quest for aristocracy—from leaving his first wife and rejecting his firstborn to seducing the granddaughter of a man who looks up to him and then refusing to marry her when she gives birth to a daughter rather than a son—Bon, too, cruelly uses those who love him—his half-siblings, Judith and Henry—in his quest for his father's recognition. The *Absalom, Absalom!* echoes in *Lonesome Dove* lead the reader to a perception of the connections McMurtry makes between the familial and the racial relationships in his novel, connections similar to the connection Faulkner draws between Sutpen's treatment of his family and the treatment of slaves in the Old South.

As Faulkner recognized the sinfulness of slavery and illuminated the consequences of the institution throughout his fiction—particularly *Absalom, Absalom!*—McMurtry recognizes the sinfulness of white usurpation of land from the Native Americans. Significantly, he has Gus, perhaps the most like-able character of the novel, place responsibility upon the white man for the violence between the two races. But also like Faulkner, whose African-American characters, though often admirable (like Dilsey), are usually underdeveloped, two-dimensional, even sometimes stereotypical (as will be illustrated further in the Gaines chapter), McMurtry creates stereotypes as he develops his Native American characters. Most obviously stereotypical is the arch-villain of the novel, Blue Duck, whom Steve Fore rightly calls "a racist carica-ture."[21] Fore explains, "Blue Duck robs, kidnaps, and murders with no com-punction and no explanations—he exists as the unknowable and lethal Other of which civilized folks are justifiably terrified" (58). Indeed, Blue Duck is so much more violent, more evil than any other character in the novel that he seems to be something "other" than human.[22] Thus, the reader may infer, that which makes him "Other"—his Native American blood—must be responsible for his inhumanity. Although Blue Duck is a "half-breed," and one might therefore wonder which race McMurtry is suggesting motivates his violence, particularly given Gus's indictment of Euro-Ameri-cans for their treatment of Native Americans, the manifestations of Blue Duck's violent nature, reminiscent of stereotypical views of the inhumanity of Native American against white settlers, would undermine any conjecture that McMurtry means us to perceive his "white blood" as the source of his violent nature. I would agree, therefore, with Fore's indictment of McMurtry for promoting such a view of the Native American: "It is inexcusable that the characterization of Blue Duck resorts to priming the pump of an undifferen-tiated fear of (cultural, racial) difference that pollutes most cinematic and televisual representations of Native Americans" (60). Either unrepentant of or blind to his crime against this race, McMurtry created more demonic Na-tive American and Mexican characters in the sequel to this novel, *Streets of Laredo* (1993), and in its prequel, *Dead Man's Walk* (1995).

In his fiction, Faulkner may have indicted the Old South for its reliance upon slavery and consequential promotion of prejudice; however, he does not suggest that the New South is any better. On the one hand, he does show how the legacy of slavery continues to infect the region, but at the same time, he suggests that the New South is less romantic than—and thus inferior to—the Old. Hence the paradox of his fiction: like his character Quentin Comp-son, Faulkner cannot seem to shake his idealistic view of that which he criti-cizes. Similarly, even though McMurtry pays lip service—appropriately through the loquacious Gus McCrae—to "politically correct" recognition of the white man's dominant role in the violence of the Old West, *Lonesome Dove* "is surprisingly nonrevisionist in its picture of the West," as pointed out by one reviewer of the miniseries based on the novel: "The good guys still perform stunning heroics with six-shooters, and Indians are faceless villains who whoop when they ride" (Zoglin 78).

A related parallel can be found between the two writers' depictions and development of their female characters. Even when Faulkner places women at the center of his novels (like Addie Bundren and Caddy Compson) or heroicizes women (like Dilsey), indeed, even when he subjects a female character to a heinous crime (as he does Temple Drake and Joanna Burden), the stories he tells still focus primarily on the male characters in the novels and these men's reactions to the conflicts of and/or crimes against these women. Although readers of *Lonesome Dove* could never mistakenly determine, as readers of *The Sound and the Fury* or *As I Lay Dying* might, that the women in the novel are central—Gus and Call are undeniably the novel's protagonists—the development and conflicts of Lorena, Clara, Elmira, and Janey are given equal time when compared to the development and conflicts of Newt, July, Jake, and Roscoe, respectively. Lorena is as sympathetic as Newt; July's developing crush on Clara parallels Lorena's growing devotion to Gus (both Clara and Gus being several years older than July and Lorena); Jake and Elmira are both self-centered; and the deaths of the likeable Roscoe and Janey are equally mourned. But just as there are no female counterparts to Gus and Call (except to the extent that Gus, who is, borrowing from contemporary phraseology, in touch with his "feminine side," qualifies as such, the matriarchal ranch owned by Clara, though already established and successful, certainly does not measure up to the male-dominated, womanless ranch envisioned by Call, though even Call knows that the reality will never live up to the ideal.

When they stop at her ranch on the way to Montana, Clara offers her home to Gus, Newt, and Lorena, but only the latter takes her up on the offer (though Dish, a minor character by comparison to Gus and Newt, returns to Nebraska after completing his duty to Call). Lorena, therefore, gives up her dream of living in California, while even Gus, who loves Clara, remains committed to the pursuance of what he claims is only Call's dream. Even after Newt finds out that Call is his father and yet has never acknowledged him—and later realizes that Call probably never will acknowledge him—he still chooses Call's way of life over Clara's offer. Rather than consider following Dish back to Nebraska where he would be treated as a son, he asserts that he doesn't want any family. In contrast to Newt and Gus, July Johnson, who, like Dish, accepts Clara's offer to stay on when he passes through in search of his wife, does not measure up to—indeed, appears clownish when compared to—Gus and Newt. McMurtry's most herolike characters are those who ultimately reject women—Call, Gus, and Newt—in favor of Call's (womanless) dream-ranch.

Even the self-centered characters Jake and Elmira receive different treatments by their author, which suggests an inclination on McMurtry's part to be more judgmental about the woman's self-absorption than the man's. Whereas both characters' self-involvement results in the tragedies of others (it is Jake's fault that Lorena is kidnapped by Blue Duck, and Elmira is ultimately responsible for the deaths of Roscoe and Joe), as well as their own deaths, one might note a contrast between their deaths that further suggests McMurtry's favoring of the male characters in his narrative. Jake is hung for being a horse thief. Not only does he die heroically—kicking the horse out from under him so that none of his friends has to do it—but also, early in the novel, Newt recognizes that stealing horses is not a hanging offense everywhere. Indeed, Call and Gus, who insist that Jake must die for his crime, had led a party into Mexico to steal horses and cattle to bring to Montana. Elmira's death, in contrast, involves no tragic scene and is no tragic loss to anyone. She is murdered offstage after foolishly leaving Clara's sanctuary while still hemorrhaging from the birth of July's baby, whom she has deserted along with her likeable, if bumbling husband. Her death seems, therefore, to be poetic justice, while Jake's ultimately emerges as another unnecessary tragedy.

Finally, turning again to Newt and Lorena, one can also see in the different last glimpses given of each of them in the novel how McMurtry suggests that Newt is to be viewed as ultimately the more heroic of the two. After rejecting any kinship to Call and claiming his desire for continued independence, Newt remains propped up by his stoic pride in the saddle of the Hell Bitch, whereas Lorena promises undying love and devotion to Gus (or rather to his corpse), stays up with his body all night, and then collapses. The reader may find the images equally tragic, but one cannot deny that the image of Newt astride Call's mare is a stronger one than the image of Lorena being carried inside by men.[23] They have both suffered the loss of a father figure, but Lorena appears debilitated by her loss, while Newt finally reaches inside himself for the strength to deal with his. Whereas earlier in the novel Newt had cried boyish tears of frustration whenever overwhelmed by circumstances, there are no tears at this time in spite of the "[d]espair in his heart" (823). "He knew the Captain had left him with too much, but he didn't say it. He would have to try and do the work, even if he no longer cared" (824).

The work, though, is as pointless as the quest, for as McMurtry reveals in *Streets of Laredo,* Newt dies in Call's absence. As Faulkner does in *Absalom, Absalom!,* McMurtry returns in the sequel (and later in a prequel) to the adventures of his larger-than-life but ultimately (like Faulkner's Sutpen) *anti*-hero, Captain Woodrow Call, who continues to seek adventure as Sutpen continued to pursue his "design." To both men, their sons are finally no more important than the women they reject; their *own* life experiences become primary. Sutpen lost sight of the inspiration for his "design" (the image of the boy he once was being sent to the back door) very shortly after setting out to pursue it, getting caught up in the dynasty over which he ruled (the *physical* dynasty of the plantation called Sutpen's Hundred). Call's focus is also increasingly secular: experiencing as much adventure as he can during his lifetime by embracing the violence of the unsettled West rather than settling on the ranch in Montana.[24] In their not so different settings—post–Civil War South and "Wild West," these novels by Faulkner and McMurtry, respectively, reflect modernist anxieties regarding the implications of the violence and destruction of war. Sutpen's failure suggests Faulkner's belief in some divine justice. Writing, if not a stylistically "postmodern" novel, at least during the postmodern, more disillusioned, less hopeful period, McMurtry leaves his character on the treadmill with his "hell of a vision."

chapter 2

Miss Jane Is Still Not in the History Books

Gender, Race, and
Class Discrimination
in the Fiction of
Faulkner and Gaines

A male-dominated theatre in a patriarchal society will project masculine values and conflicts, just as history books, having been written by men, reflect male concerns: power, aggression, battles, victories, capital.

Figes, *Tragedy and Social Evolution*

The Interests of Faulkner and Gaines: Southern and African-American HIS-Story

GAINES: . . . the women in their work did not come in conflict with the outer world as much as the men did in their work. The men competed with the white man, and there could be conflicts there. The black man competed with the white man as sharecropper and when he went into town, whereas the black woman very seldom competed. She was just a worker there. She was a worker in the big house, and she was a worker in the field. She did not have to . . . compete [by] racing to the derrick to unload the sugarcane, or go into the cotton gin to unload the cotton. In my world, it was not a competitive thing between the black woman and that outer world. She just did what she was supposed to do.

Gaudet and Wooton, *Porch Talk with Ernest Gaines*

Ralph Ellison argues in *Shadow and Act* that "the early Faulkner . . . distorted Negro humanity to fit his personal versions of Southern myth" (25), but Ellison then credits Faulkner for at least being "more willing perhaps than any other artist to start with the stereotype, accept it as true, and then seek out the human truth which it hides." Ellison adds that Faulkner may therefore be "the example for our writers to follow, for in his work technique has been put once more to the task of creating values." He further challenges writers of the different minorities to "contribut[e] to the total image of the American by depicting the experience of their own groups" (43). Ernest Gaines has taken up this challenge in his fiction and in so doing creates characters whose stories are reminiscent of Faulkner's African-American characters' stories but whose roles are much more central to the works in which they figure.

Comparisons between Faulkner and Gaines have continued since Michel Fabre's 1976 article on Gaines (quoted in the introduction). David Lionel Smith has written a provocative essay discussing "revisions of Faulkner" in Gaines's *Of Love and Dust.* In particular, he discusses the parallels between the depiction of the consequences of miscegenation in *Absalom, Absalom!* and this early Gaines novel. His argument is that "Gaines echoes Faulkner in various ways, yet he never seems merely to imitate Faulkner, because in every instance, his echoes are combined with deliberate, purposeful dissonances" (46). Smith's thesis is relevant to what my study of other parallels, between several of the two writers' works, will show. Smith's discussion of the echoes of Faulkner in *Of Love and Dust* is thorough, and he also notes briefly several comparisons between other works by the two writers, but still reason remains for another study of the intertextual relationship between their bodies of fiction. Herman Beavers has pointed out how "the African American novelist (and especially those born in the South) is invariably locked in an 'engaging disengagement' with Faulkner[:] attracted to his power of description and mastery of language, but repelled by his perpetuation of racial myth." Beavers "finds that this is most certainly the case for Ernest Gaines" (129), and this chapter will examine how Gaines deconstructs and then reconstructs Faulknerian characters, themes, and conflicts, and thereby racial myths perpetuated by Faulkner's fiction.

I once heard Ernest Gaines respond to a question regarding Faulkner's influence upon his creation of Miss Jane Pittman by saying that while Faulkner wrote about Dilsey in *his* kitchen, he (Gaines) wrote about Jane in her own kitchen.[1] The significance for Gaines of that questioner's comparison of the two characters might be perceived from remarks by David Smith on the relationship between the fiction of these two southern writers: "Faulkner is important to Gaines not just because he is the greatest writer of the South, but even more, because Faulkner addressed so trenchantly the issues of race, history, and community that so deeply preoccupy Gaines. Consequently, in order to be taken seriously, Gaines has been obligated to acknowledge the precedents established by Faulkner and to locate his own work relative to them" (47). Rather than anxiety of influence, then, as Harold Bloom might label Gaines's response to the question of Faulkner's influence upon his creation of Jane Pittman, Gaines's point of contrast between Jane and Dilsey expresses his argument with Faulkner's depiction of the South: he perceives Faulkner's African-American characters to be servants first, people second. Patricia Yaeger summarizes the conflict, which she finds throughout white southern literature, as "the difficulty white southern culture has in freeing itself from specters of ownership—from its obsessions with African Americans as objects, as things to be owned—and the question of whether whites can allow a person who has been so commodified to ascend to the status of possessive individualism" (40).

Apparently recognizing a lack of individualism in Faulkner's depiction of African-Americans, in his own work Gaines wishes to give voice and depth to these usually marginalized people. As Gaines explained to interviewer John O'Brien in 1972, "the white writers whom I had read did not put my people into books the way I knew them" (28). In several published interviews, Gaines has told about how, after moving to California when he was a boy, he missed his Louisiana home, family, and friends and so looked for books that would ease his homesickness: "I wanted to read about the South, and I wanted to read about the *rural* South. But at that time you had very few people writing anything that was in any way complimentary about blacks or the rural South. So I decided to write a novel myself" (Laney 59). Thus was a writer born, and he has indeed created a body of literature in which people like himself—African-Americans from rural Louisiana—are the central rather than peripheral characters.

In particular, Gaines's desire seems to be to tell the African-American *man*'s story, and here is where it is interesting to *compare* his focus with Faulkner's and thereby undermine the view of Faulkner's southern vision as flawed. Gaines's—and many critics'—complaint with Faulkner is that his depiction of the South is severely limited. For the most part, Faulkner explores the conflicts and concerns of the southern white male, even more particularly, of the southern white male romantic, epitomized, of course, by Quentin Compson, the prototype for several other Faulknerian protagonists. Rather than criticize Faulkner for this limitation, critics might merely acknowledge this character type as the focus of Faulkner's interest. Faulkner never claimed to be telling the whole story of the South. It was New Critics like Cleanth Brooks who viewed his canon as accomplishing such a feat. Gaines might recall his own remark in a 1969 interview that neither could he (Gaines) "fully represent the South" in his fiction (Fitzgerald and Marchant 13). Indeed, like the perspective from which Faulkner so often examines his "little postage stamp of soil," Gaines's interest in the Louisiana South is also somewhat limited—in his case, to the concerns of the African-American man. John O'Brien summed up the usual conflict in Gaines's fiction to the writer himself during an interview with him: "All your male heroes are possessed of a need to prove that they are men, and their attempts—which seem to be life-long ones—always end in death" (30). Gaines's response, then, defines his motivation and the central issue of his canon:

> You must understand that in this country the black man has been pushed into the position where he is not supposed to be a man. This is one of the things that the white man has tried to deny the black ever since he brought him here in chains. . . . My heroes just try to be men; but because the white man has tried everything from the time of slavery to deny the black this chance, his attempts to be a man will lead toward danger. So whenever my men decide that they will be men regardless of how anyone else feels, they know that they will eventually die. But it's impossible for them to turn around. (O'Brien 30)

Gaines, like Faulkner, has to some extent written several versions of the same story: Faulkner's story is that of a young white man in the post–Civil War South trying to make sense of his family's past in order to face his own future; Gaines writes of an African-American male (boy, youth, young adult, or old man) struggling to assert his manhood within an oppressive culture, even if only to stand as a man for a moment before his death.

Therefore, if we recognize Faulkner's vision to be limited, so, too, must we recognize Gaines's limitations, for his work is not, for example, nearly so concerned with the African-American *woman's* struggles. (However, in both cases, as suggested above, these *limitations* do not have to be viewed as *faults* in the writers' works but rather as the limits of each man's focus.) Surprisingly, even in *The Autobiography of Miss Jane Pittman,* Gaines is telling, through his title character, the story of several African-American men. Mary Ellen Doyle provides one explanation for focusing on men in a novel supposedly telling the life story of a woman. She reminds the reader that Jane's story is filtered through the history teacher/editor of the introduction: "The novel is a man's rendition of a woman's experience, and thus a man's concerns are reflected in the text" ("*Autobiography*" 103). She, too, notes that "[y]oung men are prominent at all stages of Miss Jane's life; no woman has an importance approaching that of Ned, Joe, or Jimmy," and she asks, "Are the omissions Miss Jane's or the editor's?" ("*Autobiography*" 102). Either way, I would point out, they are Ernest Gaines's omissions. Doyle's concluding remarks about Gaines, a male writer, writing the "autobiography" of a female character—"he had the good sense to be forthright about his viewpoint in creating a woman protagonist by also creating a male editor" ("*Autobiography*" 104)—are inadvertently supported by Gaines himself in *Porch Talk with Ernest Gaines* when he acknowledges, "I know more about the black male because I'm male myself" (Gaudet and Wooton 43). And, indeed, it is the black male whose stories he tells, even in this novel. Keith E. Byerman sums up "the basic pattern" of this novel: "an act of resistance is led by a heroic figure who is ultimately killed by opposing forces; in the aftermath, Jane is left to preserve whatever has been gained, including the legend of the hero, and to prepare a new generation of rebels" ("Afro-American" 50). Jane's role in the novel, then, is certainly more than that of Faulkner's Dilsey, a family servant in *The Sound and the Fury* who has no narrative voice in the novel, but Jane is still, as Jerry H. Bryant has pointed out, not "the principal actor in the episodes she recounts." Her role is that of chronicler, the one who tells the stories of the novel's primary actors. Bryant seems to view this role as empowering: "she is always there, speaking to us, shaping the way in which we experience events, as if she were herself those events" ("Ernest" 863). Unlike the novel's heroes, she survives (not unlike Dilsey), in large part for the purpose of telling their stories (though, again, Dilsey has no narrative voice). Apparently not disturbed by the implications of marginalization, Bryant suggests that the two roles are of equal importance: "the enduring woman and the courageous man are the critical elements in the black race's existence and embody jointly in their loving struggle of values, the characteristic features of life: change and growth" (859).

In spite of the contrasts between Jane and Dilsey, the comparisons that can also be made illuminate that, while Gaines is concerned in his fiction with removing his African-American men from the margins where he perceives Faulkner's African-American characters to be confined, he does still marginalize the black women of his novels, as is particularly evident in *A*

Gathering of Old Men (discussed in the third section of this chapter); as is also the case in his first novel, *Catherine Carmier,* the title character of which, as Mary Ellen Doyle has pointed out, is clearly not the protagonist (*Voices* 80); and as is also largely true of *The Autobiography of Miss Jane Pittman.* Gaines's remarks about Miss Jane in his essay "Miss Jane and I" suggest, however, that he was not aware of this tendency in his fiction, at least not aware of it in the novel he presented as Jane's autobiography—that is, *Jane's* life story. He writes that he "thought she could tell the story *of her life* much better than anyone else" (37; emphasis added), though in actuality, the reader realizes that she more often tells about the lives of others. With the passage of time, Gaines has apparently gained some perspective on this novel, for he has changed his view of Miss Jane's role in it. In later interviews, he reveals having realized that the novel is more about the male characters than about the title character. In a 1991 interview with Elsa Saeta and Izora Skinner, he compared his novel to Gertrude Stein's *The Autobiography of Alice B. Toklas,* which "is about everybody but Alice B. Toklas." He then pointed out about his own novel that, "as [Jane] gets older the book moves further and further away from her being directly involved in the action of the novel. . . . From the time Joe Pittman comes on the scene . . . the male characters begin taking over. She's involved, but she's not the center of the action; she's the one telling what's going on" (Saeta and Skinner 249). Later, in a 1993 interview with Michael Sartisky, he admitted again, "Sometimes I think that book is about men, not about Miss Jane" (Sartisky 269). Still somewhat unaware of the imbalance in his fiction's focus predominantly on African-American men, however, Gaines remarked in the same interview that he wrote *A Gathering of Old Men* to balance things after writing about a woman in *Miss Jane Pittman* (Sartisky 271).

Interestingly, Gaines's comment in his essay "Miss Jane and I" that he "had fallen in love with [his] title character" (37) might remind the reader of Faulkner's similar expression of his feelings about Caddy Compson, another voiceless woman of *The Sound and the Fury:* "Caddy was . . . to me too beautiful and too moving to reduce her to telling what was going on, that it would be more passionate to see her through somebody else's eyes" (Gwynn and Blotner 1). It seems, then, that both writers have, due ironically to their strong feelings for these women of their own creation, marginalized them in order to protect them, a common excuse for gender discrimination. In contrast again, however, whereas Faulkner has Caddy's story told by her three brothers, Gaines has Jane tell the story of three men. Thus, Gaines's character, though relegated to the sidelines of her own narrative, is not only still more empowered than Dilsey but also more empowered than Caddy, the white daughter of an Old Southern family. Therefore, although Gaines's central focus is still upon men, the reader can perceive some progress, for the woman's *voice* at least, if not so much her position in the text, from Faulkner's fiction to his.[2] Also in significant contrast, then, one might note that whereas the individual narrators of *The Sound and the Fury* are trapped in the *isolation* of their lives, the narrative of *The Autobiography of Miss Jane Pittman* is a *communal* effort, as the book's "editor" character (the history teacher who records Jane's story in order to provide his students with an African-American perspective of the material he teaches) explains in the introduction: while he was interviewing Jane, her visitors would help her to tell her stories. One could argue that this difference reflects progress from the still existent, isolating caste system of the New South of Faulkner's fiction, maintained in large part by the excuse of having to protect the southern lady, to the vital communal spirit in Gaines's fiction, which is attempting to break down this system, including its support of a gender hierarchy.

The main point of comparison that has been made between Gaines's perhaps most well-known character, Miss Jane Pittman, and Faulkner's Dilsey is their common enduring strength. The significant difference between the two women, however, highlights the difference in their creators' interests: while Jane's strength is directed toward taking care of the *black* men in her life—Ned, her adopted son; Joe, the great love of her life; and Jimmy, her community's chosen "One"—Dilsey's strength is directed toward taking care of the *white* family she works for—the Compsons, of course. In fact, in all of the conversations recorded in the novel between Dilsey and any member of her own family, she is either scolding them or confirming their worthlessness. Charles H. Nilon discusses Dilsey and other "faithful women servants" in Faulkner's fiction and ultimately argues, "Each of these women identifies herself with a particular white family and its fortunes and works as hard as she can to protect the family and its honor." They survive while the family is destroyed—just as Jane survives while the men in her life die one by one; however, one can clearly see how Jane's life would be more fulfilling, considering, as Nilon points out regarding these Faulknerian black women, how they "bear the burden of . . . humanity, frequently without hope or compensation" (101), while Jane receives *both* "hope and compensation" from the men she loves. Furthermore, as Gaines has remarked, Jane does not merely survive; she survives "with sanity *and love*" (Rowell 96). One might contrast the love Jane receives from the men she takes care of, as well as other people in her community, with the significant absence of gratitude, much less love, expressed by Miss Quentin when Dilsey positions herself between the young girl and Jason, or with Benjy's inability to return Dilsey's love and care.

Both women, borrowing Faulkner's summation of Dilsey's fate in his appendix to the novel, do "endure," outliving all of their charges, but while Jane is last seen defying the white man for whom she works, heading into town against his orders to stand in a protest demonstration, Dilsey is last seen in her novel settling Benjy Compson into the wagon for his visit to the cemetery and admonishing her own grandson, "En ef you hurts Benjy, nigger boy, I dont know whut I do. You bound fer de chain gang, but I'll send you dar fo even chain gang ready fer you" (*Sound* 318). She reappears in Faulkner's appendix to the novel in which she gives in to Jason Compson's decision not to do anything to help Caddy. When a librarian brings the magazine photo of Caddy with a Nazi officer to show Dilsey, who is here described as shrunken and nearly blind, Dilsey asks her what "he" has said about it, "And the librarian knew whom she meant by 'he,' nor did the librarian marvel, not only that the old Negress would know that she (the librarian) would know whom she meant by the 'he,' but that the old Negress would know at once that she had already shown the picture to Jason." The librarian responds, "When he realised she [Caddy] was in danger, he said it was her, . . . [b]ut as soon as he realised that somebody . . . wanted to save her, . . . he said it wasn't" (*Portable* 749). Dilsey then responds adamantly that she is unable to see the picture, implying that there is nothing she can do for Caddy against Jason's wishes, thereby continuing to acknowledge Jason's supreme authority over her. Whereas earlier in her life she had protected Benjy and Caddy's daughter, Quentin, from Jason's wrath, she apparently no longer has the strength to defy the "master." Although one might find appealing Philip Dubuisson Castille's view that this scene is evidence that Dilsey has finally renounced her sense of responsibility for the Compsons, Castille does not consider the whole scene in his discussion. He argues that Dilsey's refusal "to have anything to do with the photograph" "underscores the completeness of [her] break from the Compsons" (429), but he does not remark upon her question about whether Jason had been consulted, which precedes Dilsey's assertion that she cannot see it. Jane's behavior at the end of her novel offers a remarkable contrast to Dilsey's apparent continued compliance with the will of her former employer. Still spry and in good health for a woman over one hundred years old, Jane witnesses her employer evicting a woman who had worked for his family for over fifty years because he had learned that her son was involved in demonstrations in Baton Rouge. Yet in spite of such a vivid example of the consequences of involvement in civil rights activities, in the last line of the novel Jane walks right by this same employer to stand with Jimmy's spirit in Bayonne.

Interestingly and perhaps disappointingly, the reader does not see Jane go into town and protest for civil rights. The novel ends with a courageous defiance—"Me and Robert [notice the absence of a "Mr." before the name of her employer in this reference to him] looked at each other there a long time, then I went by him" (244)—but it is to some extent the first *action* she has taken in her life since rejecting her slave name when she was around ten years old (for which she was given a beating that may have resulted in her sterility). As Pauline Kael sums up Jane's story (in her article on the film version of the novel), "at an ironic level Jane's story is the story of how it takes a hundred and ten years to make an activist out of an ordinary black woman" (74). In his review of the film, John J. O'Connor comments upon the fact that "Miss Jane watches history from the sidelines" and then suggests that "the most startling aspect of Miss Jane as a dramatic characterization is her passivity. Her main accomplishment is that she has survived" (67). Indeed, Jane's ultimate *action* is left incomplete in the novel: as noted, *Autobiography* ends with her intention to go to town. In the movie based on the novel, a moving scene is added that allows the viewer to follow Jane into town where she walks up to the "whites only" drinking fountain and takes a drink. John Callahan criticizes this scene for its melodrama, and his argument—that a more critical problem with the scene is that it suggests that the racial conflict depicted in the movie is now solved, so we don't have to do anything about it ourselves—is certainly valid (61). Still, in light of the novel's focus on men and its relegation of the title character, a woman, to the position of observer, the movie's ending is to some extent more satisfying, particularly to the reader concerned with the marginalization of Jane in her own autobiography.[3] Her role in the novel, as already noted, is that of chronicler—recorder of the heroics of the black men in her life. As chronicler, she stands outside the action and observes, though of course she does experience the consequences: she is the one left behind when each of these men dies, to feel the pain and record the significance of the losses.[4] Though her endurance is more positive, more active than Dilsey's, it is still a limited achievement in contrast to those achievements of Ned, Joe, and Jimmy—even, perhaps of the young white man Robert Samson Jr. and the woman Big Laura (described in male terms: "tough *as any man,*" "could plow, chop wood, cut and load [as] much cane *as any man* on the place" [17; emphasis added])—all of whom gave up their lives in the fight for equal rights. In addition, as Jerry Bryant has observed, "though their lives are shorter than Jane's, they are lived at a higher intensity" ("Ernest" 859).

Indeed, Gaines characterizes the men in this novel, including the white man Robert Samson Jr., in completely heroic terms—so much so, in fact, that they each emerge as Christ figures: Joe's association with horses relates him to the Second Coming of Christ in the Book of Revelation; as illustrated by Albert Wertheim, Ned's "Sermon at the River" is reminiscent of Christ's Sermon on the Mount in that it "outline[s] a new testament, a new vision for his listeners" (226); Jimmy, called "The One," is, from the time of his youth, viewed as his people's savior; and "Tee Bob" (Robert Samson Jr.) develops into a Christ figure when his death is interpreted as a sacrifice for the racial sins of his family and ancestors, although, as Jerry Bryant points out, it is important that he not be viewed as "an instrument of salvation, through which the sinful may be *relieved* of their sins" ("From" 119; emphasis added).[5] In contrast to these men, Jane is a flawed human being, and her central flaw in the author's eyes seems to be her desire to protect her loved ones from violent deaths, which requires her to try to thwart their heroic activities. Examining Joe Pittman's death, in particular, it becomes apparent that this death is, to some extent, a punishment inflicted upon Jane by her creator for interfering with her lover's struggle to assert his manhood. Once Joe begins to work with horses—his life's dream—Jane suffers from the fear that he will be killed, either during a roundup of wild horses or while breaking one. Her fear causes her to try to discourage him from doing his work, particularly when she believes that the black stallion of her nightmares has arrived in the flesh.[6] She begs Joe not to break this horse, tries to conjure him to keep him away from the horse, and ultimately inadvertently brings about his death when she releases the horse and he goes after it.[7] It is Jane's role in the death of the one great love of her life that is troubling, suggesting as it does that she is being punished (by her "creator") for interfering with her lover's dreams.

It is important to note here that the horse is black rather than white. It is not a symbol of the white oppression of the black man that Joe is struggling to overcome. Rather, it seems to be a symbol of something within the black character that the African-American must also overcome in order to achieve manhood—one's feminine nature, Gaines seems to suggest (paradoxically with a stallion), that side of the character that would rather have loved ones alive, even if they must hold their heads down and/or crawl before the white man.[8] It is mainly Gaines's women characters who exhibit this preference: Amalia of "Bloodline," the title story of Gaines's collection of short stories; the wives of the old men in *A Gathering of Old Men*; and Jane Pittman, for example. Similarly, Aunt Fe in "Just Like a Tree," also in *Bloodline,* seems to will her own death, apparently preferring death over moving/change. Such a death contrasts significantly with the deaths of Gaines's male characters during their struggles to bring about change. Jerry Bryant explains of all of these women: "They find the threat of change not only repugnant, but full of forebodings of cosmic doom, the disruption of the heavens, and the onset of chaos" ("From" 110). Perhaps alluding to the Faulknerian theory of the "endurance" of the African-American woman, Bryant writes, "These old ladies have endured, yes, as the black race's adaptive mechanism for surviving the dangerous postbellum time, and they have tried to teach their young to survive, too. But the cost has been high—their youth's honor and self-respect." According to Bryant, this explains Gaines's "ambivalent" attitude toward them, which Bryant defines as "the love a son [has] for his mother . . . divided between gratitude for the mother's always welcoming arms and rejection of the dependence such unconditional love entails" ("Ernest" 853).

Repeatedly in her autobiography, Jane tells of how she tried to stop the men in her life from proceeding with behavior that might bring about their deaths, beginning with Joe's horse-breaking, then later Ned's preaching, and finally Jimmy's civil rights activities; she even discourages the white Tee Bob's love for a black Creole woman. Each time, her wishes are defied, the defiant man thereby asserting that it is more important to die as a man struggling for equality than to live as a boy satisfied with mere comfort. And certainly they each die heroically—while Jane lives on. Isn't there, then, some subliminal criticism of Jane's endurance? She has lived so long, in part, because she has learned how to get along in the world: avoid calling attention to oneself. This criticism is probably not deliberate. The author's interest is in the heroic behavior of the men, but, intentionally or not, he has, by praising their willingness to die for their causes, to some extent undermined the value of Jane's endurance—in contrast, ironically, to Faulkner, whose comment in his appendix under Dilsey's name—"They endured" (*Portable* 756)—suggests that

this is the *most* that African-Americans could do, indeed, even quite an accomplishment, given the situation in the New South.[9] Though a problematic character for the reasons noted above, Dilsey still emerges as the most
heroic character in *The Sound and the Fury.* In contrast, though Jane's final
defiance is heroic, since by participating in the protest activities in town she
risks eviction, Jimmy has already paid with his life for leading these activities.
Jane's defiance is not nearly so consequential and hence pales by comparison.

Noting other parallels between these two writers' works continues to reveal subtleties in Gaines's depiction of women that support further the notion that his vision of the struggle for racial equality is a struggle between
white and black *men* for the African-American male's right to assert his manhood. The role of the black woman in Gaines's fiction is usually either to try
to thwart the black man's attempts to achieve manhood in order to protect
him, as already discussed, or, as in "A Long Day in November," another story
in *Bloodline,* to support his struggle and thereby a patriarchal social system
within the African-American community not unlike the patriarchy of the
Old South (which was also ironically supported by women, one of the
groups severely oppressed by the system). The central conflict between Amy
and Eddie in "A Long Day in November" might remind the reader of the
discord between Faulkner's Molly and Lucas Beauchamp over the metal detector and search for gold that have obsessed Lucas in "The Fire and the
Hearth" of *Go Down, Moses.* Like Molly, Amy intends to leave her husband,
Eddie, because of his obsession, in this case, with a new car. Significantly,
whereas Gaines's story is about an African-American man struggling to learn
what it is to be a man, Faulkner's story is about an African-American man's
attempt to find buried treasure, which, he seems to think, would allow him
to move up the social ladder—that is, bring him closer to the level of the
white man, whose riches are also somewhat unearned in that they have been
largely attained via slave labor rather than his own.

Whereas Gaines's Amy supports her husband's goal and guides him away
from a false avenue to manhood, the role of Faulkner's Molly is to make apparent not only the futility of her husband's quest but also its destructiveness: it is destroying their marriage and her health. The sympathetic characterization of Molly villainizes Lucas and his desire to break out of his social
caste, while Eddie is presented as the more sympathetic character in his mis-
guided but not villainous quest for manhood. Another notable point of contrast between the two couples is that while Molly turns to Roth Edmonds, a
white man, for help in getting her "voce" (divorce), Eddie ultimately turns to

a black conjure woman, Madame Toussaint. Eddie thereby relies on the counseling of a medicine woman of his own culture rather than the preacher, who may be black but is also Christian and thus associated with white oppression since African slaves were converted to Christianity as a means of keeping them in line. Eddie finds the preacher's advice impotent and turns to the strength he perceives in the advice of the voice of his African ancestry.[10] In his discussion of Molly's choice of whom to turn to when in need of help—besides Roth, Gavin Stevens in the book's closing story, "Go Down, Moses"—Walter Taylor argues that she thereby behaves "as the epitome of the black child of plantation legend." The book therefore "closes with a stereotyped image that reflected the propaganda of the world of Faulkner's youth: the pathetic dependent and the obliging paternalist, bound together by sentiment" (Taylor 142). Contrasting Molly's behavior (seeking help from a white man) with Eddie's (rejecting the voice of the white man's religion) further supports this perception of Molly as stereotypical.

Although the author's sympathies seem to remain with Molly, Faulkner does redeem Lucas to some extent. At the end of "The Fire and the Hearth," Lucas turns the metal detector over to Roth after persuading Molly that she does not have to go through with the divorce, that he will give up his search for gold. Roth, relieved that there will be no divorce, which would leave him even more responsible for Molly's welfare than he already feels, tries to compromise with Lucas by telling him that he will hold the machine for him so that he can use it occasionally. But Lucas refuses, seemingly for a combination of reasons besides the one he gives Roth (that is, that he "waited too late to start. . . . I am near to the end of my three score and ten, and I reckon to find that money aint for me" [127]): one, he will not allow the white man to tell him when and for how long he can use his own property; and two, he has made a promise to Molly, which he intends to keep to the letter. He will not allow Roth to help him go back on his word, thereby proving that the word of a black man is unreliable. Although Faulkner ultimately shows Lucas acting rationally and thoughtfully, still Lucas never perceives the futility of his quest: no matter how much money he might have found, he would never achieve a social position equal to the white man's.

In Gaines's story, Eddie, too, gives his prize up completely, not partly, to prove his love to his wife: he takes Madame Toussaint's advice and burns the car up. And so has another of Gaines's male characters acted heroically—but at this point the story's turn is troubling. Upon returning home with her husband, Amy asks Eddie to beat her for leaving him so that he can show his face in the community. As Marcia Gaudet explains, Amy "insists on being beaten in order that [Eddie] can put her back in her place and become, once again, the man in the family" (153), for, as Jack Hicks explains (also referring to this incident), "[s]ex roles are well-defined in this world, and to be a man is to dominate" (116).[11] Gaines thereby seems to condone—and through the voice of a woman—the patriarchal rule within the black family, and even a woman critic (Gaudet) seems to have no problem with this relation between manhood and rightful authority; she even implicitly condones its achievement, if need be, through violence against women. She excuses Amy's request that Eddie beat her with a cultural explanation and stops short of condemning such a social order for its patriarchal nature.[12] Frank W. Shelton, however, offers a more satisfying reading of this turn in the story: he first criticizes Amy for "remain[ing] committed to a simplistic idea of manhood—that the man must dominate the woman, and in a physical, even brutal way"; he then credits Eddie for "not enjoy[ing], or even understand[ing] why he must give the beating" and argues that Eddie realizes by this time that "[h]is manhood does not depend on such things, nor on the attitude of the community" ("Ambiguous" 203). Although this reading lets Gaines off the hook for affirming the patriarchy through whatever means necessary, it still supports the gender hierarchy in Gaines's fiction: besides having acted heroically, the male character in this story is ultimately more enlightened than the female.

"You're a nigger!": False Liberals Unmasked in Faulkner and Gaines

FAULKNER: Well, I think a man ought to do more than just repudiate. He [Isaac McCaslin] should have been more affirmative instead of shunning people.

Q: Do you think that any of your characters succeed in being more affirmative?

FAULKNER: Yes, I do. There was Gavin Stevens. He was a good man but he didn't succeed in living up to his ideal. But his nephew, the boy, I think he may grow up to be a better man than his uncle. I think he may succeed as a human being.

Cynthia Grenier, "The Art of Fiction"

Although Gaines is reluctant to acknowledge Faulknerian influence upon his work beyond "dealing with . . . southern dialects" (Gaudet and Wooton 17), he does admit freely that he used Faulkner's *Go Down, Moses,* a collection of linked short stories, as a model when structuring his 1968 short story collection, *Bloodline* (Gaudet and Wooton 34), in which "A Long Day in November" was collected, along with four other stories. In the title story of the collection, Copper Laurent's characterization is closely comparable to Faulkner's characterization of Lucas Beauchamp in *Go Down, Moses* (much more so than Eddie's in "A Long Day in November"), and one can easily see in the echo how Gaines, consciously or unconsciously, is responding to Faulkner's development of black characters and racial themes.

Faulkner's Lucas is a descendent of Lucius Quintus Carothers McCaslin, a white plantation owner referred to as Old Carothers, and two of his slaves. Upon the first of these women, Eunice, Carothers fathered Tomasina, called Tomey; he later fathered Terrel, called Turl, upon his daughter Tomey. Lucius Quintus Carothers Beauchamp, called Lucas, is one of Turl's children. Similarly, Gaines's Copper Laurent is the direct product of a miscegenous rape. Like Lucas, he seems to view his Laurent blood—that is, the blood of his white father—as empowering. Indeed, Valerie Babb's description of Copper in "Bloodline" sounds a lot like Zack Edmonds's thoughts about Lucas. Babb writes, "the story suggests that he is more Laurent and even more imperious than even his uncle Frank [his father's brother]. Felix [the story's black narrator] characterizes Copper's bearing as more akin to the descendent of slaveholders than to the descendent of slaves" (34). Keith Byerman also remarks upon Copper's closer association with the Laurents than with the other African-Americans: "In his assertiveness, his arrogance, his forceful character, he is more a Laurent than the sickly, self-doubting Frank [and] these family qualities are accompanied by the traditional Laurentian feeling of superiority over and indifference to the blacks on the plantation" (*Fingering* 83). For example, Frank remarks at one point, "[Copper] didn't talk to me like he was talking to a' old man, he spoke to me like he was speaking to a slave" (*Bloodline* 204). Similarly, Zack Edmonds, another great-grandson of Old Carothers, but this one white, thinks to himself regarding Lucas, *"He's more like old Carothers than all the rest of us put together"* (114; Faulkner's italics). On the other hand, unlike Lucas, who rebels only subtly against his white relations, Copper overtly asserts his right to his father's legacy, beginning by acknowledging openly who his father, now deceased, was, by using his father's name, and by calling his father's brother "Uncle." Felix reports that Copper "said 'Uncle' to Frank just like he would 'a' said 'Aunt' to [his mother's sister] 'Malia" (203). As David Smith points out in his essay on Faulkner and

Gaines, in this story, the conflict of which Smith compares to the conflict between Charles Bon and Thomas Sutpen regarding Bon's desire for recognition, Gaines is dealing with the consequences of miscegeny in a racist society. Smith also compares Copper to Faulkner's Rider in "Pantaloon in Black" and to Samuel Worsham Beauchamp of the title story, both of *Go Down, Moses,* but finally contrasts him to these Faulknerian "defiant Negroes, who are all killed by white men," by pointing out that "Copper proves unconquerable" (54). He can be neither pushed nor scared off the land he views as rightfully his; he ultimately agrees to leave because, as he tells his uncle, "I only came this time to look around" (217).

Seeming to undermine this contrast with Faulkner's "defiant [though doomed] Negroes," some critics have perceived Copper as mentally unbalanced. For example, Walter R. McDonald calls him "insanely obsessed" (48); Todd Duncan believes he is "shell-shocked" (94); and Robert M. Luscher remarks that he is "on the edge of madness" (82). Gaines himself compares Copper to Jim Bond, the seemingly mentally deficient grandson of Charles Bon, great-grandson of Thomas Sutpen, though it appears from his comment that he means the emotionally unbalanced Charles Etienne St. Valery Bon (son of Charles Bon, grandson of Thomas Sutpen): "Copper is, of course, as much white as he is black, and he's caught up in a world where he's not any part of the world. He's betwixt and between, where he cannot go one way or the other. It keeps pulling him apart. Jim Bon [*sic*] in Faulkner's *Absalom, Absalom!*—that sort of thing. He says, OK, where do I fit into this whole scene? And when you don't find a place to fit in, madness can easily happen to you" (Gaudet and Wooton 56). Jim Bond is not mad, however, but seemingly retarded. One could make a case, though, that his father, Charles Etienne St. Valery Bon, has been driven mad by his situation of being "betwixt and between," of having no place where he fits in.

Gaines's apparent confusion between, which results in a conflation of, Charles Etienne St. Valery Bon and Jim Bon*d* may reflect his own ambivalence toward his character, an indecisiveness as to whether Copper is defeated like Charles Etienne, who is repeatedly driven to violence by his uncertain racial identity, or triumphant, ironically like Jim Bond, who outlives his whole family, black and white. After all, what proof is there in the story that Copper is at all deranged? Robert Luscher refers to the army Copper talks about as "shadow troops," implying that, since they do not really exist, Copper must be mad (82), but Copper himself admits that "[p]hysically, in the sense of an organized Army, no" there aren't any men already gathered (207). He explains, "All those who've been treated as I've been treated . . . [are] waiting for me" (206–7). This belief is, in fact, supported in an earlier conversation when Felix explains to Frank why the black men Frank has sent to bring Copper to his back door have not been successful: "when you lose the power of the rod, of the gun, they ain't got nothing to fear no more." Frank accepts this explanation, surmises that "they [now] fear the other man who picks up the rod or the gun," and asks Felix, "Do you think the time might come when they would join up with Copper against me?" (201). In further argument against Copper's "insanity," it is not an omniscient narrator but Felix and other characters in the story who judge Copper to be mentally unstable: Felix implies that Copper's actions are reflective of mental problems—an opinion that Frank (who equates him with a "mad dog" [216]), Amalia (who may hope that "the white man" will take his "mental problems" into consideration and not kill him for his behavior), and J. W. (who calls him "crazy" after watching him win a fight alone against several other men [194–95]) also express—seemingly merely because his behavior upsets the current social order, which is itself flawed. Surprisingly, one can turn to the fate of Jim Bond (since Gaines brought his name up while speaking of Copper) and invert the author's negative association of Copper with Jim Bond/Charles Etienne Bon, to support further the view of Copper as undeniably "unconquerable." At the end of *Absalom, Absalom!*, Shreve remarks on the inevitability of the "Jim Bonds [that is, the products of miscegeny] . . . conquer[ing] the western hemisphere" (302). Likewise Copper promises, "I'll be back. We'll be back. . . . And I'll take my share . . . or I'll bathe this whole plantation in blood. . . . Your days are over, Uncle. . . . It's my time now. And I won't let a thing in the world get in my way." He departs with one last comment, which is directly reminiscent of events in *Absalom, Absalom!*, perhaps confirming this connection between the triumphant vision for the future of the victims and products of miscegeny: "Tell my aunt I've gone. But tell her I'll come back. And tell her when I do, *she'll never have to go through your back door ever again*" (217; emphasis added).

Turning now to the central white character in "Bloodline," one can see that Gaines also seems to draw from Faulkner's Isaac McCaslin, the white grandson of Old Carothers, for his development of the conflicts troubling the central white character of this story, Copper's uncle, Frank Laurent. At twenty-one (in chapter 4 of "The Bear" in *Go Down, Moses*), Isaac "Ike"

McCaslin renounces his heritage, refusing to accept the legacy of land in protest of, in particular, his grandfather's rape of his slaves—and even more particularly, his grandfather's fathering a child upon his own daughter.[13] In
"Delta Autumn," then, Ike, now in his eighties, meets a woman who is the
lover of one of his young cousins and who carries with her the product of
their relationship. At first, Ike is disgusted with his cousin Roth Edmonds's
rejection of his lover and their child—that is, until he realizes that this
woman (who remains unnamed, reflecting Faulkner's concern, not for the
woman, but for the effect of her existence upon Ike)[14] has descended from
the "black" line of his family, upon which realization Ike "crie[s] . . . in a
voice of amazement, pity, and *outrage*: 'You're a nigger!'" (344; emphasis
added). Recovering himself, he tells her to "[g]o back North. Marry: a man
in your own race. That's the only salvation for you—for a while yet, maybe a
long while yet. We will have to wait. Marry a black man. You are young,
handsome, almost white; you could find a black man who would see in you
what it was you saw in [Roth]" (346). The reader is shocked by this outburst,
recognizing in it Ike's true sentiments. He is not of such a different mind
about race from the rest of his community as he likes to think. Suggesting
Faulkner's own recognition of this fact, the author switches from referring to
him as "Isaac" in earlier chapters and "the old man" earlier in this chapter to
referring to him as "McCaslin," thereby associating Ike with other members
of his family whose actions motivated his attempted repudiation. Indeed, as
John Pilkington points out, Ike's "practical advice [to the young woman]
sounds more like McCaslin [Edmonds]" than himself (285). Robert Penn
Warren even compares Ike's repudiation to Roth's rejection of his mistress
and son: both men have "tried to buy out of responsibility"—Ike, "by refusing his inheritance," Roth, by leaving money for Ike to give the woman—
and in neither case "can the consequences of the crime be commuted by
money" ("Faulkner" 265). More recently, in showing how Ike's "renunciation
of his patrimony . . . does not help anyone," Linda Wagner-Martin points
out that "[h]is absconding, in fact, allows Roth Edmonds to live the unexam-
ined life of his forebears, with no alternative community voice to check or
reprove him" (Introduction 6).[15] Ike may have given up the physical legacy—
the money and the land—but he still carries the name and with it the guilt as
well as the prejudices of his ancestors.

  Besides exposing—with the denigrating terminology ("nigger") and the
"outrage" that provoked his outburst before the woman—Ike's view of Afri-

can-Americans as inferior, his advice to the young woman also reveals: first, his wish for her—and the complication she brings to his carefree life (since washing his hands of responsibility)—to go far away ("North"); second, his support of the myth that all black men want a white woman, which, as Charles Nilon argues, "shows the extent to which even Isaac is controlled by his social world" (101); and third, his belief that her attraction to Roth has more to do with his race than with love. Ike also inadvertently admits that his repudiation was a meaningless gesture that changed nothing with regard to race relations in his community when he points out that any such change is still "a long while" in coming. Indeed, just before his outburst he had thought to himself, *"Maybe in a thousand or two thousand years"* (344), indicating how long he thinks it would be and what it would take before any change comes to this society (at least a millennium, when the second coming of Christ is predicted by the Book of Revelation). The reader is sorely disappointed in this false liberal who had earlier prepared himself to be a mortal savior.

The young woman—in her calm response to Ike's outburst—remarks upon having openly, like Gaines's Copper Laurent, acknowledged their relationship: "I said you were *Uncle* Isaac" (344; emphasis added), she tells the old man when he expresses his surprise regarding who she is—like Lucas, a descendent of that miscegenous rape mentioned previously. Comparing her use of familial terms with Copper Laurent's emphasizes this woman's desire to break down the racial barrier that keeps her from the man she loves and keeps her son from having a father. Ike, however, has surprisingly joined that barrier. He wants only to give her the money Roth left for her and then to send her away, after which he (Ike) can wallow in despair over the futility of his life. Again turning to Babb's assessment of Gaines's story, one finds her description of Frank's conflict reminiscent of Ike's conflict, as it is developed from his learning about the sins of his grandfather in "The Bear" to his meeting with this young woman in "Delta Autumn." According to Babb, Frank also "finds the inheritance of land and family name burdensome. Fatigued by maintaining the legacy of racial inequity, [he] nonetheless feels bound by his larger identity to defend the status quo" (34). Frank's explanation to Felix echoes Ike's words to the young woman. Frank cries, "I didn't write the rules. I came and found them, and I shall die and leave them. They will be changed, of course; they will be changed, and soon, I hope. But I will not be the one to change them" (199). In fact, as he later admits, he will continue to support them: "I'm going to defend this place with all my strength . . . to keep it exactly as it is" (216).

At the same time, however, as Frank reminds Copper, he has made some effort to ease conditions for African-Americans "to make up for what [Copper's father] did to these here in the quarter": he allows the descendents of his family's former slaves to live rent-free on his land and provides them food, medicine, a church, and a grave (216). In contrast to Ike, then, he keeps control of his land, knowing that his only surviving (white) relative would, upon taking over its management, charge rent and evict those who do not pay.[16] In spite of this point of contrast, neither man's choice is enough to be of any significant or lasting help to anyone. Frank is going to die eventually—and probably soon, given his bad heart and the shock of Copper's unconventional behavior—after which conditions will be worse for the African-Americans. Furthermore, since the actuality of the inevitable economic hardships will undermine the memory of past security, Frank's efforts will have been as futile as Ike's repudiation.

Frank's treatment of the African-Americans who live on his land is also reminiscent of Buck and Buddy McCaslin's treatment of the slaves they inherit from their father, Old Carothers, as reported in "Was," the opening story of *Go Down, Moses.* These two brothers, Ike's father and uncle, were apparently also uncomfortable with either their father's abuse of his slaves or with owning slaves themselves (or a combination of the two possibilities). But rather than free their slaves, Buck and Buddy gave them the run of the plantation house and moved into a shack to live. Each night, before returning to their refuge, they would lock the front door of the plantation house after all the slaves were inside, aware that several would exit the back door as soon as they were gone. The unspoken agreement was that everyone would be back inside when the brothers returned in the morning. The situation is presented comically, but it is still troubling. Edmond L. Volpe points out that, "despite the enlightened and sympathetic attitude of Buck and Buddy, they treat Tomey's Turl not as a brother but as a Negro" (235). The reader wonders, if they were so uncomfortable with their situation, why didn't they just free the slaves—particularly their half-brother, Turl—and let them sharecrop? The answer is probably related to not offending their white neighbors. Also, one senses that they are against slavery merely because of the trouble it causes them when, for example, they must chase the runaway Turl to the Beauchamp plantation, or even because of its disturbance to their consciences, perhaps whenever it occurs to them that they own their own brother. In any case, one does not notice any lack of prejudice on the brothers' part.

Gaines may be alluding to and mocking the McCaslin brothers' meaningless gesture when he has Frank list all he has done for the African-Americans who live on his land and then ask Felix, "What more am I supposed to do—give you the house and move into the quarters?" (188). Like Buck and Buddy, Frank at least maintains the appearance of supporting the caste system. He tells Felix, for example, that he will not let Copper (who is his nephew), or Felix (who has been a loyal friend to him), or Amalia (whom he considers to be "a lady" but who "happens to be black"), walk through his front door (199), echoing again Faulkner's Thomas Sutpen, who supposedly conceived of his "design" when as a boy he was turned away at the front door, his social status ("white trash") making it inappropriate that he use the front entrance. Supposedly, Sutpen wanted to ensure that no one else would be so treated, at least not at his home, but then, when his own son—who happens to be black if not poor—comes to his house, he treats him in the same degrading manner. This connection between Sutpen and Frank illuminates a connection between Sutpen and Ike, which further villainizes the latter "false liberal," who is more traditionally viewed positively, or at least romantically, by critics (at least in comparison to Sutpen).

Like Ike's repudiation because of his grandfather's treatment of his slave women, Frank's "benevolent" treatment of the African-Americans living on his property is a gesture toward making up for the rape of black women by one of his relatives. He tells Copper, "My brother, your father, was wrong. Not only with your mother, but with many other women—white and black alike." But then he continues, "White and black men he also destroyed. . . . I, myself, have suffered from his errors as much as you, as much as any other man" (215). Like Ike, Frank feels burdened by his legacy of guilt; however, Frank is simply wrong to feel that he has suffered "as much as" the African-Americans abused by his brother. Recognition of Frank's mistaken sense of equal suffering illuminates Faulkner's focus on the similarly "suffering" white liberal in his fiction and undermines the reader's sympathy for this character's frustration as he faces the ignorance of his community's racism. Is either Ike or Frank any better, finally, than not only Thomas Sutpen but also Faulkner's perhaps most despicable character—certainly not one of his romantic idealists—Jason Compson? Jason also feels burdened by the African-Americans who served his family, and he, too, Faulkner reports in the appendix to *The Sound and the Fury,* eventually moves off of his family's land and into town, telling people that "[h]e was emancipated now. He was free. 'In 1865,' he would say, 'Abe Lincoln freed the niggers from the Compsons. In 1933, Jason Compson freed the Compsons from the niggers'" (*Portable* 752).

Gaines takes on and further illuminates Thomas Sutpen's moral failure in his betrayal of his son in other works besides "Bloodline." One can find in Gaines's *In My Father's House* and *The Autobiography of Miss Jane Pittman* parallels to *Absalom, Absalom!* not unlike those noted in McMurtry's *Lonesome Dove* in the preceding chapter. In both *Absalom, Absalom!* and *In My Father's House,* a young man seeks out the father who deserted him and his mother, though a significant difference is that Faulkner's Charles Bon is the mixed-race son of a white man who deserted him and his mother upon discovering that she was Creole, while Gaines's Robert X is the black son of a black father who never married his mother. Thomas Sutpen, born "poor white trash," has, since leaving his first wife and son, proceeded with his "design" to become the patriarch of a southern plantation. Similarly, Gaines's Phillip Martin has straightened up his life after a wild youth and become a leading citizen and a preacher. Significantly, Reverend Martin is aided by white men when he collapses upon recognizing his son in his house. This association with men of the same race as his oppressors reinforces his comparison to Sutpen, who also associates with the kind of people whose discrimination against him is what motivated his design in the first place. Martin has lost contact with the very people he set out to help. Through this comparison, the flaw in Sutpen's design is perhaps better understood. He set out to defeat the caste system and instead supported it.

Sutpen's "design," as mentioned, originated with the desire to provide a haven where visitors would never be sent to the back door because they were not considered worthy of entering through the front door. Ironically, as Quentin Compson realizes, "after fifty years the forlorn nameless and homeless lost child came to knock at it [the front door]," the actual child being Sutpen's firstborn, Charles Bon, but by that time "nobody even remember[ed] the [imagined] child" for whom the haven was designed (215). In Gaines's novel, in contrast, Phillip Martin, upon recovering from the initial shock of seeing his son, sends word that Robert X is welcome "[a]ny time he would like to come here" (60). This invitation is significant: as Herman Beavers points out, Martin's house is "the symbol of his achievement." Thus, in further contrast to Sutpen, Martin "reassess[es] the meaning of his labor" after seeing his son (Beavers 90). Sutpen does eventually question where he went wrong, but not in connection with his treatment of his firstborn (he wonders, merely, why his design failed). Martin recognizes the significance of his rejection of his firstborn: "He [Martin] had worked hard for his family, his church, the people, and the [civil rights] movement, and he had been proud of that hard work. He thought he had done a good job, at least both black and white had told him so. But now, after seeing the boy in the house, after falling and not getting up, he had begun to question himself: What really was Phillip Martin, and what if anything had he really done?" (72).

Of course, events do not go much better for Martin than they do for Sutpen, in spite of Martin's acknowledgment of his son. According to the story Quentin puts together, Charles Bon wanted only acknowledgment from his father and did not care if it occurred between only himself and his father; so when his father failed to give him even that much, he set out to destroy his father's design through Sutpen's "legitimate" children, those who would inherit his design in southern plantation tradition (which typically left illegitimate—black—children out of bequests). Robert X does not care about his father's recognition of their relationship. He has only come to kill the man he holds responsible for his family's troubles. Finally unable to go through with the murder, he kills himself instead, thereby punishing his father in an even worse way. In final contrast, then, Martin recognizes his mistakes and regrets his treatment of his son, whereas Sutpen never can conceive of where he went wrong in pursuing his design and never speaks to anyone of regretting his treatment of Charles Bon. With this difference, Gaines illuminates the white man's limited ability to recognize his crimes against the African-American.

Another comparison can be made between Sutpen and a Gaines character: Robert Samson, Jane Pittman's last employer, who has two sons, one black and one white. In contrast to Sutpen, however, Robert does not try to hide his connection to Timmy, the son he has by one of his black servants, though he "couldn't even if he wanted to," according to Jane. Like Charles Bon, "Timmy was more like him than poor Tee Bob [his white, legitimate son] ever would be" (137). In this departure from the pattern of events in *Absalom, Absalom!*—that is, Sutpen's refusal to acknowledge in any way his black son—Gaines emphasizes the communal guilt of miscegenation: he reminds the reader that everyone usually knew about the products of white men who have forced themselves upon black women, and no one spoke out against such criminal behavior.

Reinforcing the connection between the two books, Samson coldly sends his black son away, even after his cuckolded wife subtly reminds him that this child is only half black. "There ain't no such thing as a half nigger," Samson retorts (144).[17] Whereas Faulkner asserts in his novel, through the voice of General Compson, that Sutpen's crime was "innocence"—not knowing that one could not treat people as Sutpen does in his monomaniacal struggle to achieve his design—Gaines will allow no such excuse. There is nothing "innocent" about Samson's betrayal of his son, which began at the time of the boy's conception. Like Sutpen's, Samson's crimes backfire. Before Timmy is sent away, he and Tee Bob have developed a camaraderie not unlike Charles Bon and Henry Sutpen's relationship. Tee Bob, therefore, learns to view a black man as a friend, a person. Consequently, he later falls in love with a black woman, and his realization that he cannot marry her results in his suicide. Thus has Samson lost his last heir, not unlike Sutpen's loss of his legitimate son, the only one of his children through whom his design can proceed as planned.

At the end of this episode, Tee Bob's godfather, Jules Raynard, presents to Jane Pittman his theory as to who is to blame for the young man's suicide. Raynard argues that they are *all*—including himself, a white man; Jane, a black woman; and the young Creole, part-black woman with whom Tee Bob was in love—responsible for making and supporting the rules that disallow love between the races and under which Tee Bob could not live. Blyden Jackson argues that Raynard "speaks for Gaines" (272), but the reader should question this interpretation. First of all, why would Gaines use the voice of a white man to express his views on this subject when most of the other white characters in his novel play a role in Jane's suffering? Second, Raynard's argument is flawed, for in this southern community, it is the white people who have made the rules regarding what is and is not allowed to go on between the races; those African-Americans who have cooperated have done so, in large part, in order to survive. In addition, the tone of Raynard's speech is so reminiscent of the tone Faulkner's characters use when they project upon events that they have not themselves witnessed (as do the three generations of Compson men in *Absalom, Absalom!*) that one might also wonder if Gaines is not here mocking their authority to explain the Sutpen history (or mocking the readers who have accepted as authoritative their second-, third-, and fourthhand accounts of the actions and motivations of others). Indeed, Jane asks Raynard of his theories, "ain't this specalatin?" (192), something no one points out within the pages of Faulkner's novels (and critics have only just begun to point out). Like the Faulknerian characters he emulates, Raynard means well as he theorizes but is irresponsible in his lack of consideration of the whole—that is, of the black perspective and motivation in cases like this. The black members of the community watch silently as Tee Bob falls in love with the Creole schoolteacher because warning anyone and thereby suggesting that a white man could love a black woman would be risky: the one who spoke up might be punished for his or her impudence. Raynard lessens his race's moral responsibility for (and his own conscience's prickling over) the sufferings of the black race if people will accept his view that the African-Americans have willingly supported the caste system. It is helpful, therefore, to recognize the echo of Faulkner's "false liberals" in Raynard's tone so as not to mistakenly perceive his message about equally shared responsibility as the one Gaines would have us believe.

Gender, Race, and Class Discrimination in *A Gathering of Old Men*

[I]n tragedy, which embodies all the highest aspirations and attitudes of a social group, old men must be respected. . . . Their wisdom must be listened to, their authority upheld, or ruinous disorder follows and society . . . is shaken to its foundations.

Figes, *Tragedy and Social Evolution*

Perhaps the most striking and direct echo of Faulkner occurs in *A Gathering of Old Men* when Jack Marshall rejects responsibility for the conflict going on at Marshall Plantation. To the Cajun troublemaker Luke Will's accusatory complaint, "One of your niggers did it"—that is, killed Beau Boutan, the son of a Cajun family—Jack responds, "I have no niggers. . . . Never had any niggers. Never wanted any niggers. Never will have any niggers. They belong to her" (159). Jack's renunciation of responsibility for the events transpiring on his family's land is comparable to Isaac McCaslin's renunciation of his birthright, the land he inherited from his slaveholding ancestors. As Ike turns his land over to his cousin McCaslin Edmonds and McCaslin's descendents, Jack has turned his family's land over to his niece, Candy. Like Ike, rather than *do* anything about the past injustices toward African-Americans by his ancestors, knowledge of which may be what drives Jack to drink in order to escape his sense of inherited guilt, which is not so easy to pass on to another, Jack has taken himself out of the picture and left all responsibility to a younger relative.

Before Jack Marshall dissociates himself from the events taking place at his family's plantation, the reader is given a summation of his life by Jacques Thibeaux ("aka Tee Jack"). Jack spends his days in Tee Jack's bar sitting where "he can look at the door where the nigger room used to be." Before the African-Americans quit using the room about fifteen years earlier, Jack Marshall had placed himself there, according to Tee Jack, "so he could tell when one of his niggers came into the nigger room, and . . . nod for me to go serve him" (152), a self-appointed duty that reflects Jack's earlier sense of responsibility for those who lived at "Marshall." Tee Jack wonders now why Jack "still looks there when he's drinking" and "if he's hearing ghosts in there" (153). Tee Jack's plausible explanation for Jack's behavior is reminiscent of Faulkner's sensitive white characters' overwhelming sense of suffering from the guilt and burden of the sins of the past—slavery, miscegenation, and racism. Ironically, the Cajun (and thus less affluent) narrator of the section sympathizes with Jack, even though, as Tee Jack realizes, "the only reason he comes here [is] it's the nearest saloon to his fancy house there on the river" (160). Tee Jack's sympathy may reflect his desire to connect with this wealthier man as a way of boosting his own self-image and his belief that he is more like this white man than he is like the black men whose lives are presently in danger. Such identification of himself with Jack Marshall on the basis of race served to reinforce the caste system, which may have placed men like Tee Jack on a level below the Marshalls but at least reassured them that they would never be on the lowest rung of the social ladder, where the African-Americans were relegated. Indeed, Tee Jack's social "inferiority" is reflected in his very typical Cajun nickname: "Tee Jack" means "little Jack" (he is apparently a Jacques Jr.). At the same time, Gaines emphasizes the connection between the two white men through their first names, which are essentially the same except for the different Anglo and French pronunciations. Their connection is further established by the fact that neither does anything in an attempt to stop Luke Will and his gang from going to Marshall.

Once perceived, these connections between the two white men support Tee Jack's ability to translate Jack's thoughts. Within his interpretation of Jack's opinion of the African-Americans on Marshall Plantation, Tee Jack explains why he sympathizes with Jack, a man who can spend his day drinking while most people, including Tee Jack, have to work to provide for themselves and their families:

> I sympathize with him. 'Cause you see he never wanted none of this. Never wanted to be responsible for name and land. They dropped it on him, left it on him. That's why he drinks the way he does, and let that niece of his run the place. Let her have it, he don't care. Don't care if it go to hell. He want it to go to hell. . . . He go by the name 'cause they gived him that name, he live on the land 'cause they left it there, but he don't give a damn for it . . . for nothing. . . . And I don't blame him. Things just too complicated. I reckon for people like him they have always been complicated—protecting name and land. It's just too much for most people. Feeling guilty about this, guilty about that. It wasn't his doing. He came here and found it, and they died and left it on him. . . . Maybe that's what he's doing when he looks at that door—cussing them. No, not the niggers who used to be in there singing—the ones who brought them here, the ones built that room. (154)

Tee Jack's assessment of Jack's burdensome guilt is corroborated by Jack himself when he is berated by an out-of-town patron in the bar for not doing anything or seeming not to care about what Luke Will and his gang are planning within their hearing. He responds to the professor's remark, "In the end, it's people like us . . . who pay for this," with, "Sure . . . But I've been paying my share seventy years already. How long have you been paying yours?" (164). Like Faulkner's Ike, Jack apparently sees no change ahead, only more punishment—on himself and other *white* people, ironically. There is no mention in this section of the suffering of the African-Americans who, as Tee Jack had pointed out, had been brought to this country as slaves and were still being treated as inferior citizens. Again, then, Gaines seems to mock Faulkner's sympathetic focus on the suffering of the sensitive romantic idealist who, as a white man, has not suffered much more pain than the nagging of his own conscience—or perhaps the collective *conscience*, to rephrase Jung, of his race.

Craig Werner believes *A Gathering of Old Men* is "a response to the vision of the 'new South' presented in [Faulkner's] *Intruder in the Dust*" (43); to illustrate, he discusses the parallels between the books' plots and the character development of Mathu and Lucas. Faulkner's Lucas Beauchamp of *Intruder in the Dust,* as well as *Go Down, Moses,* may indeed be the paradigm for

Gaines's Mathu, the central heroic figure of *A Gathering of Old Men*; again, however, the changes that Gaines makes that distinguish his character from the model are significant. To start, whereas Lucas's pride seems to be tied up with his "white blood" as well as his having descended from the male side of the McCaslin family, Mathu's pride comes from his untainted "black blood."[18] In connection, while Lucas looks down upon each of the Edmonds men with whom he interacts over the years for having descended from McCaslin women, Mathu looks down upon any African-American who is lighter than himself, "and the more [white blood] you had, the more he looked down on you" (51), reports Clatoo (one of the gathering old men). In his development of Lucas's character, Faulkner has exhibited his belief in the attraction of the power of the white patriarchy to the black man. In Faulkner's vision, even a black man would be proud to be descended from such power, even though that same power supported slavery and allowed the rape of, in this case, two black women, mother and daughter, that began the family line from which Lucas descended. It is not surprising that an African-American writer would find no such appeal in the white man's power. Thus, Gaines, more in the tradition of Alex Haley's Kunta Kinte than Faulkner's Lucas Beauchamp, characterizes the central African-American of his novel as proud of his "blue-black" skin (51). Also like Kunta Kinte, Mathu is disgusted by the evidence of miscegenation he sees in the light-colored faces of the majority of the African-Americans living around him. Finally, unlike Lucas, who never regrets his misplaced pride, Mathu eventually seems to recognize that, in looking down upon his neighbors with mixed blood, he has blamed the wrong people—he has held the products of miscegenation responsible for the rapes committed against their maternal ancestors. He admits then that his African pride is not so much related to his ancestral home as a replacement for the American pride he is not allowed to feel: "Put myself above all— proud to be African. You know why proud to be African? 'Cause they won't let me be a citizen here in this country." He adds, then, that the true reason for his anger at his neighbors was that, until this day, they had "never tried" to be citizens (182). He recognizes, though, that it is never too late and praises the other old men for their brave stand with him that day.

Recalling Lucas Beauchamp's condescending attitude toward the Edmonds men because of their lineage, which, in contrast to his own, is traced back to the female McCaslins, and considering the peripheral positions of all of the women in *Go Down, Moses,* it becomes clear once again that Faulkner's concern is with the southern man—in this work, with southern men of both races—or, as Eric J. Sundquist puts it, "the South's and Faulkner's lingering obsession with the legitimizing power of paternal 'blood'" (135). Considering the depiction and treatment of black women in *A Gathering of Old Men,* one perceives again that Gaines's predominant concern in his fiction is similarly limited, though to the conflicts endured by the *black* man. Although the novel (seemingly unintentionally) portrays the double oppression of the black woman—sexual as well as racial—it does not reflect upon this issue. Indeed, the black women in this novel are more peripheral than in any of his other novels or stories.

One may turn briefly to Valerie Babb's discussion of "A Long Day in November" as an avenue into recognizing the problematic definitions of masculinity in this later Gaines novel. Babb argues that "[w]hile for Eddie his car is a symbol of masculinity and freedom within a society that traditionally has denied both to black men, Amy views it as an intruder usurping the attention Eddie should give to his family" (17). Frank Shelton and John W. Roberts both remark in their discussions of the story upon the car as a symbol of masculinity in America and upon its particular significance to the black male. Shelton comments, "Eddie regards his evening activities in his car as the only glamorous, exciting aspect of his life" ("Ambiguous" 202). Roberts's more developed analysis of the couple's conflict over the car is similar to Babb's:

> The inability of the black male to provide for and protect his family has traditionally forced him to find alternative means of demonstrating his manhood. Through his car . . . Eddie attempts to define his manhood outside of his family. Amy, however, refused to accept . . . Eddie's attachment to his car as a demonstration of his masculinity. . . . By leaving him she forces him to seek a new way of conceptualizing his role as father and husband. (110)

Although Gaines's earlier story ends with the male protagonist's recognition of his mistaken association between a car and his masculinity, one is not sure whether Gaines's titular old men of the later novel ever recognize the problem with associating their masculinity with guns. Furthermore, neither Babb nor other critics remark upon the problem with a gun being perceived as a symbol of masculinity in *A Gathering of Old Men.* As Joseph Griffin argues, "Charlie sees Mathu's handing over the gun as his godfather's effort to make him, finally, a man" ("Creole" 39). After the killing of Beau Boutan, old men arm themselves to defend Mathu, whom they believe to be the only African-American "man enough" to kill a Cajun. Each man shoots his (for many, borrowed) gun in order to be able to take credit himself for the death, but the reader knows that none of these men committed the murder. Furthermore, as Mary T. Harper points out, for much of the novel the guns are empty, and "an empty shotgun is a useless weapon just as the men possessing such weapons are harmless; hence, Candy becomes the protector." Harper adds that the empty guns are also "analogous to the lives these men have lived": they "have faced life fearfully, refusing to take risks . . . becom[ing] empty shells of men" (300).

One problem with the association of manhood with guns can be found in the "paradox in defining manhood" that Suzanne W. Jones perceives in the novel: "The novel turns on an interesting paradox in defining manhood as it relates to 'race.' In order for Fix's youngest son, Gil, to be a man, he must refuse to kill the black man who has murdered his brother Beau; in order for each old black man to be a man, he must be ready to kill a white man" (47). Later in her article, Jones points out that most of the old men are not satisfied with merely "prov[ing] their manhood to themselves. . . . [T]he manly behavior that the old black men are eager to exhibit comes in part from their capacity for violence and from a desire for revenge" (52).

That the old men begin to feel like men once they are armed is problematic in and of itself, but in this case this troubling macho attitude is compounded by their turning right around upon taking up arms and threatening their wives with violence. When Mat's wife, fearful for his life (reminiscent of Jane Pittman), tries to stop him from joining the stand, he reports that he "turned on her" and that "she started backing way from [him], like she thought [he] was go'n hit her" (36). As their argument escalates, he threatens her with physical violence: "You touch that phone, woman, somebody'll be patching your head." Then he pushes her aside and violently rips the phone out of the wall. He reports in his narrative that "[s]omething in my face made her back from me. She kept backing back, backing back, till she had touched the wall" (37). As in her reading of "A Long Day in November," here again Marcia Gaudet fails to remark upon the problem with this threat of violence against a woman. She comments upon this episode only to note "the absence of women's influence on black men's behavior" in Gaines's fiction (152). Mat's wife cannot stop him from going to Marshall to stand up with Mathu and the other old men when Fix Boutan arrives (as they mistakenly assume he will) to avenge his son's death. Within Mat's explanation to his wife as to why he must take a stand, even this late in his life, he refers to "com[ing] home drunk and beat[ing her] for no reason at all" (38), apparently out of the frustration of working so hard for so little return. Perhaps one could read some positive side in this reference to past beatings: now that he is feeling more like a man than he has ever felt, he refrains from beating her and merely threatens her with a beating if she stands in his way. Still, the reader is troubled by the depiction of this woman, arguably representative of many of the men's wives, as being part of the world that tries to keep the black male from being a man, and by the depiction of the man, also representative of his peers, oppressing the woman as a means toward asserting his manhood.

Reminiscent of the earlier discussion of Jane Pittman's role in her husband's tragedy, Mary Helen Washington points out in her review of *A Gathering of Old Men* that the old men's wives "play out the stereotype of the saboteur of the male quest for danger and glory." Washington devotes about one-third of her review to delineating the problem with "the subordination of women in this novel." Within this discussion, Washington expresses concern about how, "[i]n order to prove manhood [in this novel], black men must stand up against white men, and the proof of their manhood is their ability to wrest respect from white men"—namely, the sheriff, to whom they tell their tales. Washington is troubled that "the arbiter of character is [thus] no longer the black community" in this novel ("House" 24).[19] This reading, however, does not take into consideration how Gaines undermines the power of both the guns and the white listeners in the course of the novel or the empowering catharsis the black men experience in telling their stories.

Gaines starts his deconstruction of the association of guns with power subtly, with the comic scene involving Billy Washington's futile attempts to shoot a rabbit. Less subtle, Gaines harshly satirizes Mapes's deputy from the moment he is first introduced by the reporter Lou Dimes, who observes the deputy's initial fright upon seeing so many armed black men and his attempt, then, to get his gun out of his car before approaching the "gathering." Knowing that a gun will do nothing to improve his deputy's ability to help him restore order—indeed, would probably aggravate the situation—Mapes stops him from arming himself. Further undercutting the role of the guns in the achievement of manhood, the old men are ultimately empowered by words, the stories they tell about the crimes committed against them and their families in the past. Their storytelling/confessions distract them from their focus on their guns, and they recognize at least subconsciously that being a man begins with owning up to their role in their abuse and oppression of themselves and their families. Perhaps, too, Gaines's killing off of Charlie Biggs in the end reflects some final judgment upon the association of killing and manhood. Charlie chooses to be the fifty-year-old man he should be when he stands up to Beau before killing him; after he shoots Beau, however, he regresses into a "boy" again and flees, leaving his uncle to take the blame. Thus, killing has accomplished nothing toward confirming his manhood.

Recognizing this faulty equation of being armed and being a man prepares for the tragic ending of the novel, which the few critics who have written about the novel have yet to recognize. For example, both Valerie Babb (123–24) and Frank Shelton ("Of" 27) argue that the events of the novel reveal impending change regarding the oppression of African-Americans in South Louisiana. A closer examination of the ending, however, reveals Gaines's subtle suggestion that, in spite of the proud, brave stand of the old men, very little is likely to change regarding race relations in the small Louisiana community depicted in the novel. This is not to say that Thadious M. Davis is mistaken regarding the several *individual* white characters' positive development in the course of the novel—namely the Cajuns Sheriff Mapes and Fix and Gil Boutan (143).[20] There is, however, no evidence in the novel that these individuals' experiences will have a significant effect on the overall race relations in the community. In fact, if anything, the author implies that an older social order has been restored when the aristocratic judge sentences the African-Americans and Cajuns on trial.

The restoration of order reminds the reader of the closing of a tragedy—with a twist: in contrast to such re-ordering in Shakespearean tragedy for example, the restoration of order at the end of this novel does not present an optimistic view of the future for the survivors.[21] Rather, as in the ironic restoration of "order" at the end of Mark Twain's *Tragedy of Pudd'nhead Wilson,* which also includes a trial scene, when Roxy's son is sold down the river and the true Driscoll son takes his place as the heir to the family's fortunes (or debts, rather), restoration of the "Old Order" in Gaines's novel also emphasizes the tragedy of continued ignorant prejudice.

In the judge's sentencing of the African-Americans and Cajuns involved in the gunfight that left two men dead, one from each group, power is implicitly returned to the southern aristocracy. It is interesting to note that in identifying the judge, Lou Dimes remarks that he is "very rich" (212), thus suggesting that he is a member of this aristocracy. The judge takes away the old men's guns. Given the earlier-established relationship between the men's guns and their renewed sense of "manhood," this is a symbolic castration, particularly uncomfortable in its reminder of the brutal way that so-called "justice" was exacted against African-Americans in the not-so-distant past of this novel. Indeed, a lynching is about what Luke Will had in mind when he led his group against the African-Americans, and lynchings of various sorts were what the old black men recalled to each other as they waited for the impending battle. Of course, the judge takes the Cajuns' guns away, too, and for them the actual punishment, rather than its symbolic suggestion, is harsh. Whereas most of the old men had not used their guns in a while, and some even had to borrow guns for their stand, taking away the Cajuns' guns "was like telling a Louisianian never to say Mardi Gras or Huey Long" (213), as Lou Dimes explains, apparently speaking of the Cajuns since the reader knows otherwise about the old men.

The reader might also note the irony of the punishment of the Cajuns, whose system of vigilante justice was initially instigated by the southern aristocracy who incited poor whites throughout the South to defend white supremacy by whatever measures "necessary," even though poor whites suffered themselves within the caste system. Indeed, with the same sentence for each group, the judge is implying his view that the two groups of men are the same, an opinion that, once grasped by the Cajuns, will inevitably inspire further resentment that will ultimately be directed not against their common oppressors but against their fellow oppressed. From the standpoint of the African-Americans, this sentence is far from a movement toward equal treatment regardless of race, for the judge is not distinguishing between the old men's protection of themselves and their loved ones and the Cajuns' planned lynching. Finally, although the two groups are given the same punishment, this is further discomforting to the reader who realizes that most of the firepower in the community is now in the hands of the aristocracy. "Order" has thus been restored within the community: guns are now only in the hands of the "right" people, the people with money, and the other two groups will soon be once again at each others' throats.

Further restoration of order is reflected in Candy's fate at the end of the novel, as will be discussed further later. Suffice it to say for now that it is implied that she will assume a more "proper role" for a woman than running a plantation, as she has done since her uncle Jack's "repudiation." Gaines seems to condone this return to a patriarchal gender hierarchy; there is no ironic tone suggesting that Gaines intends the characterization, development, and fate of Candy to be viewed as tragic. In contrast to the oppression and marginalization of all women, black and white, in *Go Down, Moses,* as well as to Gaines's depiction of black women as oppressed (and marginalized), one can conclude from the development of Candy Marshall in *A Gathering of Old Men* that Gaines views white women as sharing to some extent the power of (and thus the guilt of) the white man.[22] Furthermore, part of the black men's struggle for manhood seems to include putting this white woman in her place—that is, hierarchically beneath men, black as well as white.

As noted previously, Candy, a woman, is the current voice of authority on Marshall Plantation. Interestingly, Mathu has helped to raise this woman and, in fact, appears to love her.[23] Mathu's creator, however, seems to have a problem with Candy's position of authority, for just as he kills off Jane Pittman's great love (to some extent punishing Jane for preventing Joe from asserting his manhood), so, too, does he punish Candy. I am not referring here to Gaines ultimately taking away Candy's authority over the old men but to Candy's overall character development. First of all, Gaines names her "Candy," a derivative of "Candace," which is the formal name of Faulkner's perhaps most well-known female character, Caddy Compson, another strong-minded daughter of the decaying southern aristocracy in the New South and a woman doomed by her failure to uphold the values of her culture. Gaines emphasizes the connection between the two women by focusing in his description of Candy upon her clothes. The child Caddy Compson's dirty underpants obsessed her creator and her older brother; even Dilsey is upset by them. She has gotten her drawers dirty in the branch after taking off her dress, in front of her brothers and some black children, in order not to get it wet. Both the action of taking the dress off and the muddy drawers are of course signs foreshadowing her fate: she will lose her virginity before being married, and she will ultimately become a prostitute. Similarly, Candy Marshall's dress—or lack thereof (she wears pants)—bothers the sensibilities of the people around her. Upon first seeing Candy, the child Snookum (5), Miss Merle (16), and the old man Clatoo (50) all make some comment about her short hair and pants.

Like Caddy, too, Candy narrates no section of the novel, so the reader is never given her direct thoughts about the day's events. Of course, several of the other main characters are not given a voice in the novel (Mathu, Charlie, Mapes, Fix, and Gil, for example), and, recalling the earlier discussion of *The Autobiography of Miss Jane Pittman,* Candy is therefore grouped among the novel's *actors* rather than the *observers* on the periphery of the action, while Caddy is certainly kept outside of the action of her novel. In further contrast, this time to Candy's disadvantage, whereas the characters of the narrators of Faulkner's novel can be taken into consideration when evaluating their assessment of Caddy (as "a bitch," for example, according to Jason), the narrators of Gaines's novel are much more reliable, and thus the reader tends to credit their assessment of Candy and judge her more harshly than one judges Caddy. Indeed, she is not very likeable, not even in comparison with the other white characters of the novel: aside from Luke Will, one could argue that she is the least likeable significant white character.

Although, in contrast to Frank Laurent's niece in "Bloodline," Candy Marshall takes care of the people living on Marshall land, Gaines is hardly less harsh in his characterization of her. First of all, the seemingly liberal-minded Candy is another reminder of "Uncle Ike." In her case, she, like Frank Laurent, does not do *enough* to make up for past wrongs, as reflected, for example, in the description of Mathu's house, which does not appear to have been renovated to include such modern conveniences as indoor plumbing or air conditioning (and she considers Mathu as a father or uncle to her!). Furthermore, like Ike, she harbors the prejudices handed down to her, which surface by the end of the novel. Candy does not, like Ike and Jack, reject her inheritance, but neither does she "let 'her people' go." Her "protection" of Mathu is as patronizing as Jack's notion that the African-Americans living in the quarters on Marshall Plantation still "belong" to *anyone* at the time this novel is set (the 1970s). In addition, Candy reveals in her final speech that she is in part selfishly protecting Mathu in order to preserve her family's past, a heritage that includes the memory of at least one Marshall who fought to defend slavery. Trying to convince Mathu not to go with Mapes to turn himself in, she cries: "You knew the first. . . . You knew Grandpa Nate. The first Marshall. Remember from the war—the Civil War? . . . You knew them all. . . . Grew up with my grandpa. Raised my daddy. Raised me. I want you to help me with my own child one day. . . . I want you to hold his hand. Tell him about Grandpa. Tell him about the field. Tell him how the river looked before the cabins and wharves. No one else to tell him about these things but you" (176). In this plea, Candy echoes Faulkner's Dilsey—"I've seed de first en de last" (297)—reflecting, perhaps, that she would be more comfortable if Mathu would behave more like Dilsey: remain subservient and loyal to her and her family alone, serve the last as he did the first. Although her speech is moving, and in being so evokes the reader's sympathy for this young woman whose world is dropping out from under her, at the same time the reader does not wish to spare Candy this pain by having Mathu give in to her. Candy, rather, needs to face the selfishness of her desires. But, and a final point in illustrating Candy's unrelentingly negative character development, Candy is as unable to see—as Ike never saw how ineffectual his rejection of his inheritance was in rectifying race relations—that she is continuing to patronize the old men and that their stand to protect themselves will be more effective toward changing the situation that caused the conflict at hand than her method, which merely attempts to preserve the status quo. While Candy wants Marshall Plantation to stay the way it is, the way it has always been, the old men—Mathu included—are ready for change. Tragically, however, as the conclusions of both novels reveal, such change is still a long time in coming.

Candy's ultimate fate—the independent, nonconforming Candy appears to accept Lou's ultimatum to change or lose him—seems also to be a "punishment" in that it puts her back "in her rightful place" as a woman. Of course, she does need to learn that those gathered are indeed men and that they can therefore fight their own battles or at least make the decisions as to how their battles would be fought and then choose to invite her to participate if she so wished. But Gaines does not show her learning this lesson, and in comments to Mary Ellen Doyle in 1983, the author corroborates this view that Candy never gains insight. When Doyle remarks (mistakenly, as Gaines points out to her) that "Candy seems to undergo a learning process about Mathu and the people, to realize she can't be the old-time patron because they won't take her protection any more" and that in the end "[s]he understands why Mathu goes home from the courthouse with the other people," Gaines responds, "I really don't think she understands that. She knows she needs Lou for support; that's why she reaches for his hand when Mathu leaves. But Mathu's turned his back on her, and I don't think she knows why" ("MELUS" 171).

Indeed, Candy is the only character who maintains her vision of these men as helpless to the end, when she wants to bring Mathu home after the trial. Even Luke Will ultimately seems to recognize Charlie's manhood, as suggested by his final comments to Sharp—"Mapes ain't in charge no more . . . Charlie is. We got to deal with Charlie now"—and by his moving in closer to face Charlie man to man (206). And certainly Gaines shows Sheriff Mapes, another man, to be enlightened by the end of the day. Whereas Mapes eventually accepts his inability to control the situation at Marshall Plantation and ultimately agrees to call Charlie "Mr. Biggs," thereby displaying his recognition of Charlie's manhood, Candy has by this time become enraged by her loss of control over the men and threatened to kick them all off her land when they do not go along with her wishes.

The reader might here be again reminded of Ike McCaslin, whose racist outburst in "Delta Autumn" undermines his liberal voice earlier in "The Bear." Likewise is the reader of Gaines's novel troubled when Candy asserts her right as proprietor to join the old men in their meeting to decide what they are going to do next, once they learn that Fix is not going to show up. After Clatoo tells Candy, "we don't want you there this time," Rooster, the narrator of this section, remarks that "[n]obody talked to Candy like that—black or white—and especially not black" (173), revealing that though the African-Americans may recognize what she has done for them through the years, they are also cognizant of her inherent prejudices—as she herself revealed in her question to Mapes earlier in the day regarding his reason for beating the old men: "Because they're black and helpless, is that why you're picking on them?" (67). Ironically, she, too, ultimately tries to play on their "helplessness" by threatening them herself in response to being barred from their meeting: "Y'all can go on and listen to Clatoo if y'all want . . . [b]ut remember this—Clatoo got a little piece of land to go back to. Y'all don't have nothing but this. You listen to him now, and you won't even have this."[24] Mapes points out her hypocrisy: "Listen to *the savior* now. Do what she wants or you're out in the cold," he tells the old men, and he remarks to Candy, "you want to keep them slaves the rest of their lives" (174; emphasis added).[25] In Mapes's allusion to Candy's false Christ-like behavior, the reader is again reminded of Ike McCaslin, whose behavior also mocks, rather than mimics, Christ's. Ike gives away his worldly goods but still allows the Edmondses, who are the trustees of his land, and thus the "cursed" land itself to support him. He then becomes a carpenter, revealing his prideful association of himself with Christ. Nancy B. Sederberg points out the significant difference between Ike and Christ: "whereas Christ gave up carpentering to serve humanity and die young, Ike takes up carpentry, withdraws from humanity, and lives to be a useless old man" (90). Indeed, nothing he does "saves" anyone.[26] African-Americans in his community are no better off for his sacrifice. Indeed, in giving up his position in the community, he gives up the power with which he might have accomplished change. Michael Millgate illustrates this notion by pointing out "Roth's killing of the doe at the end" of "Delta Autumn," which "suggests . . . that Ike has failed to pass on to younger men [even] the practical training he received from Sam Fathers" (210–11), much less his moral codes of behavior toward people.

In contrast, Candy tries to assert, rather than repudiate, her power at this point, yet her actions also undermine her own wish to improve conditions for the African-Americans, for, as Sandra G. Shannon explains, "she . . . implies that the old men cannot take charge of their own lives." Shannon calls her "the embodiment of the well-meaning but ineffectual white liberal who, though essentially benevolent, is in fact a deterrent to the cause of freedom" (207). Candy believes that her duty as heiress of the plantation, complete with the same guilt that Ike regrets for the past sins of slavery and brutality against one group of people who have lived on this plantation, is to take care of these people, whom she has viewed as "her family's people," in the same way that her father would have had he lived. Mapes, then, had spoken accurately when he remarked to Lou upon the latter's arrival, "She still thinks she can do as her paw and the rest of them did fifty years ago" (74)—that is, decide for themselves the guilty party and whether and what kind of punishment is deserved. Candy merely wants to replace a patriarchy with a matriarchy (for the time being—until the son she mentioned earlier grows up), but as Valerie Babb implies, her "maternalism" is no better than her father's and grandfather's paternal rule (125).

Furthermore, Candy can no longer protect "her people," not only because they do not want her to but also because she has also lost control of the Cajuns. Ironically, oftentimes when members of the planter class decided that a crime had been committed by an African-American, they would call upon members of the poorer class (of white men) to do their dirty work for them: patrollers were paid to return runaways; overseers were instructed to whip slaves; poor whites were encouraged to fight for the planters' cause in the Civil War; and later, "poor white trash" did much of the lynching for the Ku Klux Klan, which was formed, ostensibly, to protect the southern lady, mainly the *planters'* mothers, wives, and daughters. Recalling this "excuse" for the vigilante violence of the KKK, Gaines has Luke Will remark before heading with his gang over to Marshall, "Somebody got to do it [settle the score for Beau's death] 'fore it gets out of hand. . . . Next thing you know, they'll be raping the women" (149). Tee Jack reports on Luke Will and his gang's reputation for being involved in the kind of activity described above:

> On the side, they did other little jobs to keep things running smoothly in the parish. Like turning over nigger school buses, throwing a few snakes into nigger churches during prayer meetings, or running niggers out of what used to be all-white motels and restaurants. Some people say they got paid as much for these little civic duties as they did at the dirt plant. But nobody knew where the money was coming from, or if they did know, they knew better than to go blabbing about it. (159)

Given the reader's knowledge of who in this community would have extra money to pay for these "civic duties," it is not difficult to guess who, again, orders such actions as Tee Jack describes to be taken and then pays for the service. Candy is thus confronted with another legacy of guilt that has gotten out of hand: at any moment she expects Fix and his family to arrive to enact the same kind of vigilante justice on the one whom they believe to have killed Beau, as well as anyone who gets in their way. Candy's authority will not stand up in the face of Fix any better than it does before the old men.

Valerie Babb discusses this transition of power in Louisiana, which Gaines depicts throughout his fiction, and compares it to Faulkner's development of a similar conflict in post–Civil War Mississippi: "The casting of the Cajuns as both an element of negative change and the representatives of a new southern order replacing the old reflects the influence of . . . Faulkner. The unstoppable Cajuns bear a strong resemblance to Faulkner's Snopes clan, and present in almost all Gaines's works, they are a breed apart, looked upon by blacks as usurpers and by the decaying southern gentility as rapacious arrivistes" (12). In "Barn Burning," Faulkner introduces the Snopes family and, while contrasting the despicable Abner Snopes with his sensitive, not yet corrupted son Sarty, is also careful to show that Abner is not much more despicable than the southern aristocracy whom Sarty at first admires. Abner's lesson to Sarty regarding the similarity between the current system of sharecropping and the past system of slavery is accurate, and it reminds the reader that Major de Spain is living comfortably from the backbreaking service of other people in a house built with the sweat of slaves. Comparably,

Gaines deals in *Of Love and Dust* with the similarity between the former slave system and Marcus serving his time for killing a man by working on Marshall Hebert's plantation. Although, as this comparison between plotlines by Faulkner and Gaines shows, these two groups of workers have so much in common—or *because of* the poverty and oppression that assault both groups—they are still the bitterest of enemies. Again, their animosity can be traced back to their treatment at the hands of the original landowners. In *A Gathering of Old Men,* Tucker, another of the old men, recalls in his narrative on the day of the stand: "After the plantation was dying out, the Marshalls dosed out the land for sharecropping, giving the best land to the Cajuns, and giving us the worst. . . . Here, our own black people had been working this land a hundred years for the Marshall plantation, but when it come to share-cropping, now they give the best land to the Cajuns, who had never set foot on the land before" (94). It is understandable that resentment would arise against those who, the African-Americans felt, had usurped their land—the Cajuns.

Gaines again alludes to the similar social and economic positions of the Cajuns and African-Americans in *A Gathering of Old Men* during the discussion of the limited access that both groups presently have to the river. When Corrine complains about current restrictions (during one of the few times one of the black women gathered around Mathu's house speaks up), Mapes points out that neither can he fish or hunt "like [he] used to," nor can Fix, who, Mapes says, is "as much victim of these times as you are. That's why he's back on that bayou now, because they took that river from him, too" (108). But the shrinking of the amount of land on the river is particularly poignant to the African-Americans, representing as it does another limitation enforced upon them. In Gaines's novel, as Valerie Babb explains, the "shrinking river space masks the severity of the larger social confinement of blacks within a dichotomized environment. The place in which these characters find themselves sequesters them through laws and customs that vigilantly regulate most aspects of their lives. Every decision—from where they may fish, to where they may work, to whom they may love—is decided for them or influenced by larger white society" (119). The significance of the "shrinking river" can be further illustrated by comparing it to the shrinking woods in *Go Down, Moses.* In Faulkner's book, the diminished forest represents the invasion and corruption of civilization, which, as the book shows, has formerly supported slavery and continues to support a caste system. Indeed, these oppressed people labored to build but do not share the prosperity of the cities and towns that have replaced the woods. Although Gaines reveals that there are groups of white people who are also discriminated against, he reminds the reader, too, that these groups have participated in the discrimination—and violence—against the African-Americans. Rejecting Mapes's remarks about Fix's similar confinement to the bayou, Beulah, another of the women gathered with the men, points out his participation in corrupting the river where the African-Americans had fished and washed; she recalls to Mapes and the others Fix's role in the drowning of black children nearly fifty years before.

Soon after Beulah's remarks, Gaines introduces Fix himself, who fails to live up to the reader's expectations. He is an old man, holding his grandchild and mourning his deceased son, the father of this baby, and he is unable to inspire his other sons to avenge their brother as he would have done as a younger man. And he will not go to Marshall without his sons. However, even if Fix has mellowed in his old age, that does not mean that the two groups will make their peace with each other, for the reader also meets Luke Will at this time, and Luke Will is ready, borrowing from KKK terminology, to "ride." Luke Will's hatred of African-Americans and the anger that Gil Boutan, brother of the deceased, feels toward Candy Marshall illustrate the consequences of the caste system in Louisiana. When the former plantation owners privileged the Cajuns over the African-Americans, they thereby reinforced the Old Southern caste system. Within such a system, the Cajuns could view themselves as superior to the African-Americans, but also they felt inferior to the aristocrats. They resented the aristocrats' demeaning glance, and, in order to maintain their own sense of self, they turned a similar eye on those below them on the social ladder. Revealing the aristocrats' snobbery, the Cajuns' resentment of the aristocrat, and the consequential prejudice against those below the Cajuns on the social ladder, in their brief encounter in the novel, Gil lashes out at Candy: "You never liked any of us. Looking at us as if we're a breed below you. But we're not, Candy. We're all made of the same bone, the same blood, *the same skin*. Your folks had a break, mine didn't, that's all" (122; emphasis added). Significantly, Candy ignores him unpityingly, even though he has just lost his brother.

Although Gil is right about the social hierarchy, he has apparently failed to realize that the Cajuns currently dominate the community: Candy's family, representative of the community's Old Southern aristocrats, is losing its power over both groups, the Cajuns and the African-Americans, as events of that day signify (though the judge's sentence, as noted, seems to restore the Old Order—temporarily at least). Candy stands alone as the voice of the aristocrats, her aunt and uncle each having escaped into a drunken stupor, while Fix and his family and friends are gathered together much like the old men on Marshall.[27]

It is important to notice Gil's ambivalence toward the African-Americans in the scene with his father. Joseph Griffin believes that Gil "has been sensitized to the evils of black victimization by whites as a result of his own experience as a Cajun living in a society dominated by a higher white class" ("Creole" 42). In contrast, Suzanne Jones associates Gil's enlightenment regarding race relations to his university experience: "While Gil's father thinks that an education at LSU should reinforce the old Southern code, Gaines suggests otherwise. An education opens Gil's mind to the racial discrimination and oppression in the rural community in which he grew up" (49). Daniel White believes that Gil's experience as half of the "Salt and Pepper" team has taught him "that cooperation [with the African-American] leads to success" and credits him with realizing "that his partnership with Cal has meaning beyond the playing field." He argues that Gil "wants to set an example of racial cooperation for the South and the entire country to see" (177). Apparently, these critics view Gil as acting for the common good when he stands up to his father against avenging his brother's death in the manner of his father's generation (that is, vigilante revenge). These critics do not, however, account for all of Gil's explanations to his father for his desire that they leave justice up to Mapes and a court of law: "Papa, I want to be an All-American at LSU. I have a good chance. . . . I couldn't make All-American, Papa, if I was involved in something against the law. . . . Even if our name was involved, the Yankee press would destroy me" (138). Gil's motivation, it seems, is as selfish as it is humanistic: he wants to be an All-American. His brother Jean, similarly, worries about his patronage: "My butcher shop is in Bayonne," he tells his father (140). This is not to say that Gil is not partly motivated by a desire to improve race relations or that Jean is not to be commended for his desire not to participate in his father's kind of justice, but the reader should recognize that both are also motivated by their own self-interests. Change of heart regarding prejudices that have been fostered for generations does not so easily come about, as further supported by Gil's coldness toward Cal upon learning that his brother has been killed by a black man and his earlier-quoted remarks to Candy about being "the same" because of their common "skin."

Suzanne Jones suggests that "Gaines has [Gil] behave this way to depict the complexity and difficulty of overcoming the racism one has been raised with. This scene shows how stereotypes can lie latent but potent in one's consciousness." But, Jones adds, "[i]n the discussion that follows among Gil and his family, Gaines makes it clear that he is no longer the bigoted young man his father raised him to be" (48). Indeed, following Gil's explanation regarding how avenging Beau's death in the traditional way would ruin his chances of being an All-American, "Christ-like," as his father mockingly responds to his words, he takes on himself the burden of the history between his family and the African-Americans: "I'm sorry, Papa, . . . [f]or what happened. . . . For Beau. For us all. That you think I've gone against you, I'm sorry. I'm sorry for those old men at Marshall. Yes, Papa, I'm sorry for them, too." Fix responds, "'A regular Christ.' . . . He made the sign of the cross. 'A regular Christ in our midst. . . . Feels sorry for the entire world'" (145). Although Jones perceives that "Gaines expects the reader to take this comparison more seriously, as a new vision of Southern white working-class manhood" (49),[28] Gil's "stand" is ultimately as ineffectual as the old men's, for little will change in the community as a result of his refusal to "ride." He thus joins the earlier list of Gaines's ineffective Christ figures, comparable most to the other white Christ figure, Tee Bob in *Autobiography of Miss Jane Pittman*.

While Fix does decide to go along with his surviving sons' wishes and leave it to the law to convict and punish his deceased son's killer, a group of Cajuns led by the bloodthirsty Luke Will set out for Marshall Plantation to avenge the murder immediately and in their own way and against the wishes of Candy Marshall, representative of the aristocrats. Just before their arrival at Marshall, Mathu's godson, Charlie Biggs, shows up to admit to being the one who shot Beau, and, culminating in his narrative of how he came to do so, the terror that seized him afterward, and his attempt to run away like a "boy," a definite sense of catharsis is accomplished as a result of the old men's stand. Even Mapes, who first walks into the novel the epitome of the southern sheriff stereotype, develops to the point of recognizing the heroism of these *men,* in particular, of *Mr.* Biggs. Each man has confessed his past guilt for not fighting for or even standing by a family member when he or she was killed or raped, and then Charlie, whose killing of Beau was ultimately vengeance for all of those crimes, dies for all of these "sins" of omission.[29] In addition, Charlie pays for the life he took with his own, and in that way the novel continues to follow in the tradition of tragedies (Hamlet's death makes up for his killing the "innocent" Polonius). Still, such compliance with the form calls our attention back to the issue of the restoration of order at the end of a traditional tragedy and the lack of a viable order to which the survivors can return at the end of this novel. Perhaps to emphasize this lack, Gaines suddenly switches genre from tragedy to comedy in the tone of the novel's ending.

In deciding to employ the element of tragedy of the restoration of the social order after the deaths of those involved in the disruption—which traditionally reflects the restoration of moral order—Gaines was faced with a dilemma: the original social order of the South was immoral, for slavery and racism were at its core. In his introduction to his interview with Gaines, John O'Brien contrasts Gaines's vision of the southern past with Faulkner's: "unlike Faulkner, who was enamored of the past because its strict social order at least offered man stability, Gaines in his fiction labors to escape the immobile past and to view change as necessary in sustaining life" (25). O'Brien continues, "Whereas in Faulkner the characters are usually trying to upset the natural order of things by stopping time or making it move backwards, Gaines, with some remorse about the loveliness of certain qualities of the past, reaches toward a future that can potentially shape the world in a more humane way" (26).

As Faulkner had shown in his fiction, descendents of the southern aristocracy had to be reminded every now and then—as Quentin is in *Absalom, Absalom!*—of the falseness of the paradisiacal vision of the Old South. In his novel, Gaines, too, has characters—surprisingly, *black* characters—longing for a past that probably never was. In one of the old men's ruminations upon the past, Johnny Paul asks:

> "Y'all remember how it used to be? . . . When they wasn't no weeds. . . .
> Remember how they used to sit out there on the garry [gallery]—Mama, Papa,
> Aunt Clara, Aunt Sarah, Unc Moon, Aunt Spoodle, Aunt Thread. . . . Everybody had flowers in the yard. But nobody had four-o'clocks like Jack Toussaint.
> . . . But they ain't here no more. And how come? 'Cause Jack ain't here no more.
> He's back there under them trees [lying in the graveyard] with all the rest."
> (90–92)

Ironically, Johnny Paul evokes a pastoral image of the quarters, and, indeed, he goes on to complain that tractors—that is, technology—ruined the idyll.[30] The reader, however, wonders at this memory, wonders what time period Johnny Paul is talking about when African-Americans lived so contentedly, peacefully, and even prosperously in this area. Given the gathered men's reported age and the date the novel is set, Johnny Paul is talking about the turn of the century. Perhaps there was a brief period in between the turbulent Reconstruction era and the disruptive industrialism of the early twentieth century (which brought the tractors he complains about), but it could only have been a moment of time.[31] Still, the time that has passed since then seems to have either resulted in romanticization of the actual past, more often typical of the *white* southerner looking back, or exaggeration of a short period of time when Johnny Paul's people were happy—or appeared to be. One should also realize that Johnny Paul would have been a child at the time he is talking about, and children are not always aware of their parents' hardships.[32] Thus, Johnny Paul is standing up for a past that probably wasn't. This point is made, not to undermine the men's brave stand but rather to show how it would inevitably fail to accomplish all they hoped for. The tragic structure of the novel emphasizes that there is no viable, just order to which things can return after the requisite purging deaths.

Still, many of the characters do achieve a catharsis by the end of Gaines's novel, in spite of the lack of a satisfying resolution to the tragedy; and yet, two of the central characters (both significantly white) seem to regress, rather than develop, even after witnessing the events: besides Candy Marshall, her boyfriend, Lou Dimes. First of all, noting Lou's actual name—Louis Alfred Dimoulin—as it appears above "aka Lou Dimes" at the heading of his first section, one realizes that Lou is probably of Cajun heritage. Therefore, Lou has, by changing his name, rejected his heritage, not unlike Jack Marshall. The reader should therefore wonder, has he chosen an easier name to remember because of ambitions regarding his job as a reporter, or does his name change have anything to do with his relationship with a woman of the original landowning class? The latter possibility would undermine any positive reading of the relationship between this apparently Cajun man and aristocratic woman as suggestive of a breakdown in the caste system. Furthermore, once the significance of Lou's final narrative is grasped, the reader realizes that, like Candy, Lou cannot so easily break away from his familial ties, for although his reporting of the day's activities may begin sympathetically and insightfully in his earlier sections, it ends quite differently.[33]

A second disturbing development related to Lou's false liberalism is his treatment of Candy toward the end of the novel. Significantly, he had not, upon first seeing Candy, noted her pants or short hair, seeming to suggest that her "unladylike" appearance does not disturb him as it does so many others. At the end of the day, however, detecting Candy's moment of weakness when the old men assert their independence of her, Lou takes the opportunity to invert the hierarchy of power within their relationship, thereby suggesting that he has been troubled after all by Candy's independence and strength, though earlier his thoughts had suggested that it was these qualities that attracted him to her in the first place. So, after the men bar Candy from their meeting, Lou gives her an ultimatum. Perhaps he feels suddenly impotent by comparison after watching these much older men refuse to be abused any longer by people like Beau and Fix Boutan, intimidated by Mapes, or used by Candy and the other Marshalls. But the reader should be troubled by the possibility of Lou's association of his relationship with Candy with the motivation for the men's stand, supported as it is by Lou's discomfort when Mapes suggests to him that he is not "much of a man" if he cannot control "his" woman (74).

One is reminded here of how, for a few of the old men as well, their manhood is somehow wrapped up in dominating women. Reminiscent of Mat's recollection of having beaten his wife in the past out of his frustration over his impotence in the face of the white man, Lou, too, turns on Candy when he perceives his own impotence by comparison to these old black men and in the eyes of Mapes. Contradictorily, he prefaces his terms for their relationship to continue by pointing out to Candy that she must let Mathu "live [his life] his own way" but then tells her she must tell him "where [their] relation is going" or he "won't be coming back here anymore" (184). Apparently, he is no longer willing to let Candy "live *her* life *her* own way." Although it is reasonable to want to know whether or not he has a future with Candy, one wonders if Lou is suddenly, again, with the example of the old men before him, embarrassed by Candy's having been the controlling force in their relationship. At this point, Lou still appears to be an authoritative voice in the novel, a position that will be undermined later. His behavior here, however, does not seem to be intended to subvert this role, though it does prepare for the subversion, at least for those readers who do not approve of his treatment of Candy toward the end of the novel.

Although Candy's immediate response to being given an ultimatum is to slap Lou, at the end of the novel she seems to accept his conditions for their continued relationship, for the last thing Lou reports is that, after Mathu tells Candy he will ride home "with Clatoo and the rest of the people . . . we watched them all pile in. Candy waved goodbye to them. I felt her other hand against me, searching for my hand; then I felt her squeezing my fingers" (214). Probably feeling deserted by her surrogate father, she takes Mathu's earlier advice, "It's time you went to him [Lou]," and turns to Lou, who can give her the child she spoke of to Mathu on the day of the stand, a son to whom Mathu could tell stories of the past and thereby, hopefully, bring back that past, which Candy now feels slipping from her (177). In this final scene, then, as well as in her final speech at Mathu's house, when she talks about passing Marshall on to a son, it becomes apparent that she, too, gives in to the patriarchal order. The independent woman who has taken charge of both her father's plantation and her personal relationship up to this point in her life, indeed who, according to Lou, had never needed anybody (58), seems to agree to accept the more traditional role of subservient wife and mother.

The implication after the trial, when Candy leaves the courthouse hand-in-hand with Lou, that a marriage will soon take place (and that the shrew has therefore been tamed) seems to reinforce the comedic structure of the book, since comedies traditionally end with a marriage ceremony or the assurance of an impending marriage. Like a tragicomedy, then, this novel "employs a plot suitable to tragedy but ends happily, like a comedy" (to use the definition of tragicomedy in C. Hugh Holman and William Harmon's *A Handbook to Literature* [508]). But analyzing the text with the aid of some Faulknerian criticism reveals otherwise: that the novel is finally a tragedy. In his reading of the opening story of *Go Down, Moses,* Kiyoyuki Ono notes a problem he has with the term *tragicomedy,* seeing it as "misleading . . . because the comic element flows through the story ["Was"] and is transformed as it is filtered through Ike's consciousness, finally turning into utter tragedy" (157). Ono explains that "[f]or Ike the events in 'Was' are neither comic nor tragicomic but deeply tragic, all the more stunning now because they first appeared comical" (163). Faulkner himself once remarked on the association between comedy and tragedy: "there's not too fine a distinction between humor and tragedy. . . . [T]ragedy is in a way walking a tightrope between the ridiculous—between the bizarre and the terrible" (Gwynn and Blotner 39). An interesting point of contrast that might be noted here between *A Gathering of Old Men* and *Go Down, Moses* is how in both novels comedy and tragedy are combined, though *Go Down, Moses* begins with a humorous tone, becomes progressively more and more serious, and ends with a funeral, whereas Gaines's novel begins and ends with a comic tone, various tragedies are reported within, and at the end there is the suggestion that a wedding will soon take place. Lou and Candy will "live happily ever after," and, as will be examined later, the courtroom audience is laughing. Of course Gaines is employing these comic elements ironically, leaving his reader uncomfortable with both the marriage and the courtroom humor, the latter of which also leaves the reader further disappointed in Lou, whose insightfulness on the day of the "gathering" seems to have disappeared in his last section.

In Lou's final section, which closes the novel (thereby giving a white man the last word, another suggestion of the restored Old Order), the novel's tone suddenly lightens as Lou describes the trial.[34] In spite of the tragic death of Charlie Biggs at the end of the day on which the majority of the novel takes place, which occurs at the end of the section immediately before Lou's closing to the novel, Lou describes the courtroom scene comedically.[35] Significant to this change of tone, the point of view for this ending is that of a white man, and this white man's perception of the old men did not apparently change as a result of what he witnessed that fateful day (or at least, he has quickly reverted to a more traditional attitude toward the old men). David C. Estes describes Lou Dimes's failure of insight as reflected in this section: "[H]is own words prove him to be an unwitting fool. Despite his sympathy for racial tolerance, he still does not comprehend the revolutionary implications of the events he witnessed in the quarters. Dimes relates the final episode from a condescending point of view, reducing all of the characters to simplistic, humorous figures" ("Gaines's" 246).[36]

Indeed, these old men, who had achieved such dignity with their own voices throughout the novel, appear in the courtroom as comic figures reminiscent of plantation fiction. For example, Lou evokes an image of the minstrel figure performing before an audience when he describes how

> every now and then one of the old black fellows [note that they are not individuals to Lou, even after spending such an incredible day with them], arm in sling, or forehead bandaged, knowing he was in the public eye, would go just a little overboard describing what had happened. Besides, he would use all nicknames for his compatriots—Clabber, Dirty Red, Coot, Chimley, Rooster. This would bring the court to laughing, especially the news people, who took the whole thing as something astonishing but not serious. (212)

Like McCaslin Edmonds, who tells the story of Turl and Tennie in the comic opening story of *Go Down, Moses,* leaving out any comment on the tragedy of these two slaves' situation of only getting to see each other every six months or so when Turl "escapes" the McCaslin homestead to go to Tennie at the Beauchamp's plantation, Lou leaves out any reference to the recent tragedy he has witnessed in his narrative of the trial. On the one hand, the reader can take this point of view into account when reflecting upon the difference between Lou's version of how the events of the day in question are told in court and the old men's earlier narratives of the crimes committed against them and members of their families living on and around Marshall Plantation through the years. On the other hand, Lou's voice is still significant for its role in developing Gaines's ultimate vision of future effects of this important day upon the lives of the people who have suffered passively for so long and who finally took a stand against their tormentors. This vision is not a comic one regardless of the ending's tone. Indeed, the tone suggests that very little will change regarding how these old black men are viewed by the white man.[37] The voice that closes the novel is a white man's, and this white man finds the events unfolding in front of him ultimately amusing. Furthermore, Lou has been a voice of reason throughout the novel and is a newspaper reporter—that is, someone who is in a position to be of help to these African-Americans. Instead, he transforms the story into a comedy, culminating in his description of Mapes's testimony, which, according to Lou, received the biggest laugh of all.

When Mapes is asked where he was during the "shoot-out," at first he refuses to answer, but when threatened with contempt charges,

> [he] answered, but only for the D.A. to hear. The D.A. demanded that he speak loud enough so that the entire court could hear him. Mapes looked at the D.A. with those hard gray eyes, as if he were about to spring out of that chair and punch him, but instead said: "The whole fight, I was sitting on my ass in the middle of the walk. Luke Will shot me, and I was sitting on my ass in the middle of the walk. Now, is that loud enough?" And he got up from the witness chair and returned to the other seat. That's when everyone in the courtroom started laughing, including Judge Reynolds. (213)

Besides illustrating again the comic atmosphere at the trial, this anecdote reveals Mapes's humiliation. The reader wonders, then, which memory will burn brighter in Mapes's recollection: the moment when he recognized the manhood of the old men or the moment when he was humiliated before the town and the press. Furthermore, what has the courtroom audience learned except that this is what happens to a white man who chooses to defend black men against members of his own race? He is reduced to a court jester.

Lou's focusing in this last section of the novel only on the humorous moments of the trial, with no reference to the tragedy of what has preceded, then, is not promising. If he has missed or can forget so quickly the tragedy of the earlier events, then there is not much hope for other white members of the courtroom audience grasping it. Recalling the parallel made earlier between this novel as tragedy and Twain's *Tragedy of Pudd'nhead Wilson,* one can see how Lou Dimes, like Twain's David Wilson, ultimately deserves the label "pudd'nhead." Just as Twain's Pudd'nhead does not address before the court the role that the institution of slavery plays in the tragic murder of Judge Driscoll by a man who would have been the judge's slave had his true identity been known but only focuses his attention on unraveling for his audience the mystery of the identity of the murderer, Lou Dimes fails in his overview of the trial to comment upon how the continued support of the caste system in Louisiana contributed to the tragic events of the fateful day.

As suggested earlier with Jules Raynard of *The Autobiography of Miss Jane Pittman,* the reader is not inclined to view a white man as *the* authoritative voice of a contemporary novel by an African-American so should not be surprised to find that Lou ultimately falls short of any such expectations inspired by the earlier sections narrated by him. Lou's failure at the end of the novel is reminiscent of Faulkner's Gavin Stevens's behavior in the title story of *Go Down, Moses,* as well as in *Intruder in the Dust.*[38] As summed up by Edmond Volpe: "Gavin Stevens, with his doctorate from Heidelberg, is continually surprised and continually exasperated by the Negroes, treating them as children, as inferiors. He is kind and gentle and generous, but he can feel no true rapport with them" (250). Recognizing the parallel between Gavin and Lou confirms the position already effectively argued by Noel Polk that Gavin, too, should not be considered as the final authoritative voice of *Intruder in the Dust* or *Go Down, Moses* (133–35, 150).[39] According to Malcolm Cowley, Faulkner himself denied that Gavin spoke for his creator, though he did call Gavin "the best type of liberal Southerner" (Cowley 110), perhaps subtly suggesting that Gavin's behavior and attitude toward African-Americans is the most one can expect of someone raised in the South. Gaines seems to agree with such a view, as reflected in his development of Lou and Candy.

From the author's perspective, then, the humor in this last section seems not intended for the purpose of "comic relief" after the tragedy of Charlie's death. As Walter Kerr argues in his book *Tragedy and Comedy*, "Comedy is not a relief, it is the rest of the bitter truth" (28); and the bitter truth in this novel is the fortitude of racism and the caste system. The comic tone, then, is as ironic as the tragic-plot restoration of the order of the Old South. With this tragicomic combination, Gaines suggests that a woman maintaining power and independence and a white man understanding the black man's plight are as impossible as the improvement of race relations in that community any time soon. Therefore, David Estes is mistakenly optimistic about the effect of the stand on "the racial hierarchy," which he perceives to be "completely reversed" by the end of the novel. Although Estes is not wrong about "the revolution in [the old] men's character, their change from comic Sambos to complex humans" ("Gaines's" 247), it would be more accurate to recognize that it is in their characters and their self-perceptions where change will be felt, for the white people around them have not developed as significantly as they have.[40] The white characters in the novel continue to prefer to see the old men as "comic Sambos." Paradoxically, the employment of comic elements reinforces the sense of the tragedy of the novel. Furthermore, Gaines seems to be suggesting that there is little else we can do but laugh at the irony of the whole situation. One might consider here Ralph Ellison's remarks upon African-American humor: "[T]here is no one who sees the absurd anymore [*sic*] than the person who has lived closest to it"—that is African-Americans, who "could not escape the absurdity . . . of the racial arrangements within the society. . . . [T]here was no escape from it: we couldn't go to Africa; we couldn't go anywhere. . . . We couldn't escape, so we developed a style of humor which recognized the basic artificiality, the irrationality, of the social arrangement" ("American" 153–54). Ellison confirms that some such situations "are painful, but it is precisely because they are so painful that they have to be comic" ("American" 155).

chapter 3

The Sterile New South

Hurston's
Contemporaneous
Deconstruction of
the Paradigm

I had a design. To accomplish it I should require
money, a house, a plantation, slaves, a family—
incidentally of course, a wife. I set out to acquire these.

Faulkner, *Absalom, Absalom!*

"So de white man throw down de load and tell de
nigger man tuh pick it up. He pick it up because he
have to, but he don't tote it. He hand it to his
womenfolks. De nigger woman is de mule uh de
world so fur as Ah can see."

Hurston, *Their Eyes Were Watching God*

Before turning to female contemporaries of Ernest Gaines who continue to deconstruct Faulkner's perception of the South, it is interesting to look back at how a female contemporary of Faulkner, Zora Neale Hurston, concurrently explored the same issues he explored in her novel *Their Eyes Were Watching God* (1937), which appeared within a year of the publication of *Absalom, Absalom!* (1936). As reflected in these two novels, the two writers' similar conclusions regarding the sterilizing influence upon the New South of the legacy of the Old South reminds the reader that Faulkner's vision is not so much skewed as it is narrowly focused upon the consequences *to the empowered* of this sterility. While Faulkner examined the failure of Thomas Sutpen's design from several perspectives, Hurston provides a perspective still missing—that of a woman (for Rosa Coldfield's perspective is diluted by that of the predominating males'—including her creator's—undermining denigration of her).

The number of parallels that can be found between characters in *Absalom, Absalom!* and *Their Eyes Were Watching God* anticipates the discussions to follow in the next two chapters of Toni Morrison's recasting of *Absalom, Absalom!* in *Song of Solomon* and of the numerous echoes of that same Faulkner novel in Lee Smith's *Oral History.* Like Morrison, Hurston shows how, as the emancipated black man struggled for equal rights, he modeled himself upon the example of his empowered oppressor. And like Smith, Hurston examines the consequences of Sutpen-like designs—whether they originate from black man or white—upon women. Unlike Morrison and Smith, however, it is not likely that Hurston was responding to *Faulkner*—certainly she was not responding to *Absalom, Absalom!* in particular, there having not been enough time after the publication of this Faulkner novel to have influenced Hurston's writing of her own. According to Hurston biographer Valerie Boyd, *Their Eyes Were Watching God* was written in seven weeks and completed December 19, 1936 (Boyd 294–95). Since Hurston had been in Haiti since September, and *Absalom, Absalom!* was published October 26, 1936 (Gresset 47), it is highly unlikely that Hurston had read Faulkner's novel before writing her own. Thus, it appears that, like her contemporary, Hurston perceived early on how the sterile vision of the Old South would continue to affect the New South. But whereas Faulkner's novel suggests that this sterile paradigm is held onto because of its romantic appeal to the next generation, who must come to recognize their naïve idealizing of the past in order to break the pattern, Hurston suggests that the model is followed because it is all that is known and because it is the seemingly successful model of the empowered, who remained in power even after the South's fall and into the post-Reconstruction, modern era she and Faulkner were living in.

It bears noting again the brief interval between the publication of *Absalom, Absalom!* and of *Their Eyes Were Watching God,* which makes all the more remarkable the corresponding characters and plots of these two books:[1] Thomas Sutpen and Joe Starks, who try to become what they perceive to be the successful white male but instead become caricatures who point out the flaws in their role models; Henry Sutpen and Janie Starks, who are largely responsible for leaving Sutpen's design and Starks's Eatonville without progeny; Charles Bon and Tea Cake Woods, who die violently, leaving "seeds" of questionable value; Quentin Compson and Pheoby Watson, the listeners to the tales who are supposed to pass the stories on to others; and Clytie and Mrs. Turner, who advocate white supremacy in spite of their own black blood. The common denominator of all these characters (with the dubious exception of Charles Bon) is sterility, caused by the mistake of trying to build a New South on the same foundations as the old—ironically, a mistake being made in these two novels by the same groups of people who were victimized by the Old South: the poor white and the black.

.   .   .

Thomas Sutpen's sharecropper heritage is comparable to Joe Starks's position as a black man in Georgia who had "[b]een workin' for white folks all his life" (27). Both saved their money in order to improve their status, and then moved into towns where they were complete strangers. Early on in their plans, their attitudes reveal that they do not disapprove of the system that relegates people into certain positions; they merely wish to move up on the social ladder so that they are no longer in the oppressed positions themselves. This notion is supported in Sutpen's case by the fact that he owned slaves. Proof can be found for its applicability to Starks in the explanation about his plans: "He had always wanted to be a big voice, but de white folks had all de sayso where he come from and everywhere else, exceptin' dis place that colored folks was buildin' themselves. *Dat was right too.* De man dat built things oughta boss it. Let colored folks build things too if dey wants to crow over somethin'" (27; emphasis added). Clearly, Starks does not lament the condition of the black man in the South in this passage, for a hierarchal world means that he has a chance to govern others. As Toni Flores explains, "Jody Starks, realizing that this world is arranged in hierarchies and that he doesn't want to be at the bottom, decides that he had better become the master, or at least as much a master as any black man can be. He accepts dominance as a way of life. He has to control everybody who might possibly be brought under his control, not only Janie, but all the people of Eatonville" (56). Like Sutpen, as Starks improves his situation he emulates his perception of the successful white man of the South.[2] Upon his first entrance into the novel, Starks is compared to a white man: "He was a seal-brown color but he acted like Mr. Washburn" (26). Both Sutpen and Starks buy land and build large white plantation homes that distinguish them from others of their own backgrounds. Their neighbors' responses to these mansions are comparably negative: a mixture of grudging respect and animosity.

While building his fortune in the West Indies, Sutpen marries a land-owner's daughter, though he deserts her when he realizes that she has black blood. Then he marries a young woman from an old southern family, whose background is therefore unquestionable, as Rosa Coldfield explains, "[A]ll he would need would be Ellen's and our father's names on a wedding license (or on any other patent of respectability) that people could look at and read . . . because our father knew who his father was in Tennessee and who his grand-father had been in Virginia and our neighbors and the people we lived among knew that we knew" (11). Similarly, Janie's appeal to Starks apparently has much to do with her white features, for she first attracts his attention with her long, black hair, which is later shown to distinguish her from the other black women in the novel. One can infer from the narration that it is Janie's hair, more so than the noise the pump makes, that stops Starks: "Janie ran to the pump and jerked the handle hard while she pumped. It made a loud noise and also made her heavy hair fall down. So he stopped and looked hard" (26).[3] In Hurston's novel, it is Janie, not Starks, who abandons her first marriage. Still, it is Starks, the more worldly of the two, who does not hesi-tate to marry her in spite of the fact that she is already married. Thus, he too, sees himself as being above the law—much as Thomas Sutpen does, first, when he repudiates his first wife by merely tearing up their marriage license and, later, when he marries another woman.

Starks describes Janie in terms of the stereotypical southern lady:[4] "A pretty doll-baby lak you is made to sit on de front porch and rock and fan yo'self and eat p'taters dat other folks plant just special for you." He notes that she "aint never knowed what it was to be treated lak a lady" (28), a state-ment that also reveals another similarity between Starks's and Sutpen's choices for wives, for, as summed up by Shreve, Sutpen chose a wife "from the lesser baronage whose principality was so far decayed that there would be no risk of his wife bringing him for dowry delusions of grandeur before he should be equipped for it" (145).

Apparently, Janie recognizes intuitively the potential problem with Starks's perception of her as a *lady* rather than a woman, for she "pulled back a long time because he did not represent sun-up and pollen and blooming trees" (28)—that is, sexual satisfaction. In Janie's hesitation, one can find an-other parallel between Starks and Sutpen, for it is Rosa Coldfield's realization that Sutpen desired her only as a means to an end that causes her to leave Sutpen's Hundred after his propositionlike proposal. Janie, on the other hand, eventually goes along with Starks because, though he did not offer the passion she longs for, he did represent "far horizon . . . change and chance" (28). These possibilities are some of the same reasons that Rosa Coldfield had considered Sutpen's offer of marriage (prior to his sexual proposition). And just as Janie soon forgets her intuition that Starks "did not represent sun-up and pollen and blooming trees" and heads out to meet him, thinking, "[f]rom now on until death she was going to have flower dust and spring-time sprinkled over everything. A bee for her bloom" (31), Miss Rosa reveals to Quentin that, in spite of her former view of Sutpen as a "demon," she was willing to marry him because "*there is a metabolism of the spirit as well as of the entrails, in which the stored accumulations of long time burn, generate, create and break some maidenhead of the ravening meat.*" Like Janie, she feels within herself the stirring of desires that she had long given up any hope of ever fulfilling, and "*lost all the shibboleth erupting of cannot, will not, never will in one red instant's fierce obliteration*" (132; Faulkner's italics). But when Sutpen proposes that they engage in sexual relations immediately to make certain they can produce a son before bonding themselves to each other in marriage, she leaves his house devastated and horrified by her own foolishness in thinking that he had *desired her.*

Sutpen views women only as an avenue to respectability and a means of reproduction. Similarly, Janie is a reflection of Starks's success. As Jennifer Jordan notes, her "sole purpose is to serve as an ornament and symbol of her husband's social status" (108). Starks regards Janie as a show-doll to put on his porch, not as a woman for his bed. Indeed, Janie's answer to his question, "[H]ow yuh lak bein' Mrs. Mayor?," indicates the absence of sex in their marriage: she asks in turn, "Don' yuh think it keeps us in uh kinda strain? . . . It keeps us in some way we ain't natural wid one 'nother. You're always talkin' and fixin' things" (43). Their sexual relationship is further hampered by Starks's treatment of Janie: as he wears her individuality down, we are told that "[t]he spirit of the marriage left the bedroom and took to living in the parlor. It was there to shake hands whenever company came to visit, but it never went back inside the bedroom again" (67). Susan Willis describes Janie's oppression as Starks's wife: "As a wife of the town's leading citizen, Janie is denied self, voice, and sexuality. . . . [S]he has, in her bourgeois life, become a domestic pet" (*Specifying* 47–48).

Willis continues her description of Janie's value to Starks: "Janie's sexuality enters into a system of display and exchange. . . . [S]he is essentially a commodity. . . .[H]er sexuality is lifted out of the economics of production. . . . Thus, appearance takes precedence over strength" (*Specifying* 50). Willis would probably agree that Starks is apparently not interested in Janie as a means of reproduction. The failure of this perfect mayor's wife to provide him with a child to inherit his big house, his big name, or his big voice does not seem to concern Starks, for the subject of children never comes up. Starks's ego thus surpasses Sutpen's in that he is not anxious about future generations. The reason for his indifference can be inferred from his recurrent expression of exasperation, "I god," which Sigrid King notes, "sounds as though he is naming himself God. Indeed, as King points out, "Once he has bought the town, Joe sets himself up as God; he creates new buildings and names them and brings light to Eatonville in the form of the lamp post" (689). And as the God of this town, Starks perceives himself to be immortal, a notion that is reinforced when, from his deathbed, he tells Janie, "Don't tell me Ah got tuh die. . . . Ah ain't used tuh thinkin' 'bout it" (82).

Although part of Sutpen's design includes having a son to inherit his dynasty, his choice between his two sons, of which one is "suitable" for his plans, results in sterility, too, for Henry, like Janie, will bequeath him no heirs. Furthermore, Henry, who lacks the drop of black blood that makes Charles Bon *un*suitable, inherits Sutpen's prejudices as well as his house, the same prejudices that infect and destroy Sutpen's garden.[5] Henry kills Charles Bon because, as Quentin determines, though Henry would have allowed an incestuous marriage between Bon and his sister Judith, he could not tolerate miscegenation. When he found out that Bon had black blood, he killed his half-brother to prevent the marriage. So Judith is left "a widow without ever having been a bride" (10) and childless. And Henry must flee his home to avoid being tried for his crime, leaving Sutpen without a son to carry his name, "*since now (if the son [Henry] still lived) his name would be different . . . and whatever dragon's outcropping of Sutpen blood the son might sow on the body of whatever strange woman would therefore carry on the tradition . . . under another name*" (148; Faulkner's italics).

While Henry is gone, Sutpen is struck down by Wash Jones, another victim of his design. Ironically, Wash is just the type of man for whom Sutpen supposedly built his house. Sutpen's plans originated after he had suffered the humiliation of being turned away at the front door of a plantation and told to go around to the back. He wanted to build a home where another like him "would never again need to stand on the outside of a white door and knock at it" so that he, "that whatever nameless stranger, could shut that door himself forever behind him on all that he had ever known" (210). And yet, rather than welcome Wash and Wash's granddaughter Milly as victims of the oppression of his own past, Sutpen treats them like animals.[6] When Milly gives birth to a girl rather than to a son who could replace Henry, Sutpen rejects her; and Wash, who had, until that moment, looked up to Sutpen for his accomplishments, kills him to avenge the insult. Sutpen has rejected the opportunity to show the compassion that inspired his design, and the consequence is his own destruction.

Similarly, Starks dies as a result of oppressing one to whom he had promised the benefits of his endeavors. This oppression culminates as, like Sutpen, Starks begins to feel the signs of aging. Seeing only himself, aged by contrast, when he looks at Janie, he strikes out at her unjustly about her age: "You ain't no young girl to be gettin' all insulted 'bout yo' looks. . . . You'se uh ole woman" (75). This scene is comparable to the scene in which Sutpen propositions Rosa "when he realised that . . . he was now past sixty and that possibly he could get but one more son, had at best but one more son in his loins, as the old cannon might know when it has just one more shot in its corporeality" (224). Like Starks, Sutpen is counting on Rosa's realization that, to use Starks's words, she "ain't no young courtin' gal." Faulkner's imagery for Sutpen's manhood here is as paradoxically light in tone and devastating in truth as Janie's rejoinder to Starks's comments about her age: "When you pull down yo' britches, you look lak de change uh life" (75). Janie has finally reached the point where she will take no more of Starks's verbal abuse, and she retaliates, cutting him down with words as successfully as Wash cut Sutpen down with a scythe.

At Starks's deathbed, then, Janie remarks on his lack of compassion for others: "Have yo' way all yo' life, trample and mash down and then die ruther than tuh let yo'self heah about it. . . . And now you got tuh die tuh find out dat you got tuh pacify somebody besides yo'self if you wants any love and any sympathy in dis world. You ain't tried tuh pacify *nobody* but yo'self. Too busy listening to yo' own big voice" (82). Cyrena Pondrom's interpretation of this speech calls to mind the inherent problem in Sutpen's design, which Sutpen never understood: "Human error has consequences; necessity . . . is inexorable. . . . Janie here explains to [Starks]—as he dies—what it means to be a human being, not simply a big voice." Just as General Compson says Sutpen's problem was "innocence," from which one can infer that the general is somewhat excusing Sutpen's treatment of others, Pondrom observes how readers critical of Janie's insensitivity toward her dying husband seem to believe that "human beings who do not understand what it means to be human until the moment of their deaths do not in any conventional social sense 'deserve' the calamity which befalls them" (192). But there is a problem with excusing an *adult* on the basis of "innocence"/ignorance about some moral issues. Furthermore, much like Sutpen's "design" for Sutpen's Hundred (in spite of what he says he wanted to provide for poor whites like himself, since that is not what he did), Starks's plan for Eatonville was founded upon self-interest alone. He is not inspired by the freedom Eatonville offers to the black men and women who live there; he has not chosen to live there to raise a family where they are free from white oppression. He has settled in Eatonville simply because it is the only place where he believes that he, a black man, could be a "big voice." Once he is no longer that "big voice," he quits and dies.

.   .   .

Like Henry, then, Janie is left with Starks's legacy. Jerome E. Thornton addresses implicitly the sterility of what Starks gave—and thus left—to Janie: "only the dead reality of material goods." Thornton remarks on the loneliness of Janie's position, from which she is separated from "the *life* that traditionally thrives" in Eatonville: "the art of storytelling, a good game of cards or checkers, or simply sitting on the front porch at dusk, gossiping with her neighbors" (265; emphasis added). I would disagree to some extent with Thompson's assessment of the vitality of Eatonville. Though these activities seem vibrant in comparison to Janie's existence, none of them involve children. Indeed, a reference to raising children is found only once in the novel, when Mrs. Robbins comes into Starks's store to get meat for her children (68). This one of only three appearances of children in Eatonville alludes to children in need. Furthermore, the other two references are, significantly, both connected to deaths: after the death of the mule, we are told of "children visiting his bleaching bones now and then in the spirit of adventure" (58); and the description of Starks's funeral procession includes "babies riding astride of brothers' and sisters' backs" (84). Implicit in this scarcity of children in Eatonville is a communal sterility that extends into Janie's life.

Janie and Henry are offered salvation from the negative influence of Starks and Sutpen by their relationships with Tea Cake Woods and Charles

Bon, respectively. Tea Cake offers Janie the chance to get away from Starks's shadow, for even the suitors who called on her—after a respectable amount of time had passed after Starks's death—continued to treat her as Mrs. Joe Starks: "They were all so respectful and stuff with her, that she might have been the Empress of Japan. They felt that it was not fitting to mention desire to the widow of Joseph Starks. You spoke of honor and respect" (88). In direct contrast to Starks, as well as to these men, Tea Cake "looked like the love thoughts of women," and Janie felt that "[h]e could be a bee to a blossom" (101). He also awakens other feelings in her besides desire—for example, "Doubt. All the fears that circumstance could provide and the heart feel, attacked her on every side. *This was a new sensation for her,* but no less excruciating" (103; emphasis added). Her ability to feel again suggests that with Tea Cake she is learning how to live again; indeed, we are told that "her soul crawled out from its hiding place" (122). Furthermore, early in their relationship, Tea Cake is seen "making flower beds in Janie's yard and seeding the garden for her" (105), which suggests that he is bringing an end to the sterility of Starks's home.

By killing his half-brother, Henry rejects the chance to stand up against his father. This is not to say, however, that Bon could have been an instrument of salvation for everyone. He has been a victim of prejudice ever since his father left him and his mother, and yet he still uses Judith as a pawn to force his father to recognize him, not unlike the way that his father uses people, particularly women. Just like Sutpen, too, Bon is willing to abandon the wife and son he already has and marry Judith. Also like his father, ironically, he justifies his actions to Henry (who does not at this point know that Bon, too, is black) with the words, "this woman, this child, are niggers" (94). Sutpen has apparently influenced his black son as surely as he did his white son.

Similarly, Tea Cake is not so unlike Joe Starks as many critics have tended to view him. First of all, his treatment of Janie distinguishes her from the other women of their race whom they meet in their travels. As Jennifer Jordan points out, "When they arrive on the muck, Tea Cake carefully picks the only place that has a bathtub and makes sure that the work in the bean fields never gets oppressive." And Jordan reminds us later that "he does not 'let her go with him to the field. He wanted her to get her rest.'" Jordan notes, too, that "Tea Cake insists that she live on what he makes" (111). Also, on the subject of Janie's money, SallyAnn Ferguson argues that Tea Cake "squanders some of [Starks's] money to prove that he could earn it back in his own way

. . . and so be as much a man economically as Starks was" (193). In Mary Katherine Wainwright's explanation for Tea Cake's actions here, one can see another comparison between him and Starks: she argues that Tea Cake "takes Janie's money after they run away together in order to bolster his own ego by throwing a big party for his friends" (283). This is much the same reason that Starks took Janie to Eatonville with him—to show off in front of his new neighbors. Notable about this episode, as well, is Tea Cake's explanation for his disappearance, in which he, like Starks, isolates Janie by perceiving her as a lady: "Befo' us got married Ah made up mah mind not tuh let you see no commonness in me. When Ah git mad habits on, Ah'd go off and keep it out yo' sight. 'Taint mah notion tuh drag *you* down wid me" (119; Hurston's italics). Most telling of all, just as Starks made Janie wrap up her hair when he noticed another man's pleasure in it, jealousy prompts Tea Cake to beat Janie: "When Mrs. Turner's brother came and she brought him over to be introduced, Tea Cake had a brainstorm. Before the week was over he had whipped Janie. Not because her behavior justified his jealousy, but it relieved that awful fear inside him. Being able to whip her reassured him in possession. No brutal beating at all. He just slapped her around a bit to show he was boss" (140). Wainwright notes how this "belief in his right and duty to abuse Janie physically" mars their ideal relationship (238). Cyrena Pondrom connects Tea Cake's jealousy to his acceptance of the superiority of white men (which also compares him to Starks): "He does not trust the superior attractiveness of his own handsome blackness and believes that a man who looks white will take Janie from him" (195). According to Pondrom, it is this same implicit perception of the white man's superiority that ultimately results in Tea Cake's death, for upon the approach of the hurricane, he and his friends "place their trust—erroneously—in the example of the white boss" rather than follow the Indians (194). Finally, as Tea Cake suffers from the effects of the dog bite, his raving echoes Starks's words to Janie on the day he died. Both men blame Janie for their sufferings. Starks berates Janie for ridiculing him in public, reminding her, "Much as Ah done fuh yuh" (81). Similarly, Tea Cake says, "Ah done went through everything tuh be good tuh you and it hurt me tuh mah heart tuh be ill treated lak Ah is" (174).[7] After recognizing these similarities between Tea Cake and Starks, one no longer finds Tea Cake acting so much out of character when during his rabid ravings he attacks Janie.

The question of how much Janie grows during her time with Tea Cake has been a popular issue in the criticism of this novel. Janie's assessment of her feelings for Tea Cake, which comes early in their relationship, may provide a clue to the answer to this question. As Janie gazes at the sleeping Tea Cake the same night of his disappearance in Jacksonville, she "felt a *self-crushing* love" (122; emphasis added). The self-destructive nature of her feelings for him apparent in this phrase is confirmed by "the *helpless* way she hung on him" (140; emphasis added) after he beat her so unjustly and by the risk she took after shooting him by catching him as he fell: she "leaped forward as he crashed forward in her arms. She was trying to hover him as he closed his teeth in the flesh of her forearm." In spite of this bite from a man infected with rabies, which Dr. Simmons has warned her could mean her own death, she then "thanked him wordlessly for giving her the chance for loving *service*" (175; emphasis added).[8] At the moment of shooting Tea Cake, "she was just a scared human being fighting for its life"; but Janie did not have enough practice at being so "humanly" self-interested, so, upon seeing him fall, she immediately reverted to "her sacrificing self" and risked her life to serve him one last time (175). These instances do not reveal a woman much altered from the passivity she exhibited in her relationship with Starks. Thus, although Janie has come out of her white house far enough to feel again the emotions that remind her that she is alive, she does so only with Tea Cake as a crutch. Apparently, then, Starks's influence upon her continues after his death. She continues to play the role of "*lady* in distress," the position in which Starks first found her on Killicks's farm. Tea Cake merely replaces Starks as her "knight in shining armor."

Soon after Tea Cake dies—and after she has had to stand trial for killing him—Janie returns to the security of Eatonville, a place where, like Starks and Tea Cake, the people think of and treat her as special. In this view of her return, one can find another comparison with Henry Sutpen, who also returns to the home he had refuted. This comparison also supports the view of Janie as not much changed and still under the influence of Starks. On the other hand, like Henry, Janie may have come home to *die* (not to resume her death-in-life existence in Eatonville), for, as Robert Haas has argued most convincingly, "Janie, clearly and in Hurston's deliberate intent, is living with the possibility that she may be dying, that after a few weeks, or months, or years of apparent good health she may suddenly succumb in the same terrible way as did Tea Cake" (206).[9] Indeed, there is no indication in the novel that she has been treated for rabies, although, as Haas has enumerated, there are many references (made by the doctor who treats Janie) to the danger of her being infected by Tea Cake (Haas 211–14). The serious nature of rabies treatment, described by Haas as "brutal (beginning with cautery of the wound with fuming nitric acid) and long (about three weeks of daily injections)" (209), makes it an experience that could not just be left out of the narration. Pat Carr and Lou-Ann Crouther remind us that "Hurston is a careful and conscious writer, and since she deliberately omits any further mention of the rabies serum, . . . it is safe to assume the shots were not administered" (55).[10] Therefore, one can conclude that Janie could eventually die from the bite that she received from Tea Cake.[11] Hurston was not silent on that point. As Carr and Crouther point out, by the time that Janie is acquitted by the white jury, "the bite on the arm has been mentioned three times, for Hurston does not want us to miss the fact that Janie has been bitten by the rabid Tea Cake" (54).

Janie's return home to die (at least believing she may soon die) can then be viewed, paradoxically or ironically, more positively than the notion of her returning to a place where she is safe from accusations of murder. As Robert Haas asks, "Who wishes to see the mighty hero, home at last, now tending the yard and feeding the cat?" He argues, "If Janie cannot be sure how much longer she will live, her behavior is no longer an act of weakness, but rather an act of strength, a courageous facing up and preparing for contingency. By giving her story and her voice to her friend she is making her testament, and passing on to [Pheoby] the meaning and worth of her life" (223), which, I would add, might lead Pheoby to learn from her experiences and thus expand her own horizons. According to Jennifer Jordan, Janie's words to Pheoby, "you got tuh *go* there tuh *know* there" (183), are a rejection of "the notion that art or the telling of the story can transform people's lives" (Jordan 115), but perhaps Janie tells Pheoby her story to motivate her friend to "find out about livin' fuh [herself]" (183).

Once Pheoby has gone home, taking Janie's story with her, Janie locks up her house and goes upstairs, perhaps to await death, much as Henry Sutpen did upon his return to Sutpen's Hundred. The significance of the last passage in the novel seems clearer when read with this notion that Janie is preparing to die from rabies: "Here was peace. She pulled in her horizon like a great fish-net. Pulled it from around the waist of the world and draped it over her shoulder. So much of life in its meshes! She called in her soul to come and see" (184).[12] She has not come home to live with her memories of Tea Cake in the big white house that Joe Starks built for her, as many critics argue to Janie's discredit, but rather to die there, after telling her story to someone who might pass it on. Thus, her return is not a regression to an easier, if not fulfilling, life. It is a means of seeing that her story—if not she herself—survives, so that others like her might learn from her life and survive as well.

Besides her story, Janie brings back with her some seeds "that Tea Cake had brought to plant. The planting never got done because he had been waiting for the right time of the moon when his sickness overtook him."[13] The reference to the moon alludes to a woman's menstrual cycle, reminding the reader that Janie was not so revitalized by Tea Cake as to make her fertile. "The seeds reminded Janie of Tea Cake more than anything else because he was always planting things" (182). And yet the seeds he planted inside of her apparently fell upon the barren ground, for, though there is no mention of practicing any method of birth control, Janie has still not conceived, in spite of her very active sexual relationship with Tea Cake. This fact points once again to the notion that Janie is not able to shake the sterility of Eatonville, even after her escape with Tea Cake. Joe Starks is dead, but his influence is apparently no less powerful than Thomas Sutpen's continued to be after his death. The sterility of Sutpen's design seems to leave Henry impotent, and Charles Bon's "seed" is ultimately as dubious as Tea Cake's, for his son is self-destructive. Charles Etienne St. Valery Bon ultimately takes revenge on the Sutpen family by further "tainting" his grandfather's design: he marries "a coal black and ape-like woman" (166), and together they produce an idiot son who is left, like Tea Cake's seeds, to fend for himself when the last of his "family" is killed in the burning house.

Barbara Christian gives a brief explanation for Janie's childlessness: "Hurston . . . was not able to render her wonderful heroine . . . as a mother, since it would severely limit her mobility" (225). Elizabeth Schultz also connects Janie's childlessness with Hurston's plans for her when she remarks that "[f]or Janie . . . work is not always a matter of necessity, and motherhood seems never a consideration; therefore Hurston can speculate on the black woman at work without the pressure of poverty and children" (321). Both of these explanations of *why* Hurston chose to keep Janie childless do not, however, explain *how* Janie remains childless. Many critics interpret Janie's infamous insult as referring to Starks's impotence. In his article on naming in the novel, Sigrid King believes that "Hurston hints at sexual problems that develop between the pair because of their separate beds and Janie's eventual verbal 'castration' of Joe in the store." He points out that "[t]he word *stark* is often used as a synonym for barren" and thus implies that the responsibility for the couple's childlessness lies with Starks. But that wouldn't explain why Janie does not get pregnant by one of her other two husbands. Were all three of her sexual partners sterile (an unlikely coincidence), or was she? Given the novel's time frame, successful birth control is too incredible an answer.

Elizabeth Fox-Genovese also questions (though does not provide an answer for) the *significance* of Janie's childlessness: "At the novel's close . . . [Janie] is returning home to other black women alone—and childless. . . . Is [Hurston] inviting us to understand black women like herself as . . . incapable of reproduction?" (175). I would answer that Hurston implies instead that the cause of Janie's apparent barrenness is, rather, a symbolic consequence of the sterility of the Old Southern paradigm, which Joe Starks and, before him, Janie's grandmother, in marrying her off to the "successful" Killicks rather than to the young man who had awakened Janie's passionate nature, inadvertently supported.[14]

.   .   .

At the end of both novels, the people of Jefferson and Eatonville are left with the stories, if not the children, of Thomas Sutpen and Joe Starks. Significantly, although the two chosen listeners, Quentin and Pheoby, hear the stories from more than one source, never is the source Sutpen or Starks. Quentin is introduced to the story by Rosa Coldfield, one of the victims of Sutpen's design. He fills in the gaps in Rosa's version with accounts from his father and grandfather, members of the aristocracy that never did accept Sutpen in spite of his achieved wealth and status. Quentin has seen for himself the living ghost of Henry Sutpen. And when Quentin and his roommate, Shreve, imagine between themselves the events that no one is sure about, their sympathies clearly lie with Henry and Charles Bon, who also suffered under the oppression of Thomas Sutpen. Similarly, Pheoby hears much of the story from Janie, who was oppressed by Starks's ideas of her role as his wife and the first lady of Eatonville. When the third-person narrator takes over, part of the reason is so that events can be told that Pheoby would already know about and Janie would not have to tell her. Pheoby would have witnessed these events as one of the townspeople whom Starks lorded over, as well as from the perspective of a woman, a sex Starks believed to be inferior by nature.[15] Events she did not witness, one can be pretty sure, she would not have heard about from Starks, again given his opinion of women. Thus, she would have heard these stories from other citizens of the town, all of whom, like herself and Janie, were oppressed by Starks.

In the course of hearing the tales told to them, Quentin and Pheoby begin to view Henry and Janie as heroic figures whom they would like to emulate. If one considers *Absalom, Absalom!* in light of the events of Faulkner's earlier novel in which Quentin plays a central role, *The Sound and the Fury,* one can perceive how Quentin would admire Henry for his apparent ability to commit incest with his sister, vicariously, through Charles Bon, and for his ability to kill for his sister's honor. In *The Sound and the Fury,* Quentin failed at his attempts to commit both acts: he could not commit incest with Caddy, and he could not kill Caddy's lover, Dalton Ames. Evidence that Quentin makes the connection between himself and Henry and views Henry as having acted more heroically than he was capable of can be found in the two times that Quentin is unable to listen to the storytellers past the point of Henry shooting Bon: at the end of chapter 5, when Miss Rosa describes the events leading up to Henry standing up to Judith and saying, "*Now you cant* [sic] *marry him. . . . Because he's dead. . . . I killed him*" (139; Faulkner's italics); and when, as he starts out to pick up Miss Rosa to take her to Sutpen's Hundred, he admits that "he had not been listening [to his father] since he had something which he still was unable to pass: . . . that gaunt tragic dramatic self-hypnotized youthful face [Henry] . . . [and] the sister facing him across the wedding dress which she was not to use, . . . the two of them slashing at one another with . . . words" (142). When Quentin meets Henry, however, the emaciated, dying man explodes Quentin's heroic image of him, and Quentin recognizes the irremediable effects that Sutpen's design has had on his son. At the close of *Their Eyes Were Watching God,* Pheoby tells Janie: "Ah ain't satisfied wid mahself no mo.' Ah means tuh make Sam take me fishin' wid him after this" (183). However, Pheoby does not yet realize that Janie may be dying. It is left to the reader, then, to wonder what will happen, if Janie dies, to Pheoby's new plans to stand up to her oppressors. Will Pheoby continue to aspire to be more like Janie, or will she come to the conclusion that the consequences—which might include risking her life—are too severe? Janie's eventual death is bound to have its effects on the "seeds" she plants in Pheoby's mind. In addition, just as no one will be there to plant or water Tea Cake's seeds, Janie will not be there to verify Pheoby's tale of a strong woman's battle against her oppressors. Critics have disagreed about how the novel's ending affects the reader's response to Janie's story of rising above the oppression in her life; if one deconstructs the novel based on the possibility that Janie has come home to die, it becomes the story of a black woman who *tried* to rise above her oppression.

.   .   .

One final noteworthy comparison in the two novels is between Hurston's Mrs. Turner and Faulkner's Clytie, both being mulattos who believe in white supremacy. Mrs. Turner tells Janie, "We oughta lighten up da race" and "Ah can't stand black niggers. . . . Ah hates tuh see folks lak me and you mixed up wid 'em. Us oughta class off" (138). The narrator explains Mrs. Turner's self-incriminating attitude thus:

> Anyone who looked more white folkish than herself was better than she was in her criteria, therefore it was right that they should be cruel to her at times, just as she was cruel to those more negroid than herself in direct ratio to their negroness. . . . Once having set up her idols and built altars to them it was inevitable that she should accept any inconsistency and cruelty from her deity as all good worshippers do from theirs. (138)

Thus, Mrs. Turner "felt honored by Janie's acquaintance" since Janie was "more white folkish than herself" (138). Similarly, when Charles Bon's octoroon mistress visits his grave, Clytie treats her with the same respect that she shows to Judith: "Clytie, who did that fetching and carrying as Judith made her, who must have perceived whether Judith told her or not that it was another negro whom she served, yet who served the negress." She even goes out of her way to serve the octoroon's son, Charles Etienne Saint-Valery Bon. Like Mr. Turner, Clytie apparently believes lighter-skinned blacks should "class off," for when she found this boy playing with a neighborhood black boy she "cursed the negro child out of sight with level and deadly violence and sent him [Charles Etienne] back to the house" (158). In her treatment of the son of Charles Bon, it is also evident that, like Mrs. Turner, Clytie is ashamed of black skin: when she bathes him she "scrub[s] at him with repressed fury as if she were trying to wash the smooth faint olive tinge from his skin" (161). And finally, as Mrs. Turner regards Janie as superior to her, Clytie places this child, who is less black than herself, on a cot, while she sleeps on a pallet on the floor. (In doing so she is also keeping the boy in a position below the only other resident in the house, the "pure" white Judith, who sleeps in a bed.) Just as Mrs. Turner's ideas about hierarchies are reminiscent of Starks's ideas, Clytie inherits her prejudices from her father, Thomas Sutpen, as surely as did Henry and Charles Bon.

Upon recognizing the numerous parallels between the two novels, one might wonder again at the coincidence of two such different writers as a white man from Mississippi and a black woman from Florida publishing such similar novels within a year of each other. The explanation seems to be simply the fact that they are both Southern Renascence writers, for both follow this tradition in southern literature of retelling the story of the fall in terms of the history of the South. In much nineteenth-century southern literature, the Old South was depicted as a prelapsarian Eden. As mentioned in chapter 1, with the Southern Renascence, the focus turned to the fall (the sin of slavery) and its consequences (the Civil War). In this analogy, the New South would be equivalent to the fallen world, a world where ideals are unattainable. And yet Faulkner's Thomas Sutpen and Hurston's Joe Starks strive to build an ideal home in this fallen world. Such an attempt, as these two novels show through the aforementioned sterility, inevitably fails.

The failure of Thomas Sutpen's design is most apparent when his home becomes a funeral pyre for his son Henry, the heir to what is left of his "design" by then, and his daughter Clytie, another product of the sin that brought around its destruction. The failure of Eatonville is much more subtly indicated within the text of *Their Eyes Were Watching God.* An intertextual reading of these two novels provides the reader with the material to fill in the silences in Hurston's novel that reflect the failure of Joe Starks's plans. Although neither Hurston's third-person narrator nor her protagonist in her part of the narration of her story explains certain absences in the novel—Janie's childlessness, the almost complete lack of children in Eatonville, and the treatment for the bite Janie received from the rabid Tea Cake—these absences are significant to the theme of the sterility of false ideals. By reading *Their Eyes Were Watching God* intertextually with *Absalom, Absalom!*, one can perceive the relationship between these absences and this theme. And once the common theme of sterility is recognized, we realize the significance of Janie's childlessness in spite of the narrator's lack of explanation regarding this factor in her tale. Starks's treatment of Janie results in the absence of heirs to his big name, much as Sutpen's treatment of his family did. Furthermore, Janie is a reflection of the sterility of Eatonville, for the only children alluded to in this town are either hungry or associated with death. Janie's pending death, then, foreshadows the end of Eatonville, just as Henry Sut-pen's death means the end of Sutpen's design.

Although in an ideal world there is no need for fruition (there being no death), the ideals of Thomas Sutpen and Joe Starks are false ones, for they are not ideal for everyone involved. All of the other characters are in oppressed positions within the ideal. But Sutpen and Starks are so caught up in their aspirations that they are blind to the effects that their treatment of others will have on their goals—the same effects that slavery had on the Old South. Sutpen denied his first son and then produced one who better fit his "de-sign"—the one he had by his white wife, who came from an Old Southern family. But this was his weaker son, and though Henry did kill Charles Bon, he left no heirs when he died, as Bon did. Similarly, Starks took Janie with him to Eatonville because her appearance fit his idea of the perfect wife, and then he treated her like a possession rather than like a woman. Consequently, he, too, died childless. At the end of *Absalom, Absalom!*, the plantation house and Thomas Sutpen's white son, Henry, and black daughter, Clytie, which are all that is left of his "design" by then, are destroyed in a fire. Surviving the fire is Charles Bon's retarded, black grandson. And yet that idiot boy is not much less than what will survive Joe Starks's town, given the few references to children in the novel. Eatonville appears to be as sterile as Sutpen's design. Perhaps, though, Hurston hoped that women like Pheoby would be inspired by Janie's story to head out to the muck to create a new, more fruitful para-digm.

chapter 4

Resounding Truths in *Absalom, Absalom!* and *Song of Solomon*

Exploring
Epistemology
with Faulkner
and Morrison

He just wanted to beat a path away from his parents' past, which was also their present and which was threatening to become his present as well.

Morrison, *Song of Solomon*

[T]o me, no man is himself, he is the sum of his past. There is no such thing really as was because the past is. It is part of every man, every woman, and every moment. All of his and her ancestry, background, is all a part of himself and herself at any moment.

Faulkner, in Gwynn and Blotner, *Faulkner in the University*

Sounding very much like the homesick Ernest Gaines, who could not find his people or his home in the books he read during his adolescence in California, Toni Morrison has said repeatedly that one reason she began writing was to tell stories that had not yet been told.[1] In an interview with Nellie McKay, Morrison explained, "I am not *like* Faulkner. . . . I do not have objections to being compared to such extraordinarily gifted and facile writers, but it does leave me sort of hanging there when I know that my effort is to be *like* something that has probably only been fully expressed perhaps in music, or in some other culture-gen that survives almost in isolation because the community manages to hold on to it" (McKay 152). And in another interview, Morrison remarked to Claudia Tate, "I wrote *Sula* and *The Bluest Eye*

because they were books I had wanted to read. No one had written them yet, so I wrote them" (Tate 161). The number of studies pairing Morrison's work with Faulkner's might suggest that someone *had* been writing these stories before Morrison, but Faulkner's version is just one perspective on their common history: they are both writing about the *legacy* of the Old South. As Patrick O'Donnell argues about the echoes of Faulkner in *Beloved,* "Morrison calls upon Faulkner not as an act of homage or in order to overturn him—to declare influence and independence—but because her writing is linked up with his, his story part of her story" ("Remarking" 326). And yet, addressing the 1985 Faulkner and Yoknapatawpha conference attendees, Morrison said that she doesn't "find strong connections between [her] work and Faulkner's" but suggested that she admires his perspective for its "courage. . . . He had a gaze that was different . . . a refusal-to-look-away approach in his writing that I found admirable." Still, she told this same audience, "I am not sure that [Faulkner] had any effect on my work. I am typical, I think, of all writers who are convinced that they are wholly original and that if they recognized an influence they would abandon it as quickly as possible" ("Faulkner" 296–97).

John N. Duvall begins his examination of Toni Morrison's 1977 novel *Song of Solomon* and Faulkner's *Go Down, Moses* remarking on the "risk" of pairing these two authors since doing so "conjures up vivid images of domination in our American past"; therefore, he reassures his audience that he has no hierarchy in mind when considering the novels together: "in positing an intertextual relation between *Song of Solomon* and *Go Down, Moses,* I am not granting the latter any privilege as master text" ("Doe" 95).[2] Nor am *I,* in pairing various works with works by one of the leading figures in the "established" canon of American literature, doing so for the purpose of showing whether and, if so, how well these writers' works stand up next to this longtime critically established writer's canon. I am more concerned in this study with the dialogic relationships between the works of such writers as Toni Morrison and various Faulknerian texts. I am, as already indicated, not the first to pair Morrison with Faulkner, and in the time since I began this chapter as a paper for the 1995 South Atlantic Modern Language Association conference, the body of criticism looking at the two writers together has grown from a couple of articles to three books: Philip Weinstein's 1996 *What Else But Love?: The Ordeal of Race in Faulkner and Morrison*; a 1997 collection of essays, edited by Carol A. Kolmerten, Stephen M. Ross, and Judith Bryant

Wittenberg, entitled *Unflinching Gaze: Morrison and Faulkner Re-Envisioned*; and Patricia McKee's 1999 *Producing American Races: Henry James, William Faulkner, Toni Morrison*. In the closing essay of *Unflinching Gaze*, Patrick O'Donnell summarizes what seem to be the intentions of the majority of critics writing on these two writers:

> we should construct Morrison's relation to Faulkner as one of a differential intertextuality wherein Morrison is neither simply "influenced" by Faulkner, nor simply troping upon or trumping the black and white figures to be found in his fiction. In her fiction, Morrison's project is quite different: there, she is intent upon inscribing black figures in other terms than those that apply to the writers she discusses in *Playing in the Dark*; she is committed in her novels to bringing those figures to the historical and narrative foreground. ("Faulkner" 227)

Certainly it is Faulkner's vision that is more often deconstructed via my intertextual readings, thereby illuminating, for example, the marginalization of his African-American characters. Andrea Dimino suggests in her essay on Faulkner and Morrison that Morrison's "revisiting of [Faulkner's] works in much of her own fiction could be seen as a tribute to his imagination and artistry and to his engagement with important cultural issues. But this revisiting also represents a continuing combat with Faulkner, a foregrounding of certain elements in his work in order to reveal problematic cultural affiliations and values" (33). Dimino shows in her essay how "[i]n general, the 'self' for Faulkner is a white male, and women and black people are seen as the other; their voices are muted or erased" and therefore, "[w]hen a contemporary writer like Morrison, as part of her own cultural project, actually expands and alters for her characters the voice of the Faulknerian other, she could be seen as continuing a process begun in his works: to assert against the voices of the past a narrative of the present" (33).

.   .   .

In contrast to Duvall, as well as the other critics who have paired *Song of Solomon* with *Go Down, Moses,* and also in contrast to those critics who have paired Faulkner's *Absalom, Absalom!* with Morrison's *Beloved*, I would pair Morrison's *Song of Solomon* with Faulkner's *Absalom, Absalom!* because of the provocative similarity between the epistemological issues of both novels.[3] To begin with, a central character of each book, Faulkner's Quentin Compson and Morrison's Milkman Dead, spends much of his novel putting together, from various narratives, the story of a family's past in search of the "true story" of the Sutpens and Deads, respectively, from which each protagonist hopes to discover how to live his own life in the present.[4]

Brian McHale suggests that "the dominant of modernist fiction is *epistemological*," explaining,

> modernist fiction deploys strategies which engage and foreground questions such as . . . "How can I interpret this world of which I am a part? And what am I in it?"[5] . . . What is there to be known?; Who knows it?; How do they know it, and with what degree of certainty?; How is knowledge transmitted from one knower to another, and with what degree of reliability?; How does the object of knowledge change as it passes from knower to knower?; What are the limits of the knowable?

McHale then shows how "there can be no doubt that Faulkner's *Absalom, Absalom!* . . . has been designed to raise just such epistemological questions." He calls *Absalom, Absalom!* "a detective story," which he considers "the epistemological genre *par excellence*" (9). Patricia Yaeger notes how the work of black women writers reflects "a longing for lost epistemologies—the names, customs, revenants, and remnants of Africa" (13), and one can hear/read the epistemological questions listed above in Morrison's *Song of Solomon* and find the epistemological themes McHale lists from *Absalom, Absalom!* also in *Song of Solomon*: "the accessibility and circulation of knowledge, the different structuring imposed on the 'same' knowledge by different minds, and the problem of 'unknowability' or the limits of knowledge." Finally, in *Song of Solomon*, one can find, too, the same epistemological devices used in *Absalom, Absalom!*, including (as also listed by McHale) "the multiplication and juxtaposition of perspectives, the focalization of all the evidence through a single 'center of consciousness' (the character[s] Quentin [and Milkman])" (9). And in Morrison's novel, as McHale points out of Faulkner's, "the epistemological difficulties of its characters [are transferred to or shared by] its readers": the novel's "strategies of 'impeded form' (dislocated chronology, withheld or indirectly-presented information, . . .) *simulate* for the reader the very same problems of accessibility, reliability, and limitation of knowledge that plague Quentin and Shreve" (9–10)—and Milkman Dead.

While exploring the story of Thomas Sutpen, Quentin discovers the flaws in the Old South he has heretofore revered, as evidenced by his behavior in

The Sound and the Fury. Quentin learns that Sutpen came to Mississippi from Appalachia as a young boy, poor and naïve, his naïveté including no experience of the plantation system or the institution of slavery. Though white and thus not subject to enslavement himself, Sutpen almost immediately experiences firsthand the injustices and cruelties of the plantation system when he is told to go around to the back door of the "big house" and recognizes that the "likes of him" are not considered worthy of entering by the front door, even to do a favor for the plantation owner (the youth has been sent to deliver a message to the proprietor). Sutpen's reaction to coming to such an awareness of the caste system of the Deep South and his place within this system is unfortunate. He determines to rise himself to the position of plantation master, ostensibly in order to welcome and shelter people, like the young boy he had been, who blunder into the community naïvely unaware of their social "inferiority"; ultimately, however, his goal is perverted by the desire to assert his own inherent "superiority" as a white man. Therefore, Sutpen models his "design" after the very prototype that so insulted him in his youth. Sutpen's crimes against his extended family as he drives obsessively toward his goal reflect the flaws within the Old South itself. Quentin's recognition of these flaws undermines any romantic notion of or regret for that historical period.

As Sutpen came South from Appalachia, Morrison sends her protagonist, Milkman Dead, to the South for his "education."[6] Also, as pointed out by Philip M. Weinstein ("David" 62; *What* 120), what Milkman learns about the history of his grandfather, Macon Dead Sr., is comparable to Thomas Sutpen's rise from poverty to prosperity: "He had come out of nowhere, as ignorant as a hammer and broke as a convict, with nothing but free papers, a Bible, and a pretty black-haired wife, and in one year he'd leased ten acres, the next ten more. Sixteen years later he had one of the best farms in Montour County" (Morrison, *Song* 235). But after this first Macon Dead is killed by white men, Macon Dead II, Milkman's father, spends much of his life striving to achieve the white man's success—also not unlike Thomas Sutpen. A deeper irony—perhaps even a deeper tragedy—can be found in this second Macon Dead's efforts, for, like Hurston's Joe Starks, he is a black man modeling himself after the very kind of man who once enslaved his ancestors and who continues to oppress the Dead family.[7] In contrast to Starks, who makes no reference to his slave heritage, Macon II arrived at his assimilating philosophy of life even after watching the murder of his own beloved father by white men who coveted the first Macon Dead's property.

In the course of learning about his family's past, Milkman must recognize the flaw in his father's "design" and develop for himself other goals than "own[ing] things," which his father has told him is "the one important thing [he]'ll ever need to know" (55). Indeed, it is not until Milkman starts to shed the symbols of his material inheritance from his father (his fancy clothes, suitcase, and watch) that he moves toward achieving his own early dream— flight—for, as his friend Guitar points out about peacocks, "All that jewelry weighs it down. Like vanity. Can't nobody fly with all that shit. Wanna fly, you got to give up the shit that weighs you down" (179).[8] As he journeys south, Milkman inadvertently trades his "jewelry" one piece at a time in exchange for pieces of his great-grandfather's story, the legend of one ancestor who was able to successfully transcend his oppression—not by modeling himself after the oppressor but by drawing from powers inherent to his African tribal roots—the ability to fly. First, Milkman ruins his city clothes on the way to and from Circe's house, where he learns, for one thing, that "Sing" was his grandmother's name and, therefore, that the ghost of the first Macon was calling for his wife rather than commanding his daughter Pilate to "sing."[9] Upon returning to town, Milkman learns that his suitcase has been lost; thus, he has given up the rest of his clothes in return for the knowledge he received from the residents of Danville of the value of "links" (229)—in particular, his own link to his grandfather's heroic reputation. After his car breaks down, Milkman is invited on the hunting trip that inspires several insights into his own "[i]gnorance . . . and vanity" (276).[10] And he leaves his watch after seeking more information about Sing from Susan Byrd.

In Faulkner's novel, Quentin Compson is summoned by Rosa Coldfield, who wants to tell him her version of the life of Thomas Sutpen, her brother-in-law, whom she considers an irredeemable "demon." Quentin soon recognizes that Rosa's biases color her objectivity and so seeks a more reliable source, his own father, to tell him about the rise and fall of Thomas Sutpen. The Compsons are not family relations of the Sutpens, have thus not been hurt directly by Thomas Sutpen's actions; therefore, Quentin probably reasons, Mr. Compson, who has heard much of Sutpen's history from his father, who had heard it from Sutpen himself, should be a more objective narrator than Rosa Coldfield. On the other hand, although Quentin's family is not related by blood to the Sutpens, what Quentin learns as he deconstructs and reconstructs Sutpen's life is that, indeed, they are more "related"—through social position—than is comfortable; thus, his father's and grandfather's interpretations of Sutpen's actions are also subjective, reflective of their own concerns. For example, Quentin's grandfather comes to the conclusion that Sutpen's crime was "innocence" (178)—that is, that he did not know any better when, for example, he treated the women in his life so cruelly and crudely. According to General Compson, Sutpen did not realize that he could not so easily desert his first wife. General Compson's opinion of the female sex as naturally vengeful is evident in his lamentations over Sutpen's "mistake" (his view of what the mistake was, that is) in thinking he could get away with leaving his wife and son. Aside from being troubled by General Compson's misogynistic tone as he expresses his shock that anyone could not know that a woman would not allow a treacherous husband to go unpunished, the reader should also notice that he seems to be "excusing" Sutpen's behavior—that is, excusing this man's development of a plantation at the expense of almost every human being with whom he comes in contact. General Compson is therefore excusing Sutpen's desertion of his first wife and son upon learning that they are not white; excusing Sutpen's contribution to the population of slaves in Mississippi; excusing Sutpen's treatment of his second wife, son, daughters (including another child of mixed race), and in-laws; and excusing Sutpen's exploitation of the poor white man who was devoted to him, even as he seduced the man's granddaughter and then rejected her, too, when she did not give birth to a son. It bears repeating: General Compson excuses all of these crimes on the basis of Sutpen's "innocence." One might apply Morrison's view of innocence, as she declares it in her novel *Tar Baby*, to such an "excuse" for Sutpen's crimes: "An innocent man is a sin before God. Inhuman and therefore unworthy. No man should live without absorbing the sins of his kind, the foul air of his innocence" (Morrison, *Tar* 243).[11] Morrison also notes the danger of innocence when talking about one of her favorite characters, Hannah Peace of *Sula*: "Hannah is uncomplicated and really and truly knows nothing about jealousy or hostility. And when you take that kind of innocence and put it in an adult, it has reverberations" (Betty Jean Parker 63).

Perhaps, as Quentin will recognize years later while piecing together the Sutpen history and himself filling in some of the blanks, General Compson perceives the origin of Sutpen's design—the origin, therefore, of his crimes—

as the very social system that he himself fought to protect; and perhaps General Compson would like to excuse his own support of this social system, too, with a plea of "innocent." His generous pardoning of Sutpen's behavior, therefore, may reflect an unconscious desire for acquittal. Philip Weinstein suggests that "[t]he innocence that Faulkner exposes registers white male consciousness blind to its own offenses" and contrasts this innocence with, using Bodwin of Morrison's *Beloved*, "the innocence that Morrison exposes [which] registers less the ignorance of specific deeds committed than the unawareness of a systemic brutality in which one is—as white—complicit" (*What* 164–65). Actually, Morrison does not so easily let her black characters off the hook either. In *Beloved*, for example, she explores the culpability of the whole community as several characters first try to blame Sethe for singularly inhumane treatment of her children and then come to recognize their own guilt for some act/crime similar to Sethe's: for example, Ella's refusal to nurse her child because it is the product of rape, and no one in the community warning Sethe that Schoolteacher is on the way. Morrison is understanding about what drives her characters to act as they do, but she is also objective in her depiction of their crimes against each other. Ashraf H. A. Rushdy explains, "Morrison is not justifying Sethe's actions; she is writing about them . . . through eyes that accuse and embrace, through a perspective that criticizes while it rejoices" (577–78).[12] In this, she is similar to Faulkner, who also "embraces" while "accusing" the white South.

Whereas General Compson was most concerned with Thomas Sutpen, who caricatured and thereby exposed the southern plantation owner, Quentin's father's narratives focus on Sutpen's descendants. The reader who is familiar with *The Sound and the Fury* will not be surprised by Mr. Compson's interest in Judith Sutpen's relationship with Charles Bon and then in the son born to Charles Bon and his octoroon wife/mistress in New Orleans. In the Compson family's recent past and during the same time period when Mr. Compson and his son are re-creating the Sutpen history, his daughter's troubles, the central concern of *The Sound and the Fury*, parallel to some extent Judith's in that both young women are dealing with familial interference in their "love lives." The present of *Absalom, Absalom!* begins in September 1909, which is just after the summer during which Caddy Compson, Mr. Compson's daughter/Quentin's sister, had lost her virginity (revealed in the earlier-published novel), and ends in January 1910. Within this same time frame, the reader of both novels realizes, Caddy, having been deserted by

her first lover, apparently engages in promiscuous sexual activity, the consequence of which, occurring not long after this latter date, is an illegitimate
pregnancy. Therefore, just as Mr. Compson's focus on Judith Sutpen's
doomed relationship may reflect his concern about his own daughter's situation, in turn, his focus on the fatherless Charles Etienne St. Valery Bon in
Absalom, Absalom! prepares for his later concern about his new fatherless
grandchild, whom he brings home to be taken care of shortly before finally
drinking himself to death.

Joining his grandfather and father, Quentin ultimately participates in the
Sutpen saga, re-creating events that took place before his own birth in an
attempt to understand them. The reader familiar with *The Sound and the
Fury* will recognize that, also like his grandfather and father, Quentin is in-
terpreting events with his own life experiences in mind. Quentin is fascinated with Henry Sutpen, with whom he identifies because Henry, too, recalling a recurrent echo in *The Sound and the Fury,* "had a sister." Max Putzel
notes the similarity between the Quentin/Caddy/Dalton Ames triangle and
the triangle including Henry and Judith Sutpen and their half-brother
Charles Bon (14). As Quentin and his Harvard roommate Shreve re-create
what they believe happened within this earlier triangle of incest and betrayal,
Quentin seems to relate to Henry Sutpen, who, like himself, is the weaker
sibling and unable to act upon his attraction to his sister's strong character,
subconsciously perceiving her strength as a complement to his own sensitive
nature. Daniel J. Singal suggests that the "Platonic incest" of these two sets of
siblings is "derived from their mutual need for self-completion" (204). He
shows how these "*three* Sutpen siblings are presented as partial beings attempting to make themselves whole by vicariously incorporating the images
they project onto one another," and he argues that "we find Henry identifying with Bon in order to be able vicariously to marry Judith," although he
adds that Henry thereby not only "merge[s] with" Judith but also "accomplish[es] his desired fusion with Bon" (205). In any case, Henry does
seem to offer Bon to Judith (or Judith to Bon) as a part of himself. This plan
does not change when Henry learns that Bon is his half-brother. In a sense,
then (and in contrast to Quentin), Henry *is* able to commit incest, if only
vicariously. In the midst of the Civil War, Henry tells his father that, yes, he
is going to let Bon marry Judith since "it won't be much longer now and then
we won't have anything left: honor nor pride nor God. . . . And when you
don't have God and honor and pride, nothing matters except that there is the

old mindless meat that don't even care if it was defeat or victory" (354). In Henry's mind, at least they "will all be together" (347) in the hell of their ancestors (the consequences of Charles and Judith's incest and his allowing it to occur). Being together, even if in hell, is a notion that Quentin had also found appealing in *The Sound and the Fury.* However, in contrast to Quentin, who believes that his particular family is cursed, Henry's words show an acceptance of the inevitable destruction of his whole society for its sins, not just of his family for theirs.

According to Quentin's interpretation of events, Henry was not only willing to commit incest (again, albeit vicariously through Charles); he was also able to kill for his sister's honor. In his employment of *Absalom, Absalom!* to illustrate how so many "classic modernist texts" are detective stories, in which the protagonist must "sift through the evidence of witnesses of different degrees of reliability in order to reconstruct and solve a 'crime,'" Brian McHale notes that in the case of this novel, "the quotation-marks can be dropped from around the word crime, for there really is a murder-mystery to be solved here" (9). Although McHale does not clarify, I believe he would agree that the mystery is not so much *who* killed Bon, as it would be in a typical detective story, but *why* Henry killed this man that he loved so much. In Quentin (and Shreve)'s version of the Sutpen saga, they determine that Charles Bon is Thomas Sutpen's illegitimate *black* son. Therefore, Judith was going to marry a man who Henry discovered had "black blood," and though Henry could tolerate (even desired) incest, miscegenation was too much of a denial of the codes of his society. Furthermore, the murder, as Quentin interprets it, was at great sacrifice to himself. Henry was able to give up a part of himself (that is, his brother and friend Charles Bon), the sister he loved, and (like Caddy) his home for his beliefs. Upon reaching the end of his re-creation of this Sutpen "romance" with Shreve, however, Quentin is still haunted by the not-so-heroic-looking apparition he met in the Sutpen home at the end of the day he spent with Rosa Coldfield, when he learned one of the main reasons she had asked for him: she needed him to help her force her way into the Sutpen house and to be a witness to what she found there. The man with "the wasted yellow face with closed transparent eyelids . . . the wasted hands crossed on the breast as if he were already a corpse" (373) does not match the romantic hero of Quentin's Sutpen scenario, the brother who had shown such courage and self-confidence as he first committed fratricide (as well as a kind of suicide) in time to save his sister's honor and then stood up to this sister to tell her, "Now you can't marry him. . . . Because he's dead. . . . I killed him" (172).

Instead, Quentin finds in Henry Sutpen another victim of the Old South, as it was reflected in Thomas Sutpen's design. Quentin is again forced to face the fact that the codes of honor and morality upon which the aristocratic South had prided itself were not enough to combat the destructive power of its caste system, as evidenced by Thomas Sutpen's purpose in life: to avenge the humiliation he suffered as a young boy when he was told "even before he had had time to say what he came for, never to come to that front door again but to go around to the back" (232). Out of that humiliation, Sutpen had formulated his design, which required "money, a house, a plantation, slaves, a family, . . . a wife" (263) but not love, nor even compassion, for Thomas Sutpen understood one thing that Quentin Compson and other "authentic" members of the southern aristocracy refused to face: that the southern practice of the relegation of people into set positions in society is a denial of love. And since Sutpen's goal was to become what General Compson and others like him represented to him, he saw no place for love in his plans.

Quentin finally understands the consequences of this deficiency of love when he recognizes the living ghost of Henry Sutpen. Had Henry's father been able to love his first son, Charles Bon, who did not fit into his design because of his "drop" of "black blood," Henry would not have had to kill Bon to "save" his sister, for, as is theorized by Quentin and Shreve, Bon would have given up all plans to marry Judith in return for any sign of paternal recognition. And the notion that Henry killed Bon to defend his sister, not from incest but from miscegenation, even though he himself had first loved this man, illustrates to Quentin the bequest of prejudice rather than compassion from father to son. Having allowed his own insensitive obsession with his family's position and honor to prevail over his sister's desire for love, Quentin sees in Henry a foreshadowing of his own fate—to die guilty and alone.

In the course of the day and night in January when he and Shreve piece the Sutpen saga together, Quentin realizes the horrifying consequences of ideals centered around what Max Putzel terms "the misremembered past" (19). Quentin had probably hoped to justify, in the course of the retelling, his defense of his home and its way of life, to his Canadian roommate and to himself, as well as, perhaps, to the absent Caddy, in order to justify, too, his denouncement of her lifestyle (in *The Sound and the Fury*). He realizes that he has built his ideal vision of the South on its chivalric virtues, and he is suddenly faced with its flaws, which are personified within the history of Thomas Sutpen, as perhaps best illustrated by Malcolm Cowley in the list he provides to support his view of *Absalom, Absalom!* as "a tragic fable of Southern history": "Sutpen's great design, the land he stole from the Indians, the French architect who built his house with the help of wild Negroes from the jungle, the woman of mixed blood whom he married and disowned, the unacknowledged son who ruined him, the poor white whom he wronged and who killed him in anger, the final destruction of the mansion like the downfall of a social order" (348).

Dolan Hubbard summarizes *Song of Solomon* similarly, calling it a "meditation on history [that] examines the debilitating effects of slavery and its aftermath on black America. . . . The Dead family becomes a trope for those blacks who migrated to the North and Midwest in the wake of Reconstruction in order to escape from oppression and in search of freedom" (288). Hubbard's summary of the life of Macon Dead II is reminiscent of Cowley's list of Sutpen's mistakes:

> The marginalized Macon Dead severed the linkage with his sister born without a navel, closed the door on his Southern roots, married the only daughter of the only black doctor in town, and became a somewhat successful businessman, albeit a borderline one. Macon makes an uneasy peace with his past, and in his hasty retreat from agrarian culture, his embrace of industrial culture made him hard and indifferent toward the needs of his family. (288)

Morrison also echoes Quentin and Shreve's re-creation of events as Milkman listens to Susan Byrd tell him about the love of Ryna and Jake: "His mind was ahead of hers, behind hers, with hers, and bit by bit, with what she said, what he knew, and what he guessed, he put it all together" (323). Like Quentin, Milkman is drawn to a romantic perception of his heritage. When he learns about his flying African ancestry, he is at first elated by the heroic image of this man who "[l]ifted his beautiful black ass up in the sky and flew on home" (328). But also like Quentin, he must recognize the not-so-romantic side to this story, the significance of Pilate's lesson: "You just can't fly on off and leave a body" (332).

Whereas Quentin seeks a more accurate version of the story of Thomas Sutpen from his father and, via his father, from his grandfather's stories to replace Rosa Coldfield's version, which he finds dissatisfying, Milkman turns to women, his aunt Pilate among others, for the "truth" about his father's history because his father's version is suspect, not to mention sketchy. After his first visit to the home of his aunt when he was twelve, a visit made against his father's wishes, upon being reprimanded for going there, Milkman insists upon being told "why" his father does not have anything to do with his own sister. He asserts his rights as a young man not to be strictly forbidden to do something, the way a child is, without explanation (50). Macon recalls that at twelve he himself was already "work[ing] right alongside [his] father" (51) and tells Milkman about his own parents and his early life with his father and sister after his mother's death and up to the time that his father was murdered. However, he still refuses to explain what occurred afterward to cause the breach in his relationship with Pilate. Rather, he leaves Milkman with the unqualified opinion that his sister is "a snake" (54) and with his own philosophy of life: "Own things. And let the things you own own other things. Then you'll own yourself and other people too" (55). Milkman is, not surprisingly, not satisfied with his father's final assessments: the Pilate he met does not match his father's perception of her, and his father's own description of the first Macon's successful farm belies the notion that property equals power, for Milkman's grandfather had not escaped being killed by "owning things." Indeed, as Milkman would later learn, his grandfather was murdered *because* he owned one of the best farms in the county. Furthermore, Milkman's personal experience will continue to teach him that "owning things" is no protection: his own life is threatened several times, even though—again *because*—he was the son of the richest and most powerful man in his community. He learns from his mother, for example, that although he was his father's last hope for a male heir (since by the time of Milkman's birth Macon and Ruth were completely estranged), his father had tried to make his wife abort the fetus. More recently, Milkman's cousin/lover Hagar has repeatedly tried to kill him after he breaks off their relationship in a letter in which he also enclosed cash.[13] And closely echoing his grandfather's fate, during his trip South, envy and resentment of his obvious prosperity leads a stranger (though in his case a black man) to try to kill him in a knife fight. Finally, while traveling through the South in search of pieces to his family's puzzle, his life is repeatedly threatened by Guitar, again because Guitar believes that the materialistic, self-centered Milkman is planning to cheat him out of his share of Pilate's gold.

Precipitating most of these threats to his life, when Milkman is twenty-two, another altercation between him and his father (during which Milkman hit his father for assaulting his mother) leads Macon to tell his son about the disintegration of his relationship with Milkman's mother. Again Milkman is dissatisfied with his father's story. First, he is not comfortable with hearing the intimate details of his parents' lives; second, he realizes that he is only hearing one side of the story. Morrison reports Milkman's musings after this conversation with his father:

> Milkman tried to figure what was true and what part of what was true had anything to do with him. What was he supposed to do with this new information his father had dumped on him? Was it an effort to cop a plea? How was he supposed to feel about the two of them now? . . . "Goddam," Milkman said aloud. "What the fuck did he tell me all that shit for?" He didn't want to know any of it. There was nothing he could do about it. . . . You can't do the past over. (75–76)

Milkman has not yet realized, as so many of Faulkner's characters ultimately come to realize, the presence of the past, perhaps most eloquently summed up by Faulkner's Gavin Stevens in *Requiem for a Nun*: "The past is never dead. It's not even past" (92). One recalls, too, Quentin's similar discomfort with what he has heard about the Sutpens, as revealed in his silent question as he pleads with Shreve not to proceed too fast toward re-creating Henry's murder of Charles Bon: "*Am I going to have to hear it all again. . . . I am going to have to hear it all over again I am already hearing it all over again I am listening to it all over again I shall have to never listen to anything else but this again forever so apparently not only a man never outlives his father but not even his friends and acquaintances do*" (222; Faulkner's italics). Milkman, too, ultimately realizes that knowledge of his father, grandfather, and great-grandfather's experiences would be helpful to his own life. Therefore, he does, as Quentin does in *Absalom, Absalom!*, eventually seek other sources on the subject of his family's past (his mother; his sister Lena; the people he meets during his trek south, particularly Circe and Susan Byrd; and, most important, Pilate), and, also like Quentin, he puts together a history of his family that works for him: though perhaps not exactly accurate, it gives him understanding and (in contrast to Quentin) peace of mind.

.   .   .

When considering Quentin and Milkman's sources of information as they try to make sense out of the histories of their culture and family, respectively, one might be struck by a significant difference, which may merely reflect the authors' different sexes but, in doing so, also illuminates authorial validation of the misogynistic attitudes of some of Faulkner's characters. Rosa Cold-field, Quentin's first source of information about the Sutpens, indeed, the person who calls his attention to the family, is not only his most unreliable source but also a somewhat unlikable and unsympathetic character. Although her story is a pathetic, even tragic one—for her whole family is swallowed up by Sutpen's "design," and she is ultimately humiliated by him himself—at the same time, she is treated to some extent as the comic relief of the novel. Emphasizing her diminutive stature within Sutpen's design, which is also reflective of Sutpen's treatment of all women, Faulkner presents a comic image of Rosa's actual small stature: when Quentin (and the reader with him) first sees Rosa, she is sitting in a chair "that was so tall for her that her legs hung straight and rigid as if she had iron shinbones and ankles, clear of the floor with that air of impotent and static rage like children's feet" (7). At their later meeting, on the very solemn night when they discover the dying Henry Sutpen hiding out at Sutpen's Hundred, the tension of suspense is again partially alleviated by Rosa's ridiculous appearance carrying the umbrella, which Quentin does not yet know conceals a hatchet and flashlight, and "trotting beside him . . . producing a steady whimpering, almost a moaning," unable to see where they are going (366).

Rosa is further disparaged when Quentin later recalls that night and implies that Rosa is to blame for Henry's death: "after almost fifty years she couldn't reconcile herself to letting him [Thomas Sutpen] lie dead in peace" (362). Apparently, Quentin resents—rather than understands—Rosa's vendetta against Thomas Sutpen, which drove her once more to the Sutpen house and resulted in Clytie later setting the house on fire so that the authorities would not come to take Henry away to prison for the murder of Charles Bon. Quentin's thoughts here echo his grandfather's misogynistic suggestion that Eulalia Bon was ultimately largely to blame for Sutpen's crimes: first, Eulalia did not tell Sutpen she was "black," and later she sought to ruin him for his desertion of her and their son. With this misogynistic echo in mind, the reader should recall that, when Quentin and Shreve re-created the events that might have precipitated Charles Bon's friendship with Henry Sutpen, they began with General Compson's opinion that Eulalia Bon would not allow Thomas Sutpen to get away with deserting her. Somewhat in contrast to his grandfather, however, Quentin seems unable to credit a woman with such an ingenious scheme as sending Charles Bon to the same college Henry was attending or with having the foresight to recognize the role that Judith could play in a scheme against Thomas Sutpen. Rather, Quentin and Shreve create a lawyer (male, of course), who is hired by Eulalia to find Thomas Sutpen but who devises a blackmail scheme of his own behind her back. Quentin and Shreve's scenarios, therefore, are as specious as Quentin's father's, grandfather's, and Miss Rosa's.

In contrast to Faulkner's characterization of this one woman to whom he gives narrative voice,[14] in *Song of Solomon*, Milkman recognizes that the women he talks to are the more reliable narrators. They do not hold back, even when the story is not flattering to themselves, as when Milkman's mother tells her side of the story about the disintegration of her relationship with her husband. Interestingly, comparable to the image of Rosa's diminutive stature, which Faulkner mocks even as he employs it to reflect Rosa's "small" role in Sutpen's design, Ruth Dead begins her story to her son with: "because the fact is that I am a small woman." Ruth, however, is speaking only metaphorically; Morrison does not, in this case at least, reflect *status* through *stature*, which would have resulted in a caricature not unlike Rosa Coldfield. Through his description of Rosa, Faulkner succeeded in undermining much of the sympathy that the character's situation might have evoked. Morrison has Ruth qualify her statement to Milkman and to her reader: "I don't mean little; I mean small, and I'm small because I was pressed small" (124). Morrison describes Ruth's appearance to Milkman at the start of this scene as "slump[ed]" (123), but there is no mockery in the narrative tone; rather, Ruth appears pitiful. Ruth's story evokes the reader's sympathy for this oppressed woman, and then, with her concluding admonishment of Milkman for his only response—accusing, *belittling* questions—Ruth achieves a kind of dignity that Rosa Coldfield never enjoys: "Ruth turned toward her son. She lifted her head and looked deep into his eyes. 'And I also prayed for you. Every single night and every single day. On my knees. Now you tell me. What harm did I do you on my knees?'" (126).

Another character who, in the hands of Toni Morrison, contrasts significantly with Faulkner's depiction of women is Pilate Dead. Ironically, then, Audrey L. Vinson compares Morrison's development of Pilate to Faulkner's development of characters like Caddy Compson through the eyes of several other characters: "Using a technique reminiscent of William Faulkner, Toni Morrison permits no unilateral view of Pilate in revealing her character. It is only through the combined viewpoints of Macon Dead, Ruth Dead, Milkman and Circe that one approximates a reasonable perception of Morrison's most enigmatic character" (63). In an interview with Nellie McKay, Morrison explains that she did not allow Pilate much voice because she "loomed very large in the book. So I wouldn't let her say too much" (McKay 143). Morrison's reasoning for not allowing Pilate too much voice contrasts provocatively with Faulkner's explanation for why he didn't allow Caddy Compson to narrate a section: "Caddy was . . . to me too beautiful and too moving to reduce her to telling what was going on, that it would be more passionate to see her through somebody else's eyes" (Gwynn and Blotner 1). In contrast to Faulkner, Morrison is aware of Pilate's potential "threat" as a strong female character: "Sometimes a writer imagines characters who threaten, who are able to take the book over. To prevent that, the writer has to exercise some kind of control" (McKay 143). Similarly, she told Elissa Schappell that, allowed to speak more, Pilate would "overwhelm everybody. She got terribly interesting. . . . I had to take it back. It's *my* book; it's not called *Pilate*" (Schappell 106). Still, Pilate is perhaps the most admirable character in the novel.

.   .   .

Another interesting point of comparison and contrast between the two novels is the role that Pilate's killer, Guitar, and Quentin's roommate, Shreve, each play in motivating his respective friend to seek the truth about the central family of his novel. Whereas Shreve and Guitar both inspire their friends to explore the past, Shreve is of course much less menacing than Guitar. Also, Guitar's role in the novel extends beyond motivating Milkman, while Shreve's role is limited to being a sounding board for Quentin's theories as the latter strives to reconcile his father's, grandfather's, and Rosa's versions of the Sutpen saga with the story told in its last chapter, which he himself witnessed. It is interesting that Quentin's response to Shreve's ultimate question, "Now I want you to tell me just one thing more. Why do you hate the South?"—the significance of his emphatic, perhaps hysterical, "'I dont hate it,' Quentin said, quickly, at once, immediately; 'I dont hate it,' he said. *I dont hate it* he thought, panting in the cold air, the iron New England dark: *I dont. I dont! I dont hate it! I dont hate it!*" (303)—is echoed by Guitar in response to Milkman's confusion about his membership in the avenging Seven: "It *is* about love. What else but love? Can't I love what I criticize?" (223). Indeed, Guitar undoubtedly loves his friend, and yet he will later track Milkman down intending to kill him.

In choosing Quentin, who had committed suicide in the earlier-published novel, to narrate his later novel, Faulkner must have intended to suggest that Quentin's discoveries about the Sutpens contribute to his decision to commit suicide, an act that leaves his sister, niece, and mentally disabled brother at the mercy of his cruel brother Jason.[15] Quentin selfishly sacrifices himself—and thereby also Caddy, Benjy, and his niece—as a last desperate attempt to make his sister's loss of virginity, that problematic symbol of southern honor, matter. His suicide, in this light, is a regression from his recognition of the flaws in the Old Order. In contrast, even if Milkman's final leap is viewed as a kind of suicide, he is thereby offering himself to his friend, which shows a development of his character rather than (continued) irresponsibility. Milkman has been strengthened by his discoveries about his ancestors. While *Absalom, Absalom!* comes to a close with the surviving black Sutpen howling in the wilderness just outside of Quentin's southern hometown, within the possibly last words of the third Macon Dead (Milkman) are the echoing syllables, "*Tar tar tar . . . Am am am am . . . Life life life life*," which might translate into a validation of his heritage: "Black Is Life." And while the last time the reader sees Quentin in *Absalom, Absalom!* he is shaking in his New England dorm room, trying to convince himself that he doesn't hate the South, Macon Dead III literally leaps off of the pages of *Song of Solomon,* reflecting his newfound generosity—"You want my life? . . . You need it? Here"—and pride—"For now he knew what Shalimar knew: If you surrendered to the air, you could *ride* it" (337).

While both family histories have been collected into some kind of logical order and meaning, the fates of Quentin (suicide) and Milkman (possibly killed by Guitar) leave the reader questioning whether or not the Truths discovered by these young men in the stories they put together will benefit anyone else. I would suggest that the stories are not lost. At a metatextual level, we the readers have read them, and so their messages are now ours to share. But even within the confines of the novel their stories are saved. Shreve was with Quentin as he put together the Sutpen saga; indeed, Shreve contributed to it. After learning about his flying African ancestor, Milkman went home and reported his findings to his father, as well as to his aunt Pilate. Pilate is killed by Guitar in the closing scene of the novel, but the final lines of *Song of Solomon* indicate that only one of the pair of men—Milkman and Guitar—

may die ("and it did not matter which *one* of them would give up his ghost in the killing arms of his brother" [337; emphasis added]); thus, even if Milkman dies, then Guitar survives to learn from the Deads' history.[16] Furthermore, as both novels teach us, while we may not determine all the *facts* within a history, the *Truth* can still be discerned. Indeed, regarding facts, Faulkner once wrote to Malcolm Cowley, "I don't care much for facts, am not much interested in them, you can't stand a fact up, you've got to prop it up, and when you move to one side a little and look at it from that angle, it's not thick enough to cast a shadow in that direction" (Cowley 89). And of the "Truth," he said during one of his University of Virginia class conferences, "I think that no one individual can look at truth. It blinds you. You look at it and see one phase of it. Someone else looks at it and sees a slightly awry phase of it. But taken all together, the truth is in what they saw though nobody saw the truth intact" (Gwynn and Blotner 273). Thus counseled by Faulkner, one realizes that, regardless of the parts of the stories that Shreve, Guitar, and Macon Dead II do not know, between what they do know and the examples of their respective friends and son, they can discern the essential Truths to be learned from the Sutpen/Solomon histories. Consider the Truth Quentin learns about the fall of the South coming about because of the sins of slavery and prejudice. This Truth holds whether or not Charles Bon is who people suspect he is—Thomas Sutpen's black son—and whether or not Charles Bon is killed by Henry Sutpen for the reason Quentin and Shreve decide upon— this black son's plan to marry his white half-sister. Consider, too, the way the Truth about Solomon's flight is recorded in the song the children sing. Milkman perceives from it the strength of his ancestor, who defied slavery, while Sweet perceives the consequences of Solomon's actions on those he left behind. A more complete Truth is in the combination of their responses.

Here one can see how *Song of Solomon* illustrates what Brian McHale shows about chapter 8 of *Absalom, Absalom!*: "Quentin and Shreve reach the limit of their knowledge of the Sutpen murder-mystery [but] nevertheless they go on, beyond reconstruction into pure speculation [thereby] . . . dramatiz[ing] the shift of dominant from problems of *knowing* to problems of *modes of being*—from an epistemological dominant to an *ontological one*." According to McHale, "the dominant of postmodernist fiction [perhaps like *Song of Solomon*] is *ontological*," posing questions (quoted from Dick Higgins) like "'Which world is this?' What is to be done in it? Which of my selves is to do it?" (McHale 10). The first of these questions, "Which world is this?" reminds the reader not to assume that Milkman's leap into the air is suicidal. Gay Wilentz argues that Morrison's ending is not so ambiguous after all; rather, it reminds us that "[i]n a multicultural society, there may be other perceptions of reality, other values, and other ways of interpretation than the ones ordained by the dominant culture." Wilentz believes that, with "the instructions of his female ancestor and aunt, Milkman flies as his ancestors flew, leaving a legacy for women's tales and children's songs." I agree with Wilentz that the question to be asked "is not whether Milkman lives or dies, but whether [he] dies or flies!" ("Civilizations" 74), but I would suggest that, should he survive his altercation with Guitar, Milkman would not, like his great-grandfather, fly *away.*

Wilentz notes more than once in her article that "the man flying away leaves people behind, most often women and their children" ("Civilizations" 72), and "it is the women who have kept track of the names and stories so that the men could soar and the children could learn and remember" ("Civilizations" 73). The reader may be here reminded of the role of Jane Pittman as chronicler of "his-stories" in Ernest Gaines's novel and the amount of heartache she suffered with each loss of a man stretching his wings. It seems to me that the loss of Pilate at the end of Morrison's novel would allow Milkman to perceive the grief suffered by those left behind (like Jane Pittman or Solomon's wife, Ryna, Milkman's great-grandmother) and thus prompt him to break the cycle of men deserting their families. Thus, I would suggest again that, should he survive his altercation with Guitar, Milkman would not fly away; rather, he would continue to seek the answers to McHale's other two questions ("What is to be done in it? Which of my selves is to do it?"), which have been part of his development through much of the book. In other words, he would explore how he must *act* to change the world in which the members of his family, past and present, particularly the women, have suffered.

We will not see this determination to effect change again until the very end of this study, with the characters created by Tim Gautreaux, but before then, we will see how other writers explore characters who behave more like Faulkner's Quentin, who is so overwhelmed by the devastating past he recovers that the only action he can take is to kill himself and thereby remove himself from the world whose history he finds so offensive. To conclude the chapter at hand, though, I would emphasize that Milkman is not so self-destructive, indeed, is likely to become more productive (if one agrees with my reading of him not flying *away* should he survive) upon recognizing "the presence of the past" (recall that early in the novel he had believed that his parents' history was *past* and thus that there was nothing he could do about it and so no reason for him to be told about it).

In her *Poetics of Postmodernism,* Linda Hutcheon suggests that "[p]ost-modernism is careful not to make the marginal into a new center," which is to some extent what Gaines did in his work, focusing so exclusively on black *his*-story. Hutcheon explains that "[a]ny certainties we do have are what [Victor Burgin] calls 'positional,' that is, derived from complex networks of local and contingent conditions" (12). Relevant to this (Morrison) chapter's focus on epistemology, Hutcheon suggests that the concept of the "'presence of the past' [which she places in quotation marks, though she does not attribute the phrase to Faulkner] depends on the local and culture-specific nature of each past," as Wilentz's reading of the novel's ending illustrates.[17] Hutcheon also notes how many postmodern theorists "seem to imply that any knowledge cannot escape complicity with some meta-narrative, with the fictions that render possible any claim to 'truth,' however provisional." "What they add," Hutcheon continues, "is that *no* narrative can be a natural 'master' narrative: there are no natural hierarchies; there are only those we construct" (13). Recall that, at the start of this chapter, I defended reading Morrison with Faulkner with the assurance that I was not thereby placing Faulkner's work in the position of "master text." Rather, reading the two together shows how Morrison's work illustrates Hutcheon's point that "[i]t is this kind of self-implicating questioning that should allow postmodernist theorizing to challenge narratives that do presume to 'master' status, without necessarily assuming that status for itself" (13).

chapter 5

No Mere Endurance Here

The Prevailing
Woman's Voice
in Lee Smith's
Oral History

I waited not for light but for that doom which we call female victory which is: endure and then endure, without rhyme or reason or hope of reward—and then endure.

Faulkner, *Absalom, Absalom!*

The preceding examination of Toni Morrison's recasting and retelling of *Absalom, Absalom!*, particularly my discussion of her depiction of women in *Song of Solomon,* illustrates Linda Hutcheon's argument in *A Poetics of Postmodernism* that it has been both "(American) black and (general) feminist theory and practice that have been particularly important in [the] postmodernist refocusing on historicity, both formally (largely through parodic intertextuality) and thematically. . . . Both black and feminist thought have shown how it is possible to move theory out of the ivory tower and into the larger world of social praxis." Hutcheon's view of how "women have helped develop the postmodern valuing of the margins and the ex-centric as a way out of the power problematic of centers and of male/female oppositions" (16) can be further explored by recognizing the Faulknerian intertexts in the work of another contemporary woman writer (this one white), Lee Smith.

When William Faulkner's Thomas Sutpen came to Mississippi from somewhere in Appalachia, he found his new surroundings completely foreign to his past experience. In light of this detail from Faulkner's *Absalom, Absalom!,* it is ironic that an analysis of Lee Smith's Appalachian-set novel *Oral History*—also the story of a particular family and spanning about the same period of time as *Absalom, Absalom!* except that it looks further into the family's future—reveals several echoes of issues and character types found in Faulkner's novels, in particular, in *Absalom, Absalom!, As I Lay Dying, The Sound and the Fury, Sanctuary, Light in August, The Hamlet,* and *The Town.* It is true that Lee Smith does not dwell on the issues of the Civil War or slavery found in so much of Faulkner's fiction; still, she does allude to both in *Oral History,* and a definite relationship can be seen between her novel and these Faulkner novels. One can find certain elements of *Oral History* that are reminiscent of his work: the use of multiple narrators to tell the story of the Cantrell family, the motif of a "curse" on this central family of the novel, criticism of the romantic heroic ideal, and conflict involving the contrast between the Old and New Souths. In addition, the character Richard Burlage, who is quite literally the central narrator of *Oral History* (that is, Smith places his section in the middle of the novel), is reminiscent of Faulkner's romantic protagonists Quentin Compson, Horace Benbow, and Gavin Stevens, as well as some of the more minor male romantics of Faulkner's fiction and even his villainous idealist Thomas Sutpen. Furthermore, the dominating character of this central section, Dory Cantrell, remains as much alive in the reader's memory because of the strength of her character as does Faulkner's Caddy Compson, and both characters are destroyed, in part by their treatment at the hands of romantic idealists. Finally, Smith's novel ends with more than the sense of endurance that Faulkner alludes to in the last line of his appendix to *The Sound and the Fury.* The strength to endure is found not in a black woman like Dilsey but within the voice of the new Appalachian woman, Dory's daughter Sally. However, borrowing the famous phrase from Faulkner's Nobel Prize speech, Sally "will not only endure: [s]he will prevail" (Faulkner, *Essays* 120). These final points of contrast illuminate what reading this Smith novel intertextually with the writings of Faulkner shows about each author: first, how much of Faulkner's fiction deals with sexual oppression, a fact often overshadowed by critics' focus on his depiction of racial oppression; and second, that in Smith's fiction, the struggle against sexual rather than racial oppression is the central concern. Writing about a region of the South where slavery was uncommon and blacks scarce, Smith takes issue, instead, with the oppression of the women. Still, examining *Oral History* as it echoes characters and events in novels by Faulkner reveals how oppression, whoever may be its victim, leads to the same kind of destruction.

The narrative structures of *The Sound and the Fury* and *As I Lay Dying* seem to be the patterns upon which Lee Smith has organized *Oral History*. As in *As I Lay Dying*, each of the chapters, with two exceptions, is headed with the name of a character, and most of these chapters are narrated by that character. Two exceptions to this latter characteristic of the chapters—the "Pricey Jane" and "Almarine" chapters—are reminiscent of the "Dilsey section" of *The Sound and the Fury* in that, though narrated by a third-person, omniscient voice, a particular character still dominates the section.

The character-named chapters that comprise *Oral History* are framed by short italicized sections that open and close the novel. In these sections, a college student descendent of the Cantrell family is visiting her mother's family in order to record an "oral history" for a class. The closing frame serves as a kind of appendix similar to Faulkner's appendix to *The Sound and the Fury*, in that, after returning to the present from which the novel started and telling about what happened to Jennifer at the end of her trip to Hoot Owl Holler, Smith provides the future of those characters who are still living by this time, as well as the future of Hoot Owl Holler. In his review of *Oral History*, Frederick Busch mistakenly suggests that the narratives within the frame are what Jennifer recorded during her visit. Not only can this not be the case since Granny Younger, the first narrator, is dead by this time, but also this interpretation does not take into account the sections narrated in third-person or the presence of Richard Burlage's journal in the novel, of which Jennifer could not be in possession, since neither Richard nor any of his Richmond family is aware of the existence of this young woman, his grandchild. Moreover, such a reading implies a cooperation with Jennifer's oral history project that she does not receive from her relatives in Hoot Owl Holler. Rather, they treat her as an outsider, withholding information from her and keeping her at arm's length. Thus, as Fred Hobson has pointed out, the achievement of the narrative structure of *Oral History* is comparable to the lesson behind the various narrators in *Absalom, Absalom!*: "the reader finally knows more of the truth than any of the individual narrators," and furthermore, as Millkman Dead as well as Quentin Compson (and the reader) learned, that "the deeper truth . . . is that truth itself is not only a relative but a highly elusive thing" (*Southern* 28).

.   .   .

Speaking, apparently, from the grave, as Addie Bundren is when she narrates her section of *As I Lay Dying*, *Oral History*'s first first-person narrator, Granny

Younger, provides much of the history of the Cantrell family. Her first sentence introduces the central character of part 1 of the novel: "From his cabin door, Almarine Cantrell owns all the land he sees. He's not but twenty-two years old now" (27). Slipping into the past tense then, she gives a brief overview of the Cantrells who preceded Almarine on this land and follows this information with a summary of Almarine's childhood. She also recalls the Civil War, in which Almarine's father fought. Its depiction in this novel reflects both differences and similarities between this part of the South and the South of Faulkner's novels. In contrast to the almost uniform allegiance to the Confederacy of the men of Mississippi, Granny tells how "some men hereabouts took up on one side, and some the other. There was nary a slave in the county. So they done what they felt to do." She follows this illustration of a significant difference between Appalachia and the Deep South, however, with a statement that was true of the effect of the Civil War on the whole country, North and South: "It split some families down the middle. . . . Churches too." But her explanation for Almarine's father's decision to join the Union army is in keeping with one of the characteristics common in southern men listed by W. J. Cash in *The Mind of the South*—that is, their lust for combat: according to Granny, Van Cantrell joined the Union army "because . . . it was the quickest army to get to." Finally, like southern women all over the country, Almarine's mother, Nell, kept up the land in her husband's absence, in spite of having "not done a thing but lay in the bed having a sick headache since the day [Van] carried her in that wagon up the trace" (29). These details reflect the "southernness" of Smith's novel, which in turn further prepares for the connections between it and Faulkner's novels.

After telling of Almarine's return home after a five-year absence, during which no one knew his whereabouts, Granny slips back into the present tense, reflecting the immortality of Almarine's presence as the dominant patriarch of the Cantrell clan. The past is just as much alive in this southern novel as is the present. Like Faulkner, Smith shows that the faults of the New South were inherent in the Old. There is a "curse" on the Cantrell family that originates with the heroic Almarine. In *Absalom, Absalom!*, the Sutpen family is similarly "cursed," and, as Quentin Compson realizes, the curse is ultimately traceable back to the South's "original sin" of slavery, which led to its "fall." Rosalind B. Reilly has remarked on the allusions to the story of Adam and Eve in Granny's narration of Almarine's past: "she [Granny] turns his life into the myth of man's intercourse with nature, reshaping the facts into a tale of witches and spells with overtones of the story of Adam in paradise" (81). I would suggest that Smith employs the story of the fall of Eden more fully than Reilly suggests, certainly more extensively than Faulkner's analogous use of it to explore the role that the history of slavery continues to play in the New South. Smith's novel takes on the Genesis story itself (and/or perhaps Milton's version of it in *Paradise Lost*) rather than using it as an analogy for the southern story. Smith explores the tradition inherent in this story of blaming and punishing Eve—the woman—for the fall of man.

The curse upon the Cantrells begins with the temptation of Almarine by Red Emmy, who is purported to be the devil's mistress (and one might note here then the appropriateness of their names beginning with "A" and "E" as do *A*dam and *E*ve). Like Eve before the Fall, Emmy is not ashamed of her naked breasts: upon catching Almarine watching her bathe, she "made no move to cover her glory" (44). Their subsequent brief affair is paradisiacal to Almarine—for a while. However, in direct contrast to the choice that Milton's Adam makes upon being tempted by Eve, Almarine chooses to stay in Eden without Eve rather than lose Eden, which is what he fears will happen, for his sexual relations with Red Emmy leave him too exhausted to work his land. In book 9 of *Paradise Lost,* upon discovering that Eve has eaten the forbidden fruit, Adam says that he, too, is

> . . . ruin'd, for with thee
> Certain my resolution is to Die:
> How can I live without thee, how forgo
> Thy sweet Converse and Love so dearly join'd,
> To live again in these wild Woods forlorn? (ll. 906–10)

In contrast, Almarine's land is more important to him than his lover is. While Adam does not consider replacing Eve—

> Should God create another Eve, and I
> Another Rib afford, yet loss of thee
> Would never from my heart; no no, I feel
> The Link of Nature draw me: Flesh of Flesh,
> Bone of my Bone thou art, and from thy State
> Mine never shall be parted, bliss or woe. (ll. 911–16)

—like Thomas Sutpen in *Absalom, Absalom!,* Almarine abandons Red Emmy and their unborn child to seek a more suitable wife. Unfortunately, Almarine learns, as Sutpen learned (that is, the hard way—through tragedy), that one cannot so easily dismiss that which does not fit into one's plans—particularly not human beings.

Even the reader who has taken Coleridge's advice, "willing[ly] suspen[ded] his or her] disbelief," and accepted Red Emmy's power to put an actual curse on Almarine would not argue with the fact that his family's troubles begin with his poor conduct toward this woman: he treats her not as a human being but as the personification of some*thing* detrimental to his ideals. Perceiving Red Emmy as a witch makes it acceptable for Almarine to desert her. As he tells Granny Younger—significantly, just after asserting his determination not to lose his land—"I won't have no witch-children in my holler" (55). Whatever Red Emmy and her child may or may not be, Almarine and his descendants continue to suffer for their priorities and consequential treatment of women as something other than human.

Corinne Dale argues that Red Emmy is actually "feared and persecuted" for her "sexual power." Apparently, Dale does not believe in Red Emmy's magical powers. She suggests, rather, that the people of Hoot Owl Holler charge Red Emmy with being "a witch and the devil's lover" because she "is neither modest nor chaste" (much as the Puritan communities of colonial times did to many of their female citizens). Dale continues, "Almarine Cantrell believes that [Red Emmy] has bewitched him with her sexuality, that she is exhausting him by 'riding him' at night—the usual sexually charged complaint against witches which betrays a fear of female sexuality" (31). Linda Tate notes that "Granny Younger, like many in her community, mistakenly believes that Red Emmy is a witch"; Tate argues that Granny Younger's "persistence in this belief is less a result of her belief in the supernatural . . . and more a result of her intolerance for Red Emmy's divergence from community standards for appropriate female appearance and behavior" (107). The earlier reference made to the false invalidism of Almarine's mother, Nell—apparently, in part, a means to escape sexual relations with her husband (since she got up after he left for war and worked the land in his absence, she has apparently not taken to her bed to escape hard work)—becomes significant as one explores the role of sex in the novel. This seemingly minor detail about a character mentioned only that once prepares the reader for the significance of attitudes toward female sexuality in the novel. Ironically, Nell's attitude is closer to the accepted norm than the passion of Red Emmy is. While Granny Younger mentions without censure Nell's false invalidism, she condemns Red Emmy as a witch in large part for her voracious appetite for sex. Linda Byrd points out, "Granny establishes her reliability by telling us about her age and experience, assuring us that the story she tells is 'truer than true,' but the reader should recognize early in her tale that even though she is a woman, she colludes with the patriarchy in her judgment and condemnation of Red Emmy" (121). Byrd calls Granny "one of Smith's female characters who has chosen to suppress her own sexuality" and notes how, although Granny is sexually aroused by witnessing Almarine and Red Emmy making love in the storm, "she is unable to view another older woman's sexuality as normal. Instead, she chooses to accept the community-validated explanation for Red Emmy and Almarine's behavior in labeling Emmy a witch and insisting that she cast a spell on Almarine" (121–22). Indeed, Granny Younger not only "accepts" this view, but, as narrator, she passes it on and, as counsel to Almarine, she supports his desertion of his lover and their baby.

Not long after kicking Red Emmy out of his bed and his home because she distracts him from his work, Almarine marries a "safer" woman: the reader hears about the way Pricey Jane keeps Almarine's house and yard but not about their sexual relationship. Indeed, the reader is given no glimpse at all of Almarine and Pricey Jane's sex life, whereas the passionate relations between Almarine and Red Emmy were provided in detail.[1] Again, Granny Younger speaks approvingly of Almarine's second choice while condemning Red Emmy and wins the reader over to her way of thinking by presenting the romance between Almarine and Pricey Jane in fairy tale terms: a relationship with the potential for happily ever after but destroyed by the wicked witch still hovering in the margins.

Noting a parallel between the experiences of Faulkner's Eulalia Bon, also rejected for a more suitable wife, and Red Emmy with Thomas Sutpen and Almarine Cantrell, respectively, not only illuminates Smith's criticism of the treatment of women as far back as Eve; it also calls the reader's attention to Faulkner's similar depiction of sexual oppression. The comparison between Almarine's abandonment of Red Emmy and Sutpen's abandonment of Eulalia Bon leads the reader to consider the suffering of Sutpen's first wife, which is often overshadowed by the usual focus on Charles Bon, the abandoned son. Indeed, that Sutpen never learned how to behave toward women contributes as much to the destruction of his "design" as does his treatment of his "black" son. The reader is reminded, too, therefore, that although critics more often focus on the sin of slavery as that which Faulkner's fiction blames as the cause of the fall of the South, another of Faulkner's "cursed" families—the Compsons—is also rendered heirless by their handling of their daughter/sister and granddaughter/niece in *The Sound and the Fury*. This and other Faulkner novels reflect that he was concerned with the oppression of women as well as the oppression of African-Americans.

In the second and third sections of part 1, Smith employs a third-person narrator to pick up the story of Almarine and his wife, Pricey Jane, where Granny Younger leaves off, much as Faulkner does in the last chapter of *The Sound and the Fury*. One reason for this method is also in keeping with Faulkner's structuring of *The Sound and the Fury*. By not giving his heroine Caddy Compson a voice, Faulkner allows her to remain otherworldly, separate and different from her siblings, certainly more admirable than her brothers, who expose their egocentric selves as they narrate the novel. Similarly, in her section of *Oral History*, Granny Younger describes Almarine as some kind of "super hero." She tells how he was not afraid to climb higher than anyone else into the mountains surrounding their valley and how he talked to animals: "he could scream in the night like a painter until the painters all around were screaming back," and he "trained a crow one time, till it could talk" (28). She stresses his uniqueness among the mountain people: "he had growed up into the finest-looking man you ever laid your eyes on, that's a fact. All that pale gold hair and them light blue eyes, and so tall and so straight. Everybody else around here is mostly dark complected and mostly slighter than Almarine" (36). According to her description, he was a beautiful, golden-haired loner, sweet but independent, daring and seeking.

Likewise, Granny draws an image of Pricey Jane in romantic terms: "this was about the prettiest gal you ever laid eyes on. She was slight and just as dauncy as a little fancy-doll, the smallest, whitest hands and the littlest ankles. She had that blue-black hair they [her family] all had, excepting hern was all in curls, and a face like a heart, with them big blue eyes" (59). The seemingly fragile nature of Pricey Jane's beauty, as well as the focus on her beauty without mention of her sensuality, are reminiscent of the romantic heroines of nineteenth-century sentimental novels, the ideal, virginal beauties of such romantics as Chateaubriand, Goethe, Shelley, and Hawthorne. Also like so many of these writers' heroines, she dies tragically.

The third-person narrator of the next two sections provides Pricey Jane's and Almarine's thoughts, without giving to these transcendental characters actual voices, which would declare their physical reality and thereby diminish their legendary stature.[2] Pricey Jane's section reveals the depth of her love for Almarine, and Almarine's section links him with the tradition of tragic heroes. His tragic flaw—pride—keeps him from rushing home to his wife after going into town for supplies, a delay that factors in her death. He does not want the townspeople to think that Pricey Jane has also cast a "spell" upon him, so he stays in town to play cards with the men, while Pricey Jane is home drinking poisoned milk and feeding it to their son. Returning to the comparison made between Pricey Jane and the female manifestations of the ideals of romantic heroes in the writings of Goethe, Poe, and Hawthorne, one recalls from works by these writers that the romantic heroines pined away while their lovers focused on them as ideals rather than as women. As James D. Wilson explains in *The Romantic Heroic Ideal*, "The romantic poet/ hero usually prefers the 'frozen maiden'—the embodiment of his intuitive understanding of divine truth—to the living, warm, and fertile woman" (102). One might view Pricey Jane's death as resulting from a similar cause— being treated as an ideal rather than a lover. She dies as a result of Almarine's failure to come home to her.

Wilson illustrates and elaborates upon the consequences to the female manifestations of the hero's ideals with, among other works, Shelley's *Alastor*: "*Alastor's* Visionary ignores the loving entreaties of the Arab girl to pursue the veiled maiden" (102)—as Almarine rejects Red Emmy and pursues Pricey Jane. Wilson continues, "A disturbing undercurrent emerges as the infatuation with the narcissistic projection spells doom for the hero and for the woman as well. Such a perception of woman proves debilitating and ultimately self-destructive; the woman loses feminine identity or individuality as she becomes undifferentiated from the male, and the social order potentially suffers from the ensuing sterility" (103). Indeed, the son of Pricey Jane and Almarine, obviously a product of their sexual relationship, of which the reader gets no other evidence besides the two children, dies with his mother, symbolically suggesting (like Sutpen's unreproducing heirs and Janie and Joe Starks's childlessness) that such a passionless relationship does not produce enduring offspring. Though the daughter of Pricey Jane and Almarine survives, she ultimately becomes the victim/manifestation of another romantic's ideals and also dies tragically.

Rather than facing his responsibility for the deaths of his wife and son, Almarine seeks a scapegoat to blame for his misfortunes, and Red Emmy is targeted as such. After the deaths, he storms out of the cabin and into the mountain, apparently to find and kill this "witch" whom he holds responsible for his losses, and when he returns bloody no one investigates the possible murder. The town thus participates in the scapegoating, suggesting their fear and condemnation of passionate women. It is significant that the possible murder is not investigated, reflecting as it does the vulnerability and voicelessness of women in this community. Red Emmy, who has no father or brother to defend her honor, is on her own against Almarine's rage, not only when/if he sought to kill her but also earlier, when Almarine put her out, pregnant with his child. Again, though, Almarine is fated for retribution for his behavior (or rather, the sins of the father are visited upon his daughter Dory: later in the novel, Aldous Rife warns Richard Burlage that he will have to answer to Dory's brothers and father (Almarine), but Dory waits to come to Richard after her father is killed and her brothers on the run for avenging the murder. Consequently, Richard is also able to leave her with impunity, not even knowing that she is pregnant, and his desertion haunts her until she finally commits suicide upon the same tracks on which Richard rode a train away from her.

Given the fact that Almarine views Red Emmy (rather than himself) as the one culpable for his tragic loss, the reader is not surprised that he apparently does not learn from Pricey Jane's death that he cannot get away with deserting women, even temporarily as he did when he delayed his return home to his wife. He later coldly rejects Rose Hibbits, who was sent by her mother to keep house for him and take care of his children, apparently with the hope that he would eventually take up with her.[3] Although the Hibbits women are taking advantage of Almarine at a vulnerable time in his life, when viewed together with his treatment of Red Emmy and Pricey Jane, Almarine's behavior toward Rose becomes reminiscent of Sutpen's treatment of Rosa Coldfield, who served him similarly and who was also not offered a proposal of marriage (and the similarity between the two women's names suggests that Smith may have intended this comparison). For the most part, both men ignore these women's service to them. Briefly, Almarine comes out of the fog he had been in since Pricey Jane's death and notices Rose's presence—perhaps even notices that Rose, whose homeliness will inspire neither passionate lust nor romantic love, is an even safer replacement for Red Emmy than Pricey Jane was. But then, when his deceased brother's part-Indian wife shows up at his door one morning, Almarine casually takes up with her, instantly forgetting about Rose. Sutpen, too, notices one day that Rosa is an eligible woman and proposes to her but then replaces his proposal with a proposition. When she will not merely "breed" with him to make sure she could give him a (white) male heir before they bonded themselves to each other in marriage, he casually turns from her to Milly Jones, the daughter of a man who worked for him, a woman he eventually compared to his mare when she provided him with a "filly" instead of a "stallion."

Consequently, both Rosa and Rose become agents of these men's respective diabolical reputations. To hide and avenge her rejection, Rose reports to her mother that Almarine told her Red Emmy had put "a curse on the whole holler . . . before he kilt her" (87). This outright lie, as well as Rose's developing madness—her behavior not unlike the behavior of Red Emmy witnessed by those who have seen her since Almarine sent her away—also provides further insight into how Red Emmy's reputation as a witch came about, and it is interesting to note that once again a woman suffers more from the act of retribution than does the man who committed the "crime." In Faulkner's novel, Rosa Coldfield summons Quentin Compson to tell him about the "demon" Thomas Sutpen, ensuring that her side of the story is passed on. Ironically, though both women's versions of the legend of their respective nemeses are presented as specious, there is more truth in them than even the tellers realize. Thomas Sutpen's behavior toward women is so reprehensible that demonic is not too harsh a term to use, and it is suspected by the community that Almarine, who returned bloody from the mountains whence he'd fled in his rage at Pricey Jane's death, killed Red Emmy and her baby.

The comparisons already noted between these men lead the reader to recognize a final surprising similarity between Thomas Sutpen and Almarine Cantrell. To Sutpen, sex is only a means toward procreation and then only valuable if the product is male, an attitude at first seemingly far different from Almarine's, whose passion Granny Younger witnessed unleashed in the middle of his fields during a storm. But upon a second look, one realizes that since his relationship with Red Emmy, Almarine has adopted an attitude toward sex similar to Sutpen's, as reflected in his sexual relationship with Pricey Jane, which we know exists only by the presence of their two children, and then in his taking up with Vashti, with whom he produced several sons, though the reader is privy to no sexual activity and witnesses no declarations or expressions of love between the two.[4] The degeneration of Almarine is more clearly perceived when one compares his depiction in Granny Younger's narrative as the romantic hero of a tragic fairy tale to Richard Burlage's depiction of him as a hillbilly bootlegger in part 2.

.　　.　　.

The whole of part 2 of *Oral History* consists of Richard Burlage's journal, an inferior medium given the novel's title and the opening section's mockery of writing.[5] Richard is a descendant of the aristocracy of the Old South, like Faulkner's Compsons and Benbows. Indeed, the prototype for Richard's character might be said to be Quentin Compson, who is also the prototype for Faulkner's other romantic heroes Horace Benbow and Gavin Stevens. Indeed, at various points in the novel Richard's behavior mimics each of these three as well as other similar Faulknerian characters. In the beginning of his journal, Richard announces his plans to make a journey, which he regards as "a pilgrimage back through time, a pilgrimage to a simpler era, back . . . to the very roots of consciousness and belief." His sense of the superiority of his own self-awareness over the level of self-awareness of those he will meet is evident from the start: "I make this pilgrimage fully aware of the august company I hereby join: all those pilgrims of yore who have sought, through their travels, a system of belief—who have, at the final destination, found also themselves. I seek no less. *I seek no less,* I say, even though Victor's slurred denouncements still ring derisively in my ears" (97; Smith's italics). Richard's view of himself as superior to the common man is reflected in his diction and tone and, ironically, supported by his brother Victor's assessment of him as a chivalric hero "going forth to slay the dragon" (99). In addition, Richard's account of his "gentleman's education"—"a passing acquaintance with classics, . . . a haphazard knowledge of Latin and French; some sense of history; a love of literature; and last, but by no means least, how to hold my liquor, look a man in the eye, and play . . . the ukulele" (101)—recalls perhaps the original prototype for the sentimental romantic hero, Goethe's young Werther, as well as, with the notion that learning how to hold his liquor was part of a gentleman's training, the much less romantic Gowan Stevens of Faulkner's *Sanctuary.* Richard may here be mocking himself but not to the extent that Smith is mocking him. She is also, by calling to mind these other characters, warning the reader of his potentially destructive nature.

Richard reports Victor's impatience with his plans to seek a "simpler," more fulfilling life: "How many times do I have to tell you? . . . This is it, this is it, and this is *all there is to it.* You might as well stay here and join the firm"

(97). A short while later, Victor clarifies his words: "*That's it.* . . . That's all there is. There is pain, and the absence of pain." Victor's response to Richard's ideals echoes the fatalism of Faulkner's Mr. Compson, an attitude that Richard, like Quentin, is unwilling to accept. Richard reports that "Victor lost his soul in the war . . . along with certain ideas of conscience and decency I hold dear" (99), reminding the reader of how Mr. Compson treats casually the issue of Caddy's virginity (or lack thereof), while her sexuality obsesses Quentin. Also like Mr. Compson, Victor drinks, possibly to help him live with his view of life. Of course, both men's drinking also undermines their cynicism. If Caddy's loss of innocence means so little to Mr. Compson, why is he drinking himself to death? Victor admits at the end of his conversation with Richard that he does wish him well in his romantic quest, thereby suggesting that he does not discount the *idea* behind Richard's pilgrimage. Rather, it is Richard's *ideals* that trouble him: "Your expectations are so high . . . [t]hey're ridiculous," he tells Richard, adding that Richard's nature—his "assiduousness," the fact that he "think[s] about feeling rather than feel[s]"—will compound the consequences of seeking an ideal (99–100).

Contemplating his home and family, Richard thinks of their "Beauty, sadness, *decadence,*" a summation that is followed by and thus seems to be a response to the images of Victor's drinking and the subservient position of the black woman Mary to their mother, with whom she grew up. A few moments before, he had called Mary "Mother's eternal shadow" (98), alluding (deliberately or not) to the notion of the shadow of slavery upon the image of the Old South. Now, he dwells more fully on the "decadence" of the past. Describing his home, he writes, "Huge white columns support that house—Grecian columns [the reference to Greece again alludes to the issue of slavery]. It is a house supported by the past, and the past, as we all know, is dead. Yet we perpetuate its anguish, preserve its romance, and appreciate, by God, its beauty" (98–99). The belief that "the past is dead" reveals Richard's naïveté. The reader will see, in Richard's section as well as in those that follow, how Almarine's actions, related in part 1 of the novel, continue to affect the Cantrell family long after Pricey Jane's death and Red Emmy's subsequent disappearance, much as Thomas Sutpen's actions early in his life continue to affect the lives of his descendants. In contrast to Almarine, who suffered the consequences of his actions, and Sutpen, who at least witnessed the consequences of his, although Richard's actions continue to affect his descendants, his refusal to accept this notion of the presence of the past allows him to live untroubled by his irresponsible behavior toward Dory Cantrell, never recognize that he destroyed her, and never know how a daughter he never knew he had was also affected by his actions. Ironically, at the end of his contemplation of the presence of the past in the South of his upbringing, he reveals that it is just that—the presence of the past—as well as the responsibility that it implies, which he wishes to escape by leaving home: "My consciousness of these things produced in me again that claustrophobia which has caused me, finally, to flee" (99). And he will "flee" again, this time back to Richmond, when he feels oppressed again—by Dory's passion and the pressure from her family and friends to treat her respectfully or give her up. Unfortunately, Dory, a naïve young woman without any honorable means of support besides a husband, can only escape her oppressive life through suicide.

Aboard the train at the beginning of his journey, as he anticipates living among "the common people," Richard begins to remind the reader of Faulkner's Horace Benbow. In *Sanctuary*, Horace first leaves his wife and wanders out to the Old Frenchman's Place, where a "family" of bootleggers lives, and then, against the wishes of his sister, defends Lee Goodwin, a member of the class termed "poor white trash" by the likes of his sister, and takes care of Goodwin's lover, a former prostitute, and their baby while Goodwin is in jail. Richard, too, will eventually become involved with a family of bootleggers, for that is how the Cantrells are by this time supporting themselves. Already his response to the young coed on the train taking him away from Richmond is reminiscent of Horace's response to women—for example, Horace's association of Temple Drake with his stepdaughter, Little Belle, in a fantasy involving a train. Richard calls the girl he watches "an incipient vamp," notices "her full red lips" turned down "in a pout," and relates how "[s]he settled herself with a flourish, pulled a compact from her purse, and powdered her nose," all of which remind one of the mannerisms of Temple Drake. Richard then recalls that "[a]fter this pointless exercise in vanity, she treated me to a brilliant meaningless red smile before turning her attention to a fashion magazine. I felt that I was nothing more than an object to her, unworthy of respect or even proper notice. This rankled" (102). Such are the same feelings that contribute to Horace's leaving his wife. Her daughter from a previous marriage, Little Belle, shows him neither the respect of a daughter for a father nor the interest of a woman for a man. Furthermore, Richard's feeling like "an object," a position typically felt by a woman, anticipates the role reversal to come. He will find himself the seduced rather than the seducer. A similar role reversal occurs in *Sanctuary* when would-be hero Horace becomes the victim of his sister Narcissa's machinations. Ultimately, then, both men will desert their ideals when their socially "normal" hierarchal positions of authority are threatened by women.

Although Narcissa Benbow Sartoris seems to be an empowered woman in *Sanctuary,* the novel also emphasizes the helplessness of Temple Drake as she is passed around from Gowan Stevens, to Popeye, to Horace, to her father and brothers. Also, the noted comparison with Dory reminds the reader of Narcissa's earlier experiences with men, central in *Flags in the Dust,* and later experience of being exploited herself, narrated in "There Was a Queen," which reveal that she suffers as much from being a woman in a patriarchal society as do Dory Cantrell, Temple Drake, Caddy Compson, and Eulalia Bon. Apparently, she is only momentarily empowered in *Sanctuary* by her brother's weakness as a romantic idealist. And Horace's inability to protect Temple reflects how that weakness is also destructive, as one can see, too, in the eventual fate of Dory as a result of her relationship with another romantic idealist, Richard Burlage.

As the title of *Sanctuary* implies, Horace is seeking a haven from the difficult truths about the world he lives in when he stumbles upon Popeye and gets caught up in the lives of the people of the Old Frenchman's Place. When his ideals are destroyed during and following Lee Goodwin's trial, he again seeks refuge from the harsh world by returning to his wife. Much earlier than Horace does, Richard anticipates the flaws in his idealistic plans to live among these people and teach at their school. After arriving at his destination and looking around at the people, he confesses that he "shall need a restorative haven, a refuge, in the months to come" and rents a room at the Smith Hotel to which he can go in between staying in the homes of his students (113). Furthermore, it is not long before he sets up housekeeping at the school, breaking altogether the tradition of the schoolmaster boarding with the families of his students.

In particular, Richard is disturbed by the women he sees during his first journey through the mountains: "The women were a sad, downtrodden species, from what I could tell. They appeared to be quite subservient to the men, speaking only when spoken to. Some of the girls were remarkably pretty, and yet it was apparent that they age quickly here—the men appearing, by and large, much less the worse for wear" (108). This passage from

Richard's journal prepares the reader for much of what is to take place during Richard's tenure in the mountains. First of all, his reference to women as a "species" suggests a dissociation from them similar to Almarine's treatment of Red Emmy as something other than human and prepares, therefore, for Richard's similarly callous treatment of Dory Cantrell. Also, given this description of the mountain women and apparent recognition of the ephemeral nature of their beauty, Dory's eventual seduction of Richard is somewhat surprising. He cannot see past her amazing beauty as he could the "prettiness" of the girls he'd seen on the train. On the other hand, in comparison to these women, one can see why he is so struck by his first sight of Dory:

> I must say without preamble that she is the most beautiful woman I have ever seen, with an *ethereal, timeless, other-worldly* quality about her. Her alabaster face is framed by the finespun golden curls, almost like a frizz, about her head—hair like a Botticelli! Her eyes are deep, limitless violet. Her lips are red and full. When she smiles, a blush and a dimple grace her smooth fair cheeks. Her rough attire . . . served only to accentuate the delicacy of her beauty. The sun streamed in the schoolhouse door behind her, turning her curls into a flaming gold *halo* around her head. (118–19; emphasis added)

Again Richard's diction echoes that of a sentimental novel. In fact, one review of the novel describes this passage as "the stuff of Silhouette romances" (Vigderman 282), seeming to miss the point, however, that Smith is purposefully parodying such sentimentality with Richard's journal in order to show his overly romantic nature. In Richard's defense, though, his description of Dory does not differ essentially from Granny Younger's description of Dory's father and mother. And as happens when the reader listens to Granny's fairy tale account of the courtship between Almarine and Pricey Jane, the reader once again gets caught up in the romance Richard sets up, for such is the seductive nature of romance. Hence, the reader begins to envision (along with Richard) the knight sweeping the damsel in distress up on his horse and carrying her back to Richmond where she will live as the princess she naturally is. Of course the reader is prepared by the fate of the romance between Almarine and Pricey Jane (and between Almarine and Red Emmy for that matter) for the less than happily-ever-after ending to this fairy tale.

Immediately upon seeing Dory, Richard assesses her situation of living among such inferior people as that of a "maiden in distress" and decides that he will be her savior. This perception of himself is evident—as is his superiority complex—in his shameless identification with Christ: "I felt as if I were Jesus, and the stone door to my tomb was rolled away!" (119). The reader recognizes the danger in Richard's association of himself with Christ and his perception of Dory as some kind of "other-worldly" goddess, for he is, in reality, a quite fallible man, and, like her mother, Pricey Jane, as well as the doomed heroines of romances, Dory is, in reality, quite mortal. Furthermore, although Dory is not given a section in the novel to tell her own story, her diction and the content of her speech, as she is quoted by Richard, betray her to be a more typical native of this area than he accepts (in spite of her unique beauty). For example, she is completely ignorant of the ways of the rest of the world, while she does know that the wooliness of a caterpillar is evidence of a hard winter ahead. When she remarks upon this fact of nature, Richard is struck by her "oneness with the natural things of the earth" (130), but rather than coming down to earth himself with his assessment of her, he becomes even further enamored with her. Recalling that thoughts of Dory lead the idealistic Richard to read Christopher Marlowe's "The Passionate Shepherd to His Love," one can perceive from Dory's comment about the caterpillar that, like the shepherdess in Sir Walter Raleigh's response to this poem (his poem "The Nymph's Reply to the Shepherd"), she is more pragmatic than her would-be seducer. She, too, realizes that spring will not last forever, winter will come, and one must prepare for it. Hence, her ultimate demise is evidence of the extent of Richard's negative effect on her nature. After instilling in her the desire to see the world outside and to experience its luxuries, he leaves her dissatisfied with her present life. Consequently, she eventually takes her own life, in compliance with the traditional "romantic" fate of the romantic hero's ideal.

The characterization of Dory is reminiscent of Faulkner's Eula Varner of the Snopes trilogy, who is also paradoxically earthy and otherworldly. Like Richard's first vision of Dory, Eula's introduction in *The Hamlet* includes golden imagery: she is compared to "honey in sunlight" (*Hamlet* 95). Unlike Richard, the schoolteacher Labove, upon facing Eula for the first time, recognizes immediately that "there was nothing in books here or anywhere else that she would ever need to know, who had been born already completely equipped not only to face and combat but to overcome anything the future could invent to meet her with" (*Hamlet* 114). Labove apparently understands that he has nothing to teach this girl that she will need to learn for her life. Richard, on the other hand, believes that "in [Dory's] eyes [he is] some supe-

rior being from another place, with a fund of 'knowledge' beyond her ken."
He follows this notion thinking he therefore "understood [his] position and
[his] responsibility" (130); however, his actions eventually prove this false insight to be further evidence of his lack of self-knowledge. He ultimately does
not live up to his professed "responsibility" and thereby proves himself
Dory's inferior, particularly in his devotion to their love.

Faulkner's Labove comes to realize that if he had the chance to be intimate
with Eula, as Richard does with Dory, "[h]e would be like a young girl, a
maiden, wild distracted and amazed, trapped not by the seducer's maturity
and experience but by blind and ruthless forces inside herself which she now
realised she had lived with for years without even knowing they were there"
(*Hamlet* 119), an assessment that aptly describes Richard's reaction to his
sexual relations with Dory. He finds the essence of himself, the depth of his
heretofore thwarted passions, while he is with her, which is what he had
claimed he wanted to find during his pilgrimage. Anne Jones connects the
way Richard's journal entries "run on" without regard to punctuation with
how his "lived sexual and emotional experience" has come to dominate "over
the control of the mannered Richmond way" (119). However, recalling the
similar incoherence reflected in the failure to heed to rules of punctuation
and capitalization toward the end of Quentin Compson's section of *The
Sound and the Fury*, one may also see this degeneration in Richard's writing
as a bad omen for the lovers' future. He does have with Dory the chance to
live the simpler life he claimed to long for, but so did Thomas Sutpen have in
Charles Bon just the kind of boy he envisioned when he first developed his
"design" in *Absalom, Absalom!* And, as Sutpen denies his son, so does Richard
desert Dory.

One should note here that in spite of Richard's high-minded reasons for
leaving home, he reveals early in his journal that he has recently been jilted
by a woman. Perhaps, then, his affair with Dory has reinstated his confidence
in his desirability to women. Now he can return home and find a "suitable"
wife—again like Sutpen and Almarine. Ironically, Almarine's betrayal of Red
Emmy is thus harshly revenged upon him by Richard's betrayal of Almarine's
treasured daughter, though by this time Almarine has been killed and therefore cannot suffer further regret. Finally, then, Richard's actions again repeat
those of Horace Benbow in *Sanctuary*. Just as Horace returns to his wife at
the end of this novel and thereby to the lifestyle he had rejected in the beginning, Richard returns home and eventually marries the daughter of an Epis-

copal bishop. Neither man can handle the raw passions that he finds in himself and in others. One might apply Daniel J. Singal's reading of Horace Benbow to Richard: "The root of Horace's problem lies in his simultaneous fascination with and terror of that psychic netherworld of animal drives from which his bourgeois ethos has severed him and that he associates with 'reality'" (160). It is "reality" that Richard ultimately chooses. Such passion as he experiences with Dory leaves Richard physically drained and emotionally out of control, so he repeats Almarine's (and Thomas Sutpen's) offense of deserting a woman who loves him, ultimately because of the uncontrollable passion her sexuality stirs up in him. Further, unbeknownst to Richard, like Red Emmy, Dory is pregnant when he leaves. Unlike Almarine (and Sutpen), then, the only consequence to himself is the loss of the woman he deserted—and he has convinced himself that his leaving is best for all concerned. Therefore, he is never to know how his relationship with Dory continues to affect his children (she ultimately gives birth to twins he has fathered) and at least one grandchild.

Richard's connections to Quentin, Sutpen, and Horace reveal these three men's connection: like Richard, they are all romantic idealists, and it is that quality of their nature that is destructive to those around them. To be fair to Richard, there is a point when he determines that he will take Dory with him in spite of his misgivings, but this plan is thwarted by Dory's cousin Ora Mae, who, it turns out, kept his letter from Dory. Still, when Ora Mae tells Richard that Dory is not going with him, he accepts her word for it rather than return to the mountain to hear it from Dory herself.

After Richard's departure, in a conversation with Reverend Aldous Rife, Justine Poole exonerates Richard from culpability—presumably for Dory's illegitimate pregnancy, since at the time of this conversation, no real "tragedy" has yet occurred.[6] She calls Richard a "fool" and implies that, as such, he could not have stirred people up as much as he did—or perhaps seduced Dory (she is never clear about what exactly she is excusing)—without the help of the "curse" on the Cantrells. But Aldous, Richard's one friend in the community, disagrees with Justine: "He was not a fool, Justine, not exactly. . . . He was something much more dangerous, . . . a total innocent" (182). Aldous here echoes General Compson's excuse for Thomas Sutpen's treatment of women in *Absalom, Absalom!*; however, it is important to note that he is not excusing Richard for being an innocent, as Compson, Sutpen's one friend in his community, does. "Innocence" is "dangerous," Aldous realizes, which is why he had tried earlier to explain to Richard the ways of the community—before Richard did anything that could not be undone and that might lead to violence. In noting the difference between Aldous's and General Compson's views of innocence, the reader realizes that in her novel, Smith, like Morrison, more directly suggests that, as an adult, one is responsible for considering possible consequences before one acts. Aldous had told Richard stories that illustrated the violent codes of the mountain people—how they avenged those who crossed them—but Richard dismissed these stories:

> "When was this?" [Richard] asked.
> "Twenty, thirty years ago. . . . The time doesn't really matter."
> "Of course it matters. This could be a fact of history, or it could be a county myth, a folk tale. . . . "
> "It doesn't matter," [Aldous] said. "Nothing ever changes that much." (151)

First of all, Richard has not yet realized, as the reader of *Absalom, Absalom!* (and *Song of Solomon*) comes to realize, that truth is not just about getting the facts. More consequential, he has rebuffed the opportunity to become more "educated" about the community in which he has chosen to live. Thereafter, his "innocence" became a crime for which he is culpable, for he had the chance to lose some of that innocence (/ignorance) and rejected that chance in order to keep his conscience clear as he continued in his pursuit of Dory.

The tone of Richard's later section in part 3 of the novel reveals that he has learned very little since his departure eleven years before. He is still as self-deluded as ever, though he believes that his eyes are "no longer startled and wild, but melancholy and wise . . . betraying a knowledge beyond [his] years" (217). Following such an arrogant self-assessment, the reader is amused when Justine Poole, recognizing him immediately upon seeing him, cries out, "Richard . . . You haven't changed a bit" (219). On the other hand, though still self-deluded, Richard has apparently learned something by this time about the presence of the past even in such a "simple" place as Hoot Owl Holler: "Everything that had happened to me seemed to have happened a million years ago, or seemed to be, in some inexplicable way, *still* happening, over and over again as it has, I suppose, been happening on some level ever since these events took place, *as all events that ever happened always do, are never ever over*, I realized, surprised" (223; Smith's italics). In this passage, ironically, it is the naïve Richard Burlage who accounts for the present tense Granny

Younger used in her section—indeed, who accounts for Granny Younger's voice from the grave. But he remains blind to the implications of this notion, does not connect it to his actions during the time he spent with these people, and therefore is not able to recognize that the two girls who appear on Dory's steps are his own two daughters. Furthermore, he is clearly still the romantic idealist, as is evident in his thought that the "indistinct, stooped shape, the posture of an older woman" in the photograph of Dory that he took from his car was "simply the angle of her head and the way she stood at the door." Although he recalls that "they age so fast in those mountains," he excuses the image of an "older," "stooped" Dory with the notion that "the light had gone by then" (228).

.   .   .

In Faulkner's *The Town,* Eula Varner becomes the obsession of Gavin Stevens, another character whom Faulkner developed from the prototype of Quentin Compson. At the end of this novel, Eula commits suicide after Gavin convinces her that she cannot leave her husband and run off with her lover, Manfred de Spain, for, whether or not she brings her daughter with her, such actions will destroy the girl. Faced then with staying with Flem Snopes for the rest of her life, Eula kills herself. Flem is the obvious villain in this novel; however, Gavin, too, has failed Eula. Like Richard, he had taken the position of her "savior" and had appeared to promise fidelity to his devotion to her; then, when she comes to him with her plans for escape from her desperate existence, he pulls them out from under her. Similarly, Dory lives for many years with the dream of escaping to a better life, the one Richard described to her, but finally, unable to listen to the whistle of one more train that does not carry Richard returning for her, she lies down on the track to wait for the train to take her away itself. Or perhaps her decision to take her life is further evidence that she has been a good "pupil" to Richard's teachings.[7] As a result of her relationship with Richard, she has developed from a pragmatic naturalist to a romantic idealist. The one side of her married Little Luther Wade and was even happy with him. But the other side of her could not be satisfied with such an "ordinary" love and marriage and still listened for the train whistle. Perhaps, too, this romantic side of her shared Quentin Compson's fear that she would eventually forget her sorrow, for, like Quentin, she kills herself in the midst of having gone on with her life without the object of her affection but while she still remembers her loss.

Richard's legacy to Dory takes on physical form in the twin daughters she has by him, and the girls' synonymous names reflect Dory's divided self since her affair with Richard ("Maggie," the name of one twin, is a diminutive of "Margaret," which means "Pearl," the name of the other): Maggie recalls the naturally beautiful and pragmatic Dory whom Richard found in Hoot Owl Holler, and Pearl personifies the dissatisfied, romantic Dory whom he left there. According to the twins' half-sister, Sally, "Maggie chose to be beyond the gossip, and all the talk of bewitching" (251). Maggie pays no attention to a townswoman's innuendos about the bad luck associated with her grandmother Pricey Jane's earrings, which she inherited after Dory's death. Pearl is not so carefree. Her habits of reading magazines and pasting on the wall pictures from them of people and places from all over the world reflect a dissatisfaction with her own home similar to that which apparently festered within Dory after hearing Richard tell of life in Richmond. Significant, too, Pearl covets the earrings. Not only are they something else that belongs to someone other than herself, but they also represent the romantic aura surrounding their mother—and Pearl "want[s] to be *in love*" (258; Smith's italics). Sally, Dory's daughter by Little Luther, suggests that it "was right" that Maggie should have the earrings passed down from Pricey Jane to Dory because "Maggie took after Mama the most" (250), and Sally is right in her suggestion here that the ingenuous side of Dory, reflected in Maggie, is more natural to her character than her discontented yearning. Sally's description of Maggie in light of this comparison, however, becomes somewhat ominous: "she had a sweet smile, *like an angel*" (251; emphasis added), and indeed, soon after receiving the earrings Maggie is stricken by polio and seems to be dying. But Maggie defies the "curse" that has fallen upon those who wore the earrings before her. She takes them off, rejecting the legacy of doom, and gives them to her twin, who is more interested in such romanticism.

Dory is the last romantic heroine in this family saga. Those she leaves behind are citizens of the less romantic New South emerging even in Hoot Owl Holler. Reviewer David Bradley remarks upon the decline of the Cantrell line from the "larger than life" Almarine to the "diminished state" of his descendents after Dory, "people who have lost the stature required for tragedy": "That Jennifer uses her family to impress an academic voyeur, and Al, the Amway magnate, plans to turn the family homestead into 'Ghostland' . . . represents an attenuation both in blood and imagination, a loss of the strength of old ways, old passions, a commercialization of self" (39). On the other hand, the women of this next generation, except for Pearl, survive: Maggie, for example, gets up from her deathbed, marries, has four children, and moves to a brick house in Georgia. And Sally, who narrates all of part 4, thrives. She describes herself and her husband, Roy, with emphasis, as "*down to earth*" (234; Smith's italics), a quality particularly significant in light of her mother's and grandparents' otherworldliness. The life Sally makes is a happy and satisfying one, if not the kind from which legends arise. Her relationship with Roy is passionate but not obsessive. Her attitude about her family's history is similar to Maggie's: "That's the *past*. . . . It's nothing to talk about now. Now it's you and me. It's what happens after this" (278; Smith's italics). Although her words also sound uncomfortably like Richard's, she is not forsaking any responsibilities in this statement. She has dealt with her past mistakes before adopting this attitude, and when her half-sister Pearl needs her help, she is there for her.[8] She merely refuses to allow the past to lead her to self-destruction. Similar to Maggie's attitude toward the "curse," and in preparation for her narration of what befell Pearl after receiving the earrings, Sally defines the curse on her family in *secular* (rather than supernatural) terms as being "all eat up with wanting something they haven't got" (235). Here, too, then, one can see the parallel between the Cantrells and Thomas Sutpen. Sutpen's design grew out of his sudden awareness of all that he did not have when, as a boy, he spied upon a planter lounging in a hammock, being waited upon by a slave.

Unlike Smith, Faulkner could apparently not envision how the oppressed in his novel (*Absalom, Absalom!*) could ultimately produce a descendant like Sally who would defy the limitations imposed upon her. Sally rejects those men who would change her to suit the domestic norm for a wife and maintains a passionate relationship with her husband that appears to leave them both satisfied. (Roy, incidentally, in contrast to Almarine and Richard, is not intimidated by or afraid of Sally's enjoyment of sex.) Although Faulkner did go back in his appendix to *The Sound and the Fury* and declare that Dilsey and, implicitly, her family "endured" (*Portable* 756), such endurance of the oppressed—whether it be African-Americans or women—is not clearly delineated in his canon. Indeed, in the same appendix, Faulkner shows Dilsey powerless to save Caddy: recall how Dilsey asks what Jason had to say about the photograph she is shown of Caddy with the Nazi officer and, hearing that when Jason "realized that somebody . . . would try to save [Caddy], he said it wasn't [her]'" (*Portable* 749), Dilsey remarks upon her own blindness

and thus inability to identify the woman in the photograph, thereby not defying Jason's will.[9] Dilsey may "endure," but she does not "prevail." As discussed by Diane Roberts in her book on *Faulkner and Southern Womanhood*,
"*Enduring* implies no rebellion, no real resistance, only acceptance." Roberts
argues that in Faulkner's novel, which she terms "a white text," Dilsey is
"congratulate[d] . . . for colluding in a structure that imprisons her in a narrow definition of possibilities" (66). In contrast, in the last part of Smith's
novel, Sally rejects the confines of the other women in her family and still
achieves her mother's stature, not through a similarly tragic tale of her own,
but with a resounding voice that does prevail over the story she tells about
Pearl.

In contrast to Maggie and Sally, Pearl strives for a more glamorous lifestyle. But in the less romantic-tolerant New South, her destruction is, at
most, tragicomic. She is a perversion of Blanche Dubois living in Scarlett
O'Hara's gaudy Atlanta mansion. Having surrounded herself with the en-
trapments of the southern lady of her father's South and having failed to find
the happiness she sought in material things, she reaches out in desperation to
human beings. She is, by this time, estranged from her husband, so she se-
duces a high school student and flaunts herself in front of an electrician making a service call to her home. Her explanation for her actions reveals that she
is making the same mistakes her father made, though her perception of reality is even more distorted than his: according to Pearl, the student "looks like
a Greek god" (272), and "all in the world I ever intended to do was just give
him a taste, one taste of the finer things in life, show him what it was like, I
never meant to touch him at all" (273). The boy's name, Donnie Osborne, so
close to the name of the 1970s teen idol Donny Osmond, contributes to the
comedic elements of her narration of the events that lead up to and follow
the public's discovery of her desires. Still, in spite of the comedy, tragic consequences ensue from Pearl's romanticizing, as they did from her father's. She
dies following complications during her pregnancy, having also conceived
during the affair, and her young lover, like Pearl's mother, gets caught up in
the fantasy and kills Pearl's cousin Billy for no clear reason.

One can see tragic elements in the "comic" fate of the Cantrell land, too.
Like Maggie and Pearl, Sally and her brother Lewis Ray have each moved
out of Hoot Owl Holler, leaving their land to Ora Mae and Little Luther,
this couple's son named Almarine, and his family. Though the Cantrell land
seems, therefore, to have been usurped by those who have married into the

family and their descendants, who will capitalize upon the legends, much as Faulkner's Snopeses capitalized upon the errors of the Old South, in reality, it has, in a sense, gone back to its rightful heirs. Ora Mae is the daughter of Almarine's older brother, who disappeared soon after their father died and never returned. As mentioned earlier, his wife, Vashti, appeared with Ora Mae shortly after the death of Pricey Jane. Ora Mae's son, then, is the grandson of the oldest Cantrell son of Almarine's generation; thus, in the tradition of tragedy, order is restored at the end of the novel when the grandson of the firstborn inherits the Cantrell land. But there is significant irony attached to this restoration of order, which reminds the reader that the "old order" (of the Old South) was not necessarily a better order and that it contributed to the character of the new order (of the New South). This Almarine, the great-nephew of Almarine Cantrell, is called Al, reflecting the diminished stature of the current Cantrell patriarch. He has also inherited the stories along with his first name, and though he will not share them with Pearl's daughter, Jennifer, great-granddaughter of the first Almarine, who could perhaps benefit from knowing about the past mistakes made by her ancestors, he will use them for monetary profit by making Hoot Owl Holler into a haunted theme park. He, too, then, is more concerned with the value of the land he lives on than with the humanity of the characters in these legends, which he is violating through exploitation.

Although Al sends his niece Jennifer, Pearl's daughter, away with her tape recorder, she is more akin to those left in Hoot Owl Holler than they seem to recognize. In contrast to Sally's healthy rejection of the presence of the past is Jennifer's obliviousness to it. Significantly, Jennifer is the granddaughter of Richard Burlage, and Michael Kreyling wonders if she is "a Quentin Compson," who, as I have argued, is the prototype for Richard. Contemplating Jennifer in this role, Kreyling asks, "Does the meaning of the South, the meaning of history itself, hinge on her findings? Is she dancing on the railing of the bridge over the Charles River? Or, like Isaac McCaslin, is she on the threshold of a genealogical discovery that will 'unman' her, unfit her for history?" He decides, "For Jennifer the past is dead as a mackerel" (113). Later, Kreyling also compares Jennifer's future husband, the professor of her oral history class, to Quentin's roommate, Shreve, "an outsider who sees the South as a vast entertainment" (114). Sadly, the novel shows with Al's decision to develop the holler into a theme park that it is not only outsiders and academics who exploit the appeal of the culture's "romantic" history.

In his review of *Oral History*, Frederick Busch relates the fate of Almarine's land to that of some of the Compson land in *The Sound and the Fury*: Al's Ghostland is comparable to the golf course, which is developed on the land sold by the Compsons to send Quentin to college. Michael Kreyling also notes the comparison between the golf course and the theme park but then makes a point of distinction: "The transformation of Quentin's native ground from southern birthright to golf course ate away financially and psychologically at the Compson scion; in *Oral History* no one seems to care very much" (114). One is also reminded of the Compsons by Busch's assessment of the Cantrells as "doomed to lose sight of its values, cursed—by time at least, and maybe by a mountain witch—to sell the past away" (15). Like the niece they drive back down the mountain, the Cantrells still living on the land that Almarine, in essence, traded Red Emmy to save, do not share Almarine's devotion to it. Or perhaps their behavior reveals the problem inherent in Almarine's priorities, placing more value in his land than in a woman (and their child), and the consequences of such priorities upon the generations to follow.

.   .   .

What Faulkner does in several works—showing the decline of the South as it is manifested in the decline of the southern family, from the Sartorises and the Benbows, to the Compsons and the Sutpens, to the Bundrens and the Snopeses—Smith does in this one book. Like Faulkner, she moves from the Sutpen-like tragic hero Almarine to the antihero Al, a 1970s Flem Snopes, for the patriarchal figures of the Old and New Souths of her novel. In between, she focuses on the romantic hero Richard Burlage, reminiscent of Quentin Compson and his descendants in Faulkner's canon, for more evidence of the cause of this decline: the high ideals and moral values of the southern patriarchy are not effective against its members' irresponsible behavior toward their social subordinates—who are, in the community of this Appalachian-set novel, women, rather than African-Americans. The destruction of Pearl and the static character of her daughter, Jennifer, reflect the continuing negative effect of a patriarchal structure upon the South. Although Jennifer never knew her mother and is not told the story of her grandmother, she seems destined to make the same mistakes they made. Already, the purpose of her "*pilgrimage*" to Hoot Owl Holler is only to gather information that will impress a professor with whom she is enamored. Her journal and the conclusions she draws about the *"primitive people"* she met during her visit echo her grandfather's justification for leaving the Holler—and Dory—behind (284; Smith's italics). In the closing frame section of the novel, Smith reports that Jennifer *"will never get around to going back"* (285; Smith's italics), thereby bringing to a close her life as a Cantrell.

This summation is not to suggest, however, that all of Smith's women are either destroyed by men—as are Pricey Jane, Red Emmy, Rose Hibbits, Dory, and Pearl—or follow husbands and lead mundane lives in the outside world, as do Maggie and Jennifer. It is important to realize that the legend of Dory ultimately predominates—even over the legend of her father—in the novel. When his story is told, Almarine must share the stage with two quite heroic women characters, Red Emmy and Pricey Jane, whereas Dory's heroic stature is enhanced by the presence in her story of the weak romantic Richard Burlage. Just as many of Faulkner's women remain his strongest characters throughout his canon, the legend of Smith's Dory Cantrell will not soon be forgotten, and Dory's daughter Sally emerges in the last section of the novel as a prevailing voice of endurance. Perhaps Faulkner's Isaac McCaslin did get one thing right—his assessment of the optimism of women: "women hope for so much. They never live too long to still believe that anything within the scope of their passionate wanting is likewise within the range of their passionate hope" (*Go* 335).[10]

chapter 6

Rape Fantasies vs. Rape Realities

More Skeletons
Coming Out of
Southern Closets

The point is that if Southern literature is to continue to
play so important a role in national letters as it has
done since the 1920's, it will have to be constructed on
new foundations, based on markedly different conditions of experience, and will thus constitute a recogniz-
ably new and different phase of the Southern Literary
Renascence. Its writers, forced to find new responses to
new situations, cannot write in the forms developed by
Faulkner and his contemporaries, without first subject-
ing those forms to an extensive remodeling and
alteration. The new Southern writing will have to be
. . . substantially different in its values, its attitudes,
its techniques, from that of the previous generation.

Louis Rubin, *Writers of the Modern South*

The most familiar poster advertising the movie version of Margaret Mitchell's *Gone with the Wind* includes the images of Clark Gable and Vivien Leigh
from the scene in which Rhett sweeps Scarlett off her feet and carries her up
the grand staircase to make passionate, though apparently violent, love to
her. One recalls then the cat-that-ate-the-canary-like smile on Vivien Leigh's
face in the next scene of the movie, reflecting her satisfaction with the previous night's activities. Surprisingly, the sexual encounter that has left her so
content is commonly referred to by readers and viewers as a rape. Whatever
happened after Rhett and Scarlett disappeared behind closed doors, the en-

counter undeniably began as an assault: the struggling Scarlett in Rhett's arms implies that he is forcing himself upon her. Yet neither viewers nor readers seem troubled by Scarlett's euphoria the next morning. This sexual assault is depicted not unlike the way that rape is romanticized in popular romance novels, and, as in such books, the victim falls in love with the rapist: it is not long after this scene that Scarlett realizes that it is the brutal Rhett, rather than the gentle Ashley, whom she loves.

The movie version of *Gone with the Wind* premiered in 1939, and apparently audiences were not offended by the "rape" or the "rapist." Indeed, that an image from this scene is included on a movie poster suggests that the producers did not even worry that audiences would be bothered by these events in the movie. Absurdly, the censors were instead upset by the use of the word "damn" in the unforgettable final scene of the movie. One might venture to connect the censors' ultimately allowing the line to remain in the movie to the fact that it turns the tables on the untraditional, rebellious heroine and puts the hero in charge of their relationship once again—that is, as he is only on the night he assaults Scarlett. Further, one might then find troubling that this line is perhaps the most famous line of the movie.

Just over a decade before this film, William Faulkner reported that his editor blanched at publishing *Sanctuary,* which included a violent rape of a young woman. In contrast to Mitchell's glamorous "rapist," the (actual) rapist in Faulkner's novel is not the novel's hero, and certainly he does not have the sexual charisma of Rhett Butler. Indeed, Popeye is impotent and must use a corncob to rape Temple Drake. This aberrant phallus and the blood seeping from Temple as Popeye drives her from the scene of the rape to a brothel in Memphis substantiate the violent nature of the crime, reminding the reader not only that rape is not about love, and often is not even about sex, but also that it is not in any way romantic. As so much of Faulkner's fiction deromanticizes the South, so does *Sanctuary* take the (false/romanticized) thrill out of rape.

Although Faulkner's novel reflects upon the heinousness of the crime of rape, it does not explore the nature or effect of the crime upon the actual victim. Rape is merely a plot device in *Sanctuary,* a symbol of the depravity of the villain, which the male protagonist must come to recognize as a depravity he, to some extent, shares. Furthermore, the effect of the crime on the victim in Faulkner's novel is not very insightful; indeed, it supports somewhat the attitude, which society is only just beginning to reject, that the victim somehow asked to be raped and may even have enjoyed it. In his 1931 review of the novel for the *Saturday Review of Literature,* Henry Seidel Canby shows no compunction about perceiving that Temple "invites" rape "by her own depravity, which even in her climaxes of terror keeps her hovering like a soiled moth near the danger." Indeed, not so unlike Scarlett, Temple eventually becomes infatuated with the next tool the impotent Popeye uses to rape her— the young man he brings into her room to have intercourse with her while he watches. Canby concludes that Temple develops in the course of the novel into "a menace to society." Contrast this view with Canby's description of Horace Benbow as "a kindhearted, liberal man, fascinated by the injustice of human misery [and m]oved by instinctive generosity" ("School" 57), and the effects of Faulkner's focal point are illuminated: the male protagonist becomes more sympathetic than the female victim of the crime. Indeed, David Williams even suggests that, reflected in Horace's train vision (of a composite Temple and Little Belle bound to a train going through a tunnel) is the notion that "Horace has himself become the terrified victim"—that it is he who becomes the "supine sacrifice": "For in a curious reversal, he has become passively feminine . . . taking the place now of Temple and Little Belle, himself assaulted by the dangerous potency which is borne within them" (140–41).

   In ironic contrast to the perception of a victimized Horace, reviewers and early critics maintained their opinion that Temple "asked for it." Sounding much like a rapist's defense attorney of the era might have sounded in a courtroom, Lawrence S. Kubie wrote in 1934 (also in the *Saturday Review of Literature*), "That Temple invited the assault with her provocative, if unconscious, exhibitionism, is unquestionable" (27). His description of Temple then reads like an accusation against the victim and, implicitly, a defense of the crime: "Temple Drake, whose lean and immature body exists in the book only to taunt and tantalize men with promises which are never fulfilled, until finally the fulfilling of the promise is taken out of her hands and worked upon her with savage and sardonic vengeance" (30). Literary critics concurred with this perception of Temple well into the 1970s; for example, David Williams (who had perceived Horace as a victim) calls Temple "a glittering and hovering coquette who is raped in cringing terror through grossly unnatural means and carried off into virtual prostitution, meanwhile discovering that she has all along consented to it, even enjoyed it, and that her affinity for evil is absolute, to the point of aiding, abetting, and even willing the evil end of men variously involved in her debauching" (142). He continues to blame Temple for "the evil end of men": "By failing to exercise her power to absent herself, she leaves a trail of continuous carnage behind her" (144); and he calls Tommy "her earliest victim" (146). Even female critic Olga Vickery describes without questioning Horace's realization that "victim though she may be, Temple is also the cause of her victimization. The responsibility for the rape and hence for Tommy's murder is as much Temple's who provoked it as it is Goodwin's who did not act to prevent it or Popeye's who actually committed it" (113).

It is somewhat reassuring that, as André Bleikasten has pointed out, "after decades of extremely harsh judgment, [Temple] is now being reexamined with warm compassion, and feminist critics have been particularly eager to exonerate her from any responsibility for what happens to her . . . and . . . to exempt Faulkner from the charge of misogyny" ("Faulkner" 207). In one more recent study, for example, Daniel J. Singal defends Temple as "not inherently more corrupt than other people; rather, her entry into the criminal underworld serves to unleash a host of natural instincts that she has had little experience in controlling. It is thus not her affinity for evil but her very innocence that makes her so vulnerable, giving rise to the intricate mix of terror and fascination, resistance and surrender that she displays" (155). But Bleikasten questions the validity of such readings, pointing out the effect upon the reader of the author's tone: "Whatever the 'facts' about [Temple's] bourgeois family background . . . our responses to her as a character while we read *Sanctuary* are manipulated throughout by the novelist." Bleikasten explains that "Faulkner's portrayal of Temple is pretty harsh, and one must be deaf to his shrill and savage rhetoric to turn the raving nymphomaniac of the final Grotto scene into the martyr-saint of male-oppressed womanhood" ("Faulkner" 208). Indeed, Singal's sympathetic attitude, reflected in the quotation above, is somewhat hardened just a few pages later in his study when he qualifies Temple's "innocence" as "entirely a surface matter bound up with cultural conditioning and social image. Beneath that surface, she is a natural human being, replete with animalistic sexual drives, a voracious ego, and other attributes supposedly absent in the southern lady. Even before her rape, Faulkner is saying, Temple's purity was an illusion" (158).

Besides Faulkner's condemning tone toward Temple Drake, his attention is, for much of the novel, not focused on her, the victim of the crime, but on her sensitive southern would-be rescuer, Horace Benbow, who is troubled (perhaps even more than he is troubled by the rape) by his introduction to the fact that people like Popeye who commit crimes like rape not only exist but could also appear at the same place at the same time as he, and thus, that they could actually affect each others' lives. Besides the focus on Horace's reaction to the crime, as Laura E. Tanner points out, "[t]he sensational crime around which *Sanctuary* revolves is never described in the novel," the effect of which, Tanner argues, is that the novel thus "assert[s] the purely literary nature of the violence enacted [only] in the reader's mind" (18). Consequently, Robert R. Moore argues that "Faulkner *uses* [the rape of Temple] as the central metaphor for *his* understanding of *man's* ineffectuality in protecting *himself* from the encroaching reality of evil" (120; emphasis added).

The use of rape as a metaphor to explore the concerns of the empowered rather than of the victim calls to mind Toni Morrison's complaint about the metaphorical role of blackness in white-authored texts: "Race has become metaphorical—a way of referring to and disguising forces, events, classes, and expressions of social decay and economic division far more threatening to the body politic than biological 'race' ever was" (*Playing* 63). Indeed, Sondra F. Guttman recognizes how Temple's subsidiary role in *Sanctuary* transforms the novel's treatment of female oppression into a symbol for something else entirely: "although Faulkner in *Sanctuary* demonstrates an awareness of female oppression across classes, the text is ultimately unable to convincingly condemn it because it uses the white female body as a symbol in order to express anxiety about the encroaching industrialization of the South. Temple's rape epitomizes this symbolic use of the female body" (24). Laura S. Patterson has pointed out, however, that "the resonance of Southern rape changes from the 1930s to the 1990s," which change is revealed by more recent writers "[p]ositioning rape as an event rather than a metaphor or a fixed precursor to male-on-male violence" (41).

.   .   .

Before turning to the role of rape in more recent southern novels, and having been reminded of two of the most well-known rapes in southern literature,[1] the reader is asked to call to mind other rapes in this region's literature prior to the 1980s. To start, one should consider the countless rapes committed against black women by white men, which are acknowledged in southern literature since the Renascence period, though not so much before this period (and then only vaguely alluded to). Although these rapes do not fit the scope of this chapter, these crimes are certainly no less serious just because the social system of the ante- and postbellum periods did not recognize them as rapes. Indeed, I would argue that the support of society-at-large compounds the horror of these crimes. The plantation owner, the overseer, and, for that matter, any white man who had the inclination, could, with impunity, rape a black woman in the South until some time after the civil rights movement. Although many "decent gentle-folk" were disturbed by such practices, I contend that they should also have felt guilty for not speaking out against these crimes.[2]

Reflecting upon these crimes against black women, one notes the irony in how preserving the purity of the white woman was used as an excuse for such violence, even as it was used to support slavery and the Ku Klux Klan and to "excuse" the lynching of black men. Indeed, one incident of rape that occurs in early postbellum southern literature is the rape of a white woman by a black man in Thomas Dixon's *The Clansman* (1905), a propagandistic novel for the KKK. This literary rape is counterbalanced by the attempted seduction of a black man by a white woman in Harper Lee's *To Kill a Mockingbird* (1960), for which the black man was accused of a rape that never occurred—or rather, of which the woman's father was actually guilty.

Recalling the image of the chaste southern woman, the flower of the South, in southern literature of the postbellum and then Renascence periods, it is not surprising that there are so few occurrences of actual rapes of white women (by white men). One realizes that protecting the virtue of the southern woman was a primary goal of the southern white man, so raping her would not "make sense." But when *does* rape make sense? And certainly in real life, if not in literature, white women were raped in this region, probably as often as elsewhere. However, the occurrence of violence against women not motivated by racial difference and privilege is one skeleton that few southern writers allowed out of the closet until the last decades of the twentieth century when such books as Lee Smith's *Black Mountain Breakdown* (1980), Alice Walker's *The Color Purple* (1982), Jill McCorkle's *Ferris Beach* (1990), Dorothy Allison's *Bastard Out of Carolina* (1992), and (to be discussed in this chapter) Elizabeth Dewberry's *Many Things Have Happened since He Died and Here Are the Highlights* were published. Interestingly, in all of these novels, following in the tradition of *A Streetcar Named Desire* and *To Kill a Mockingbird,* the rape is committed by an acquaintance of the victim, many of them by family members; *and in none of them does the victim fall in love with her rapist.*

Before examining the deromanticization of rape in works such as these, I back up for a moment to make some more general comments about the Southern Renascence and the second flowering of literature in the South since the 1980s, in order to explain how I can make the above distinction even after naming several works and alluding to several more, written much earlier in the twentieth century, in which an incident of rape is central. The point of contrast is simple: rape occurred in those earlier works, but, as we have seen, it was used as a plot device more than as a means of exploring the oppression of women.

After World War I, America's attention began to be repeatedly drawn to the new literature being published by southern writers, and soon readers worldwide began to acknowledge the Southern Renascence. The quality of the literature coming out of the South during this period is often accounted for by the distance from their southern homes that many of the post–World War I writers had achieved while overseas, distance that allowed them to develop a more objective perspective upon the South than could be detected in the work of earlier southern writers. As J. A. Bryant summarizes the change, "the South had finally begun to see the Civil War as something more than an ancient culture's finest hour" (35). Another reason for the quality of the literature is that much of it was being written by people who had previously been denied a voice: women and African-Americans. One result of the new objectivity and the new voices is that these writers' literature brought the issue of race relations out of the closet and treated it more realistically than had much of earlier southern literature, acknowledging that the image of the content, even happy, slave who mourned his secure, even comfortable, life on the plantation before the Civil War ruined his Edenic home was a myth, as was the image of the bestial black man whose sole desire was to rape the white woman and kill her family. This new fiction deconstructed the Old South and showed how its sin of slavery continued to haunt the New South.

Southern American literature is currently enjoying a second flowering, one possible reason for which is the willingness of contemporary southern writers to take other skeletons out of closets and thus develop not new, but previously silenced, conflicts in their literature. They continue to deal with the issue of the oppression of African-Americans in the South but have begun to deal more fully with the oppression of women as well. In both cases, the difference from, for example, Faulkner's development of these two issues is that these writers examine the issue, not from the perspective of the sensitive white liberal-minded man out of place in and trying to change the social system that would support such oppression but from the perspective of the victims of the oppression. In other words, exploration of the violence enacted against these groups is not just another avenue through which to understand the development of the consciousness of the southern white male.

Examination of Elizabeth Dewberry's 1990 novel *Many Things Have Happened since He Died, and Here Are the Highlights* illustrates this point of contrast. This novel is told from the point of view of a victim of recurrent domestic violence, which culminates in the rape of the narrator by her abusive husband, which may, in fact, have been a gang rape by her husband and two of his friends. The reader cannot tell for certain what exactly happened for the narrator never recounts the incident in detail. At one point, though, she recalls a dream that suggests that the two friends who visit her husband, Malone, in their apartment may have participated in the rape: "I'm in the kitchen drinking a glass of water and Malone comes in and turns on the oven and opens it and I start saying no no you'll let all the heat out and then there are three Malones and they all have a casserole or something I can't really remember what it is but they want to stick them in the oven but there isn't room for all of them and I just keep saying no" (114). Later, she remarks of the baby she is carrying, which was apparently conceived on the night she was raped, "I hate this baby. I hate its *fathers* [plural]" (186; emphasis added).

The novel is structured as a collection of transcriptions from Dictaphone tapes, on which the unnamed narrator/protagonist recorded piecemeal the story of her marriage from soon after her wedding day to shortly after the death of her husband and birth of her child. From the opening entry, which ends with her thoughts about how she might kill herself or someone else nonviolently, she hints that her husband is physically abusing her:

> If I had to kill myself or somebody else it would not be bloody. You can stick a
> nail in somebody's ear when they're asleep and they won't be able to figure out
> what did it if you pull it back out. A gas leak when they're asleep is also a good
> idea because it looks like an accident and doesn't leave a mess. I would never
> use a gun or a knife. I am against violence.
>   Malone is not. (7)

Since she believes divorcing her husband would be a sin and murdering him would damn her to hell for certain, the narrator spends a great amount of time trying to think of a way to commit suicide, which, according to the narrator, "is a sin but not a mortal sin" (17). The difficulty lies in finding a method of killing herself that will not damage her beauty, for she apparently agrees with Edgar Allan Poe that, in her words, "there is something wonderful about a beautiful young woman who is dead" (32). Her attitude suggests that she is well versed in the tropes of a traditional romance: the beautiful heroine dies in the end, leaving everyone remorseful about the tragic loss. Furthermore, in considering how she will translate the tapes she is making into a novel, she thinks about what she will change and what she will leave out so that her novel will be more of a traditional romance than her life is turning out to be. Eventually, however, the narrator accepts that there is nothing "romantic" about her situation. Her injuries have escalated from a broken finger and black eye to a brutal rape, which, like the "rape" in *Gone with the Wind,* occurs behind closed doors, but in this case the closed doors are to the narrator's memory of the night. She wakes up the next morning, not smiling with satisfaction but baffled and bruised, unable to recall what happened or how she came to be at her mother's house. Furthermore, unlike Scarlett or any of the other so-called heroines of romances, she does not fall in love with (or in her case remain devoted to) her rapist. Rather, her husband becomes less and less appealing to her as the book—and his abuse of her—continues.

The narrator's first solution to not living happily ever after with her new husband is to rewrite her life when she transforms her taped journal into a novel: "I feel a certain strange power. Like I can rewrite the past and start over and certain things will never have happened and certain things will have and I will be beautiful and other people will know it they will say she was very beautiful I will never forget how beautiful she was" (84). The reader is here reminded of one means of dealing with distressing events typical of the traditional southern woman: selective and creative memory, what Ellen Glasgow called "evasive idealism" (Glasgow, *Certain* 50). The falseness of the narrator's sense of empowerment in being able to so easily change the past by rewriting it is reflected in the fact that she is still apparently seeing herself dead by the end of her "novel"—though whether as a result of finally succeeding in finding a way to commit suicide that will not affect her appearance or at the hands of her husband is not clear. Furthermore, her next comments contradict her belief that she can change what has happened by rewriting it differently: "Scars are what makes it hard to rewrite. You can rewrite why you got them into an accident but you cannot wipe them away.

This is all garbage you cannot change the past you cannot change anything you can only forget. You can erase the memory of them but they still leave a trace behind" (84). Twice in the novel she will repeat these sentiments to remind herself not to try to change the past: first, after Malone dies of a drug overdose she remarks, perhaps in response to the guilt she feels since she had often wished him dead: "I can't go back and redo it. You can't rewrite anything the past is unchanging unchangeable now I never rewrite anything what happens happens" (159); second, in response to her pregnancy, a consequence of the rape, she asks:

> how can I go forward when I am pregnant with the past. I am not married to Malone anymore but I am still married to Malone's past I can't take a shower I can't look in the mirror I can't find something to wear I can't try to get out of bed in the morning without the past being here in the present. . . . It's like I'm being haunted by this . . . vestige of the past this intrusion from the past . . . so he is dead only not quite buried. (186–87)

Like so many of Faulkner's male protagonists who feel overwhelmed by the burden of the past (from their slave-holding ancestors' sins back to the innate depravity of all human beings), this female creation of a contemporary southern writer comes to understand the presence of the past. But she is not making excuses for her own inadequacies and troubles by taking upon herself the sins of her ancestors. When she realizes the presence of the past, it is a step toward healing and away from the idea of committing suicide. Before she can put the past behind her, she must acknowledge its presence, including not only the rape but also her role in her victimization: that she had accepted without question the tenets of Christian fundamentalism, particularly those defining the role of the wife as subservient to the authoritative husband.

A large part of Dewberry's agenda with this novel seems to be to take on the fundamentalist Christians, so prevalent in the South, who continue to advocate obedience and submission to the husband regardless of his behavior. Dewberry shows how supporting a hierarchy within a marriage could lead to condoning physical abuse of the wife who fails to meet her husband's demands. Within the novel, the narrator blames herself for inciting her husband's temper—that is, until he rapes her. She has lapses after this incident, when she looks back and wonders how she might have been a better wife to Malone, but she can never excuse this violation. Soon after he appar-

ently raped her, in one of her entries on the Dictaphone, the narrator pon-
ders the issue of obedience and within her rumination reveals to the reader
what happened on the night she refuses to talk/write about:

> I said at our wedding I would obey him and I do that was a solemn oath to God
> and I take that seriously. . . . But it seems to me there ought to be limits that
> there are still certain things that belong to me . . . there ought to be certain
> times when I could say no and he would have to stop that he could order me to
> submit but I could say no it's still my body that I could say no about the things
> that are mine and I wouldn't be breaking my oath to God. Malone says *no you
> said love honor and obey* he says obey real loud *you didn't say obey when you feel
> like it* but I still say there's a problem. (67–68; Dewberry's italics)

Her guilty conscience, a by-product of Christian fundamentalism, causes her
to consider in her next entry her own culpability for having been drinking on
the night of the rape (which she still does not acknowledge outright), but
again she ultimately rejects any blame for Malone's violence: "I was drunk
and I have admitted that but he was worse than that and I said no and husband or no husband you don't do it when the other person says no when I
said love honor and obey I'm not sure exactly what I meant but I know what
I didn't mean I didn't mean that" (73).

Surprisingly, it is Malone who suggests that the two of them seek marriage
counseling; however, what he has in mind begins with a couples' retreat at
her mother's church where she will be reminded that her "role is like a support beam, make him look good and when he looks good you look good"
(109). The narrator reports that when the couples are divided into two
groups, the "girls" are given

> a talk about submission all of which I have heard a thousand times before . . .
> wherever they get women alone they tell us this. Sorry bad attitude. It doesn't
> hurt to hear it again actually I even learned some things. Part of the problem is
> apparently I haven't been submitting enough to Malone. Look at any troubled
> marriage and you'll see a wife who is not submitting to her husband and a
> husband who is not submitting to God. The whole Christian life is one of
> submission. (109)

Although the narrator here suggests that she is accepting this opinion of a
woman's duty to her husband, she concludes the account of the retreat with
the question, "How can I possibly submit any more to Malone and survive"

(112). Apparently, she can no longer accept on faith a dictum that puts her life in danger.

The counseling only helps Malone to curb his temper for a short time; soon, he is lashing out at the narrator again, though at this time only verbally. Typical of the abusive husband, after one such outburst, he is extremely remorseful, not only about this temper tantrum but also about the past incidents of abuse. He even alludes to the rape in his apology: "*what kind of monster would do to his wife what I did to you I just can't get over it*" (135; Dewberry's italics). His focus on *his* pain at this time reminds the reader of Faulkner's focus (in *Sanctuary*) on Horace's distress upon learning about Popeye turning Temple—who reminds Horace of his own stepdaughter (of whom he has had lustful thoughts)—into a kind of concubine. Faulkner appears not as concerned with Temple's reaction to her rape and subsequent internment in a brothel as he is with Horace's distress upon finding out about it. Dewberry's scene deconstructs such misplaced concern. She has her narrator refuse to comfort her husband for raping her in the first place or for reminding her of that night, which she is trying to put behind them so that she can go along with his wishes to make the marriage work: "Malone cut this out I can't keep going through this" (134). Surprised by his wife's failure to comfort him, Malone then accuses her of having no compassion—a particularly ironic accusation coming from a rapist: "*Christ can't you have some compassion . . . a person tells you he feels like an utter failure in life and you tell them to cut it out*" (134; Dewberry's italics). Dewberry here shows how misplaced concern, like Faulkner's concern for Horace rather than Temple, can lead to blaming the victim for the crime. Recall Faulkner's suggestion that Temple ultimately enjoyed, to some extent, her time in Memphis. The narrator of Dewberry's novel closes this journal entry expressing what her creator might say to Faulkner regarding what he inadvertently asks of his female characters and what the author's reaction might be to Faulkner's male characters: "I feel sorry for him I really do but good grief I shouldn't have to be the one he hurts and the one who comforts him because he feels bad about hurting me. He is a sensitive person that was one of the first things I liked about him but he has gone overboard" (136).

Dewberry's narrator decides not to keep her baby, the product of the rape. Now that Malone is dead, she is ready to begin a new life and wants the baby to have a life unburdened by the past as well. She is worried that since the baby is a boy he is doomed, given the history of the men in her family. She

hopes that growing up in another family will help him to defy his biologi-
cally inherited destiny. To further aid him, she also writes a letter for him to
read when he gets older, in which she rejects that part of her own upbringing
that gave Malone the right to abuse her, took away her right to defy him, and
thus nearly brought about her own destruction: "The Bible says husbands
love your wives and wives submit yourselves to your husbands but I think it
works both ways like wives also love your husbands and husbands also submit yourselves to your wives. I think it means love isn't stubborn not love is a
fool" (211).

.   .   .

As mentioned, several other contemporary southern writers include incidents of rape in their novels and treat them from the perspective of the victim or, as in the case of Jill McCorkle's *Ferris Beach,* from the perspective of
another young woman who could be similarly victimized if she came out of
the hiding place from which she witnesses a gang rape to try to help her class-
mate. Besides Dewberry and McCorkle, writers like Alice Walker (in *The
Color Purple*), Lee Smith (in *Black Mountain Breakdown*), and Dorothy
Allison (in *Bastard Out of Carolina*) are not concerned with the men who
have been unable to protect their mothers/daughters/sisters/wives from this
crime. Their interest/focus/concern is with the victims—or rather with how
these women can rise above and perhaps against their victimization.[3]

In contrast, one might take a look at the rape incident in Pat Conroy's *The
Prince of Tides* to see, as we did in the chapter on Barthelme and McMurtry,
how some writers—another white male writer in this case—continue in,
rather than react against, the tradition of Faulkner. One might apply here
Fred Hobson's theory regarding the appeal of Faulkner's influence to earlier
twentieth-century southern writers, whom Hobson believes "wrote . . . with
an eye very much on past southern giants." These writers, according to
Hobson, "could not seem to escape, did not seem to *want* to escape, the influence of Faulkner and Wolfe." Hobson names William Styron, pointing
out how his "*Lie Down in Darkness* [1951] was *The Sound and the Fury* cast in
Tidewater, Virginia" (*Southern* 5). Similarly, Conroy's novels develop South
Carolina protagonists in the Faulknerian tradition.

Throughout his fiction, Conroy returns to the Faulknerian source of conflict, the impotence of the sensitive white southern man as he tries to reconcile the continued discord between the vestiges of the Old South and the

representatives of the New. The impotence of the liberal-minded white male in *The Prince of Tides* is most fully realized in a rape scene. Not only is Tom Wingo unable to rescue his mother and sister from their rapists but he, too, is raped, even as he listens to their pleading for him to save them.[4] Reading the account of the nightmarish violence from Tom's perspective, the reader is inclined to direct most of his/her sympathy toward him; his physical suffering and psychological humiliation are rendered more significant than his sister Savannah's and certainly more traumatic than his mother Lila's.

While the main conflict of the novel's present develops from the emotional instability of Tom's sister, which has led her to several suicide attempts, it is not Savannah's mental health that ultimately interests or concerns Pat Conroy. She is, like Temple Drake, merely a catalyst for the development of the protagonist toward the resolution of *his* conflict. Indeed, the first two sentences of the novel's prologue focus on Tom Wingo's "wound": "My wound is geography. It is also my anchorage, my port of call" (1).[5] As the novel opens, Tom is called away from his home in South Carolina by Savannah's most recent suicide attempt, which brings Tom to New York and prompts him to tell *his* story of the Wingo family to Savannah's psychiatrist, Susan Lowenstein. Ultimately, it is *Tom's* mental health, not Savannah's, that is most central to the novel, indeed, that eventually most concerns *Savannah's* psychiatrist, as Dr. Lowenstein falls in love with Tom.

During his sessions with Susan Lowenstein (intended at first to help her to help Savannah), Tom proceeds from one family horror story to another, beginning with his father's violent beatings of his wife and children; seeming to culminate in the rape of Lila, Savannah, and Tom; followed by Tom's brother Luke's rescue of his mother and siblings and the murder of the rapists, none of which will Lila allow the children to discuss, and thus deal with; but then ultimately culminating in the death of Luke years later, betrayed by his beloved mother as he tried to save his town from destruction. Whether Conroy intended it or not, it becomes clear to the reader that one is to consider the ultimate tragedy to be Tom's "impotence." First, he could not save his mother and sister; rather, he is aligned with them as a third "lady in distress" whom Luke, their knight in shining armor, must rescue. Then, when he has the opportunity to even things with Luke years later by rescuing his older brother, he fails, and Luke is killed. Tom's grief and guilt have driven him to a nervous breakdown, after which he lost his job and perhaps his wife, who is having an affair. Savannah's suicide attempt, then, becomes a means of shaking him up so that he will do something to put his own life back in order.

Not only is the reader not led to be too concerned about Savannah's mental health and survival as we are directed instead to follow Tom's recovery, neither is the reader allowed to be very sympathetic with Lila Wingo as rape victim or as a physically abused wife. Indeed, Tom's mother is so villainized in the novel, not unlike Narcissa Benbow Sartoris in *Sanctuary*, that the reader is led to believe that, since no rapist could penetrate the shell of her ambition, which is much more important to her than the body that the rapist does violate, then there is no need for concern about her after the rape. In his exploration of Faulkner's transition from Victorian to modern writer, Daniel Singal determines that Faulkner's "real target" is not "*all* women" but rather, "a specific type of woman highly prevalent in the South of his day . . . the southern lady." One can see in Conroy's depiction of Lila Wingo a continuation of Faulkner's criticism of this character type's "obsession with respectability" and "shallowness" (Singal 157).

The reader is not even allowed to pity Lila for very long after the beatings she endures at the hands of her husband, since she ultimately deserts him, taking everything from him at the same time and betraying her children in the process, as she sells the family's island, which she receives in the divorce settlement, and thereby sells out their whole county, which will be the site of a nuclear manufacturing plant. This act ultimately leads to the untimely death of her oldest son, Luke, the son who rescued her from many of her husband's beatings as well as from her rapist. It may be that, in his characterization of Lila Wingo, Conroy shows how a victim of domestic violence may become hardened by her oppressor, may herself become a victimizer. Certainly her inclination toward joining rather than beating her oppressors is reminiscent, first of all, of Temple Drake's behavior in Memphis; as Singal explains, Faulkner's "main purpose in dragging Temple Drake out of her sheltered world was to make manifest the tissue of lies on which her persona of false innocence rested" (157). One might therefore use Robert Moore's reading of Temple to understand what Conroy is doing with Lila Wingo: "She is, nonetheless, a victim of evil as well. The process by which victim becomes victimizer is the story Faulkner tells in *Sanctuary*. Temple's unexpected, inappropriate behavior is not the enigma it has too often been made out to be. It is, instead, a key to understanding Faulkner's vision of evil" (113). One can also see how Lila Wingo's "if you can't beat them, join them" attitude is also reminiscent of Thomas Sutpen and Macon Dead II; but still the reader is discomforted by Conroy's unrelenting villainization of this woman while simultaneously making her husband, the abusive Henry Wingo, more and more pathetic—even sympathetic—as the novel draws to a close. Perhaps Conroy's vision is too reminiscent of the male-centered gaze of William Faulkner, a focus less excusable in a writer of the supposedly more enlightened late twentieth century.

One of the subplots in *The Prince of Tides,* which is also a subplot of *The Great Santini* (1976)—another novel in which Conroy deals with the issue of domestic abuse—and a central plot of his *The Lords of Discipline* (1980), involves the liberal protagonist's attempt to deal with race relations in his South Carolina settings during the period of integration. In his development of these conflicts, Conroy reminds the reader of Faulkner again, although in these cases he seems more aware than Faulkner of his characters' cowardliness as they try to follow their consciences without calling too much attention to themselves. It is interesting that in two of these cases—*The Prince of Tides* and *The Great Santini*—Conroy has female characters shame their brothers into standing up for the black characters being tormented. Conroy seems, therefore, to recognize the identification between white women and African-Americans as victims of oppression and their common frustration with the white man who feels impotent when, by comparison to them, he is so socially empowered.[6]

Philip M. Weinstein summarizes Faulkner's canon thusly:

Faulkner tells the story, in myriad ways, of the lost homeland, the disenfranchised white son. The ordeal of innocence wounded and transformed to outrage is his signature event. . . . In figuring out the ramifications of that young man's pain—the cultural dysfunction that underlay it, the women and blacks that necessarily suffered its fallout—he became one of America's most provocatively diagnostic novelists. The drama he narrates is at once patriarchal and Oedipal, and Faulkner emerges as the American writer who best sees through, without pretending to see past, the twentieth-century unworkability of this drama. (*What* 192)

Pat Conroy also sees through but continues to find "unworkable" the patriarchal paradox that Faulkner sets up in his fiction: whereas the South is a patriarchy, many men do not feel empowered enough by their dominance to right the wrongs around them. Rather, they are paralyzed by the enormity of the problems and begin to feel like victims themselves as they recognize their own responsibility for bringing about change. The next chapter examines, first, Faulkner contemporary Ellen Glasgow's frustration with this paralysis and then the work of a white male writer who also has white male characters at the center of most of his fiction—white men of less blue blood but more backbone than Faulkner's liberal white male Hamlets.

chapter 7

Don't Just Sit There; Do Something

Frustration
with Faulkner
from Glasgow
to Gautreaux

I was so sick of reading about the alienated hero of superior sensibility that I thought I would write about just the opposite!

Bobbie Ann Mason, quoted in Wendy Smith

As suggested in chapter 1, some postmodern writers, like Donald Barthelme, have become more pessimistic about the perpetuating dominance of the patriarchy. The works of writers like Donald Barthelme, Larry McMurtry, and Pat Conroy continue to focus on the father/son conflicts found in Faulkner's fiction; to objectify women as victims of the patriarchy but still focus their attention on the men's "suffering" within the system; and to marginalize African-Americans (and other non-Euro-Americans, as in McMurtry's fiction), also recognized as victims but who are still not the concern that the white male romantic hero is who is continuously frustrated in his endeavors to change the system and thus "save" the "Other." Ernest Gaines brought African-American men, at least, into center ring as the twentieth century moved into its last decades. At the same time, Gaines's depiction of the snail's pace at which his native Louisiana is changing its way of life lays much of the blame, one might determine from his fiction, upon the defeatism of the liberal white male's sense of impotence. How frustrating it must be for this African-American man to witness the socially empowered white man wringing his hands helplessly! Indeed, one can find in Gaines's development of Frank Laurent in "Bloodline" evidence of his frustration. As described by Jack Hicks, "Frank has inherited a legacy of racial devastation: though he realizes the cruel history of the institutions around him, he professes himself powerless to undo the past" (121).

Such frustration is neither new nor limited to black writers. By listening to echoes of Faulkner's "A Rose for Emily" in the work of Faulkner's contemporary Ellen Glasgow and Gaines's contemporary Tim Gautreaux one can trace this frustration with such hand-wringing by the socially empowered from Glasgow, a southern white aristocrat, but a woman, to Gautreaux, a southern white man, but not an aristocrat.

A Rose for Eva, Too: Two Sheltered Lives

Always, from his earliest childhood, he mused, with a curious resentment against life, he had been the victim of pity. Of his own pity, not another's. Of that double-edged nerve of sympathy, like the aching nerve in a tooth, which throbbed alive at the sight of injustice or cruelty. One woman after another had enslaved his sympathy more than his passion.

Glasgow, *The Sheltered Life*

Miss Glasgow . . . is one of the very few writers upon the old and the modern South who understands tradition, who comprehends the intricate values of the life of a "gentleman" or a "lady," and yet never writes sentiment when satire is called for, never perfumes the "bad smell" of decaying gentility.

Henry Seidel Canby, in a 1932 review of *The Sheltered Life*

It is not surprising that critics have not remarked upon the echoes of Faulkner's "A Rose for Emily" (first published in 1930) in Ellen Glasgow's 1932 novel *The Sheltered Life*. One cannot at first imagine two more different characters than Faulkner's grotesque Emily Grierson and Glasgow's romantic Eva Birdsong, although Glasgow biographer Susan Goodman has made one point of comparison: "Like Faulkner's Miss Emily [Glasgow's Eva] belongs to the public, which regards her less as a person than a 'memorable occasion'" ("Memory" 248).[1] Recognizing the roles of Emily and Eva in their respective communities, as well as similarities between the authors' descriptions of these two works' settings and the cover-up in both works of the murder that each of these two women commits reveals the common guilty party: the community whose ideals—or need for ideals—ultimately drive these women mad.

In narrowing her guilty party from the communal voice that Faulkner uses in his story to the characters directly involved in her novel (the Archbalds in particular), Glasgow further reveals an impatience not only with the community that holds on to its ideals but more particularly with romantic idealists like General David Archbald (including, perhaps, Faulkner himself).[2] General Archbald can be perceived as Glasgow's (perhaps unintentional) satirical manifestation of the character who received most of Faulkner's sympathy—characters like Quentin Compson and Horace Benbow, and eventually, though not yet created by the time Glasgow's novel was published, Isaac McCaslin and Gavin Stevens. As has been shown in the previous chapters, Faulkner's liberal-minded romantic heroes sympathize with the oppression they witness (but do not themselves, as white men, experience) but bemoan their own impotence to relieve this suffering (being part of a minority themselves, as liberals). I suggest that Glasgow's satire of this character type in her creation of General Archbald may be unintentional because, according to Glasgow biographer E. Stanly Godbold Jr., Glasgow "never read the complete works of [Faulkner]" (224), and Glasgow's only recorded complaints against Faulkner have to do with the "violence and decadence" of his depiction of the South (Godbold 187). However, one might think of this Faulkner character type as "the futilitarians" Glasgow mentions in a 1934 review of Stark Young's *So Red the Rose*:

> Some critics . . . may object that this book is written from the point of view of the Southern planter and does not, therefore, survey the past from the flat proletarian angle. But these people had a point of view. . . . Certainly they are entitled to be heard in their own defense. They merit at least a share of the attention paid to the sodden *futilitarians* and corncob cavaliers of the literary South. (Raper, *Ellen* 98–99; emphasis added)

And directly suggestive of Glasgow's problem with this Faulkner character, in a letter dated the same year as her review, in which she expresses the same sentiments about Young's new novel, almost verbatim, she ends the passage referring specifically to "the sodden futilitarians and the corncob cavaliers *of Mr. Faulkner*" (Rouse, *Letters* 154; emphasis added), revealing by her word choice her annoyance with Faulkner's impotent idealists. This frustration might be traced back from 1934 at least as far as her creation of General Archbald for the 1932 novel *The Sheltered Life*. The general would certainly qualify as one of these "futilitarians" and thus could be perceived as an earlier response to Faulkner's then still-new prototype.

On the other hand, Frederick P. W. McDowell remarks on how Glasgow's manifestation of this character type actually predates Faulkner's. Of her 1904 novel *The Deliverance,* McDowell writes, "Here obtrudes a hint of *that aristocratic debility* which was later to be more completely exploited in Southern literature, in the failure, for instance, of some of Faulkner's characters such as Thomas Sutpen or Jason Compson III and his son Quentin to command circumstance" (70; emphasis added). Similarly, Blair Rouse concludes her study of Glasgow's work also noting the two writers' similar depiction of this character type: "Like Faulkner, Ellen Glasgow treated her Southern aristocrat with mixed admiration and regret. She, like her younger contemporary, recognized the worth of the aristocratic individual at his best, as well as the fallacies and weaknesses of his manner of life and his beliefs when they had ceased to be supported by individual strength of character" (*Ellen* 140). Glasgow may have written about debilitated male aristocrats of weak character even before Faulkner, but the point is that her depiction of the character type by the time of its manifestation in General Archbald reveals her frustration with a white man of privilege feeling so powerless to do anything to alleviate the suffering of others. (Faulkner, in contrast, shared the frustration of the supposedly impotent rather than of the more truly impotent—the unempowered woman or African-American.)

I therefore disagree with Frederick McDowell's assessment of General Archbald as the only character in *The Sheltered Life* who is *not* self-pitying (191). I would argue that he is the *most* self-pitying character in the novel. While McDowell's admiration of the general is not atypical of the early reviews and criticism of the novel, postfeminism readers are much less inclined to regard the general with approbation. Rather, more recent readers may find themselves sharing Glasgow's annoyance with (not feeling sorry for) the adult David Archbald who pities but does not *do* anything for Eva Birdsong, in spite of his deep admiration for, even infatuation with her—that is, until he covers up a murder for her and thereby, as Julius Rowan Raper argues, "restores the false order of their sheltered lives" (*From* 148). In like vein, Linda W. Wagner-Martin perceives General Archbald as largely responsible for the tragic events of the novel. "It is [he] who assigns the women of his family to conventional roles [and] keeps them locked into those roles." Wagner-Martin also notes the general's passivity. Not only is this characteristic what keeps him from seeking his desires, but it also keeps him from helping Eva: he admires her, but "never takes any action to improve her life," Wagner-Martin writes. His life, like Eva's, may be one of "self-abnegation," but Wagner-

Martin suggests that he has the power to change things (Wagner[-Martin] 88). Instead, he sends his granddaughter Jenny Blair on the same course as Eva.

Glasgow describes early in her novel the physical changes that have occurred in the old southern community since the turn of the century: "One by one, they saw the old houses demolished, the fine old elms mutilated. Telegraph poles slashed the horizon; furnaces, from a distance, belched soot into the drawing-rooms; [and] when the wind shifted on the banks of the river, an evil odour sprang up from the hollow" (6–7). Her description recalls Faulkner's "A Rose for Emily," in which "garages and cotton gins had encroached and obliterated even the august names of that neighborhood; only Miss Emily's house was left, lifting its stubborn and coquettish decay above the cotton wagons and the gasoline pumps—an eyesore among eyesores" (*Collected* 119).[3] And from this house a portentous odor eventually emanates.

Faulkner's narrative style and tone contribute to the reader's developing sympathy for the last Grierson left in this house. Before the nature of the bad smell is revealed to the *reader* (the townspeople, I believe, have known the source all along), one reads about how Emily's father chased away her suitors, thus leaving her all alone when he died; then about how the townspeople interfered with her more than likely last chance to have a husband, resulting, it seems, in his having left her, too. The reader also learns about how Emily has been alternately resented (for her father's snobbery) and pitied (when he died), judged (for forgetting "noblesse oblige") and pitied again (when Homer Barron disappears). Whereas the town intrudes into her business to call relatives to put a stop to her scandalous affair, they do not, significantly, intrude themselves or call anyone when she buys poison with which they believe "[s]he will kill herself." Rather, they determine, "it would be the best thing" (126). As Isaac Rodman notes in response to these two lines, "[w]ithout a qualm or a tear, the town is willing to dedicate Emily on the altar of Southern gentility, making of their idol a blood sacrifice" (10).

The narrator's "rose for Emily"—telling her story in such a way as to indict the town for the discovery made upon Emily's death—reveals Faulkner's usual awareness of the consequences of oppression, including the oppression of women, as has been shown in earlier chapters.[4] It is the limited life opportunities allowed a woman like Emily that ultimately drives her mad enough to fulfill as much of her role as woman as she can by killing her suitor rather than risk his leaving her. The perverse detail of the iron-gray hair that reveals Emily's necrophilia suggests her motive: to have her husband by whatever means she had to get him, wife being the only role allowed a woman of her class.[5]

The macabre story of Emily Grierson is surprisingly echoed by the romantic tragedy of Eva Birdsong. Eva may be as beautiful as Emily is grotesque, but like Emily, Eva is an icon for her community, a representative of their past glory. Hence, her community does not interfere in Eva's life in any way that might relieve Eva's unhappiness, yet they do intrude upon her daily life in such a way as to contribute to its burdensomeness. The whole community participates in Eva's blindness to her husband's affairs, thereby contributing to her romanticized view of her marriage. One wonders how much happier Eva would have eventually been if someone had pricked her bubble by exposing one of George's affairs openly. But just as Eva uses her ideal perception of her marriage in order to waylay any misgivings about having given up a possible opera career and having lost the family fortune, all for nothing if she were not happily married to her ideal mate, so, too, does the community expect Eva to maintain her ideal beauty and stature in order to hold on to their own romantic perception of their past. Perhaps the most poignant illustration of how Eva must always be self-possessed comes with her entrance into the novel:

> Thinking herself alone in the street, unaware of the row of admiring spectators, Mrs. Birdsong had permitted her well-trained muscles to relax for a moment, while her brilliance suddenly flickered out, as if the sunshine had faded. The corners of her mouth twitched and drooped; her step lost its springiness; and her figure appeared to give way at the waist and sink down for support into the stiff ripples of taffeta. Then, as quickly as her spirit had flagged, it recovered its energy, and sprang back into poise. As the first whisper reached her, her tired features were transfigured by an arch and vivacious smile. (16)

In that brief moment during which Eva had forgotten herself, Cora Archbald had noticed her droop and "wonder[ed] what [was] the matter now" (16). And at the ball later in the novel, when Eva sees George go outside with the young debutante Delia Barron, Mary Peyton tells her to "sav[e her] pride. . . . It is much wiser to pretend that you didn't [see them]. Even if you know, it is safer not to suspect anything" (87).[6] These women are apparently aware of the truth of Eva's marriage, but they encourage her to ignore it—for her own peace of mind, as there is nothing to be done about it, divorce not being a viable option at the time.

So, too, does General Archbald support Eva's evasive idealism, in spite of his apparent love for her, which should have inspired him to defend her honor. In his position as a community patriarch, the general might have spoken to George about his infidelities, threatened George in some way—in other words *done something* for the woman he loves, which might have waylaid the eventual tragedy. And David Archbald, Glasgow reveals in part 2 of the novel, had the *potential* to be someone who stepped in and *did something* against an injustice. As a youth, he once helped a member of another oppressed group, a runaway slave, an act that went against the ideology—and laws—of his community. And he not only got away with breaking the law in this manner, but *how* he got away with it—his parents sending him to Europe to protect him from the possible repercussions of his crime—would have shown him how a son of the southern aristocracy would be protected from the consequences that another citizen might suffer for breaking the law. Given his youthful courageousness and his early awareness of the privileges of his class, the general has no excuse for doing nothing for Eva later in his life—except that he has long since given in to the stronger cowardly side of his nature. The same boy who refused to kill a wild animal in spite of his grandfather's chiding and who helped a runaway slave returned to Virginia as a young man to kill other men in defense of the institution of slavery.[7] And after that war, General Archbald settled into his role as a southern patriarch, doing what was expected of him even when those expectations did not match his own ambitions. Thus, he finds himself in the novel's present dwelling on his past, trying to figure out what it was all about.

Faulkner returns to his story's present, the death of Emily Grierson, in the story's last section, noting how some of the men at her funeral "talk[ed] of Miss Emily as if she had been a contemporary of theirs, believing that they had danced with her and courted her perhaps, confusing time . . . as the old do" (129). Their confusion reflects Emily's role in the town as an icon. One might flash upon Faulkner's "gathering of old men" (borrowing Gaines's phrase) toward the end of Glasgow's novel, when Jenny Blair passes through a similar gathering upon leaving her house:

Downstairs on the back porch, sheltered from the sun by the grey-and-purple awning, General Archbald sat with a group of old men who had dropped in for a smoke. Though all were upwards of eighty, there was *nothing impressive* about their long lives except that they had been able to live them, that they had been young once and were now old. . . . As they had *accepted fate without thinking about it,* so they clung now to the empty hours that were left over from life. (231; emphasis added)

Strangely, these men serve no purpose in the advancement of the novel's plot. They appear only in this brief passage as the reader follows Jenny Blair through them on her way to the Birdsongs' house, and then they are dropped and forgotten. But their presence *is* significant: in this brief passage, Glasgow pointedly condemns the inaction of men like General Archbald and Faulkner's similar romantic idealists and mocks the impotence of their lives. These men may have lived scores longer than Quentin Compson, but they have done no more good than he did—and probably more damage—as much damage as Isaac McCaslin would do through inaction by the time he reaches his eighties, as was discussed in chapter 2.

One cannot imagine the reader familiar with Faulkner's prototypical sensitive southern white male aristocrat not being reminded of the type when eavesdropping upon General Archbald's ruminations in part 2, "The Deep Past." His obsession with time throughout the section echoes the prototype himself, Quentin Compson, and, like Quentin, toward the end of this section, General Archbald thinks to himself, "I do not wish to forget" (118), referring to a lost love. Unlike Quentin, of course, he does not commit suicide out of fear of forgetting; he seems to know that men like himself—as well as Quentin and the various subsequent manifestations of the Faulkner prototype (none of whom commits suicide)—do not forget because they dwell on the painful past throughout their lives. And as the general dwells on his own past, the reader is reminded of Henry Sutpen (also sickened by violence as a boy), Horace Benbow (also repeatedly disappointed in love), Isaac McCaslin (also haunted by the eyes of the hunters' prey), and Gavin Stevens (also unable to save his ideal woman). Subsequent readings of *The Sheltered Life* reveal Glasgow's impatience with the general's self-inflicted impotence: once the reader knows the general's full story, a whining tone emerges from his self-centered reverie at the beginning of part 2 as he prepares to visit Eva in the hospital, concerned more about his own discomfort with seeing her incapacitated than about her life-threatening disease.

In contrast to the general and the various Faulkner characters so much like General Archbald, Eva Birdsong, like Emily Grierson, ultimately takes action. She kills her husband, in part at least, I would argue, to protect her young protégée, Jenny Blair, from him—or rather, from an ideal vision of him that would limit Jenny Blair's life in the way it has limited Eva's. And just as the Faulknerian community covers up Emily's crime until her death—refusing to connect the dots when Emily does *not* kill herself with the arsenic but Homer *does* disappear just before an odor emanates from the Grierson homes[8]—so, too, are General Archbald and John Welch quick to begin covering up Eva's crime, transforming George's death into an accident. Given the social position of both the Archbalds and the Birdsongs (and the general's devotion to Eva), it seems likely that, had the truth been revealed, and even if Eva had gone to trial, she would not have been given a sentence of much consequence for her "crime of passion." At worst, she would probably have been sent to a sanatorium—to which she is likely to have to go anyway given the collapse that is imminent once she realizes what she has done. So what would it have hurt to allow the truth to come out? Or rather, wouldn't it have helped to put a stop to the romantic idealizing that leads to such tragedies? Thus, wouldn't the truth have done more for Jenny Blair than the cover-up? Consider how young David Archbald came out of *his* parents' cover-up of his role in a "crime": not empowered by his recognition of his privileged status and thus ready to do more deeds of good will but rather a man who would always evade responsibility for his actions—or for acting. Already we see history repeating itself, as Jenny Blair closes the novel shirking responsibility: "I didn't mean anything in the world!" (292).

Giving More than Just a Rose: Gautreaux's White Men of Action

"Years ago we in the South made our women into ladies. Then the War came and made the ladies into ghosts. So what else can we do, being gentlemen, but listen to them being ghosts?"

Faulkner, *Absalom, Absalom!*

"Now it's going to be blue-collar workers."

Ellen Gilchrist, *In the Land of Dreamy Dreams*

Though Ellen Glasgow early on reflected her frustration with an impotent white male depicted as a romantic hero on a hopeless quest, another Faulkner contemporary, Robert Penn Warren, created a similar character to narrate his *All the King's Men* (1946). J. A. Bryant describes Jack Burden's development in terms that echo my description of this recurrent Faulkner character type: "The effect of Burden's maturation is that he accepts and consents to live in a world which he cannot change" (110).[9] In contrast, fifty years later, a southern white male writer would introduce white male characters *not* debilitated by a sense of impotence but, rather, determined to make change that would ease the suffering of those around them.

In many of the short stories of his two collections, *Same Place, Same Things* (1996) and *Welding with Children* (1999), Louisiana writer Tim Gautreaux presents characters who do accept responsibility, reflected in their willingness to help others, both when they are responsible (even if only tangentially) for the trouble and when they just happen upon it. These heroic characters are, more often than not, southern white men, but unlike the sensitive white men of Faulkner's fiction, sons and grandsons of the Old Southern aristocracy, Gautreaux's compassionate characters wear blue collars.

I don't know if Tim Gautreaux was or is consciously frustrated with the impotence of Faulkner's gentry (or with Faulkner's depiction of poor whites and "white trash" in his fiction). I do know that for every two men who stumble upon a "victim" in Gautreaux's fiction, one of them *does something* about the situation. Thus, while Gautreaux does not romanticize all Cajun "day laborers" into knights in shining armor, he does allow many of these blue-collar workers to do what they can to alleviate the suffering of others.

A story with one such hero is Gautreaux's "The Piano Tuner" (from *Welding with Children*), which one might read as a revision of "A Rose for Emily" in which the anonymous first-person narrator is replaced with a man willing not just to stick his nose into the business of a lonely heiress by reporting it but also to stick his neck out to help her—before it is too late to *do anything* for her. Answering a service call, the title character, named Claude, finds Michelle Placervent in need of more than a piano tuning: the woman is seriously depressed. Her situation directly echoes that of Emily Grierson: she is "the end of the line for the Placervents, Creole planters who always had just enough money and influence to make themselves disliked in a poor community." After her mother's death, she had to take care of her father, who had started drinking, and after his death, "it was just her, the black housekeeper [who has since died], the home place [which is in disrepair], and a thousand acres the bank managed for her" (80). Michelle has a music degree but "had never done anything, never worked except at maintaining her helpless mother and snarling old man" (81–82). The stasis of her life is reflected in her desire for a new piano, which is thwarted by the condition of her house, so rotten that the steps wouldn't hold to move the old one out. Claude suggests that she move, but she "can't afford to," and besides, the house is the only family she has (84).

Moved by Michelle's talent when she plays for him and troubled by the waste not just of her talent but of her life, Claude does not just brood about her situation; he eventually gets involved. During his first service call, he asks outright, "What problems you having, Michelle?" (82); when she calls him about more stuck piano keys, frantic that he come right away, he again asks her directly "if she had any relatives or friends in town" (87), makes her tea, then, after adjusting her piano, continues to pry, coercing her to see a doctor. Once she is on medication, Claude finds her a job playing the piano in a motel bar, even advises her about what to play and how to dress, and promises to be there on her first night. Whereas Michelle's ultimate triumph occurs upon her own initiative, certainly it is Claude's prompting for her to get out of the house that sparks her later intentional or fortuitous break out of her confinement.

Returning to the perception of this story as a retelling of "A Rose for Emily," one finds beneath Michelle's depression as much rebellion as displayed by Emily Grierson, who defied her town regarding paying taxes, putting street numbers on her house, and being courted, as well as, of course, getting away with murder. The image of Emily watching from the upstairs window, thus literally looking down on the men who "slunk about the house like burglars, sniffing along the base of the brickwork and at the cellar openings" as they spread lime to cover up the smell (122), suggests her insurgency. One might then see Emily's triumph in the gray hair left on the pillow next to the corpse of Homer Barron. As Renee Curry suggests, Emily may have "artfully le[ft] the hair and craft[ed] a pillow indentation to signify the possibility that she could have done so [slept with Homer's corpse] behind the backs of the community and behind the discourse that symbolized her" (402).[10] Whether her triumph is in having her "husband" despite the town's trying to stop her or in mocking with this perverse suggestion of necrophilia their iconic view of her as a southern lady in need of their protection, still she ultimately defeats her community, even if her triumph is questionable (it is difficult to find triumph in madness or even loneliness). In Gautreaux's recasting of this story, the triumph is not so ambiguous, for Michelle

Placervent ultimately escapes succumbing to madness, ironically with a somewhat mad (but more rash than deranged) act of rebellion against her dead father and the social position that has not prepared her to support herself in the real world.

When Michelle first comes to see Claude about helping her to find a piano-playing gig, while he is pleased by her progress, there is something troubling about her countenance: "her eyes showed so much happiness, they scared him" (89). He is concerned that this "happiness" is too much connected to her medication. Then, during her first night's performance, the manager remarks to Claude, "She's smiling a lot. Is she on something?" (93). More portentous, at one point that night, just after Claude leaves, he hears her break into Hungarian Rhapsody no. 2, and when he goes back in to find out why she was suddenly playing such inappropriate music (for a lounge setting), she tells him, "I couldn't help it. I just got this surge of anger and had to let it out. . . . I've been sitting here thinking that I would have to play piano five nights a week for twenty-three years to pay for the renovation of my house." And then she asks, significantly, "What am I doing here? . . . I'm a Placervent" (93). Significant, too, when she pulls herself together, she returns to the piano and sings, "Crazy . . . crazy for feeling so lonely" (94).

But Michelle continues to play in this motel lounge as well as at the Sheraton and the country club—though she also continues to end many nights somewhat hysterical, "laughing out loud between the verses as though she were telling jokes in her head. Laughing very loudly," and when he hears of this, Claude "wonder[s] if she would ever get on an even keel" (94). Upon finishing the story, the reader wonders if she might have been devising her escape from her imprisoning house and thus laughing in anticipation of the scenario described in the closing pages.

The next time Claude is called to Michelle's house, it is to tune a new piano—she'd done just enough renovation so that her house would support a delivery. But the music store didn't want her old piano and wouldn't haul it away for her. Perhaps it was only then that circumstances inadvertently led to the story's end (rather than it all having been premeditated), although the cheap ugliness of the new piano, noted by Claude, suggests that it could have been part of her scheme. By the time of Claude's arrival, Michelle is preparing to pull the old piano out the back door—by hitching it to the tractor her father forced her to learn to drive when she was a child.

The earlier tractor reference in the story, which seemed insignificant at the time, suddenly becomes very significant, reminding the reader of how a good short story writer does not include insignificant details. After his first service call to the Placervent house, when Claude told his wife about how depressed he'd found Michelle and shared his opinion that she should go to work, his wife responds, to his surprise, "Well, she knows how to drive a tractor" and explains that she "heard that [Michelle's] father forced her to learn when she was just a kid. . . . Maybe he was mad she wasn't born a boy." Then, foreshadowing the story's end and suggesting how we are to interpret the events that ultimately transpired—as intentional demolition rather than accidental destruction—Evette responds to Claude's hyperbolic "I wouldn't have thought she could operate a doorbell" with "It might surprise you what some people can do" (86).

What Michelle ultimately does is single-handedly tear down her prison. After hitching the piano to a "locomotive"-sized tractor, "the only [tractor] in the barn that would start" (or so she says), Michelle tells Claude, "*I've planned this through.* You just stay on the ground and watch" (96; emphasis added). What follows *seems* like an accident: the piano turns broadside enroute, and when Michelle gets down off the tractor (presumably so that she and Claude can turn the piano sideways again so that it will fit through the door), her raincoat catches on the clutch, engaging it. Claude pulls Michelle out of the way and then the two watch as the tractor continues to drag the piano out of the house, from its broadside position, so that it brings with it the entire back wall. The back rooms then collapse, then the roof, all while the tractor continues to drag the massive piano, and while Claude wonders if he should go try to stop it but then stays to support the collapsing Michelle, a fire erupts from where the gas stove would be, underneath the rubble.

Michelle seems genuinely shocked—it's hard to believe she could have imagined such a scene even if she did plan any part of this debacle—but when she is questioned by the fire chief (who perhaps feels bad since by the time the firemen arrived it was too late for them to do anything but wet down the camellias and live oaks on the property), she responds, "The only good thing the house had was insurance" (98), again leading the reader to wonder about her intentions (recall, too, the new piano inside, which is presumably destroyed, was "cheap" and "ugly"). Then later that evening she says to Claude and Evette, "Look at me. I'm homeless," and the narrator follows her words with, "But she was not frowning" (99). She even laughs when they hear a story on the news about a runaway tractor that tried to pull a piano up the steps of a Catholic church, and she declares of the piano, "It escaped" (100). Whatever her intentions were, the result was the same: like the piano, Michelle has escaped her prison.

Michelle may remain a little "off" even after her escape (she still does some odd talking at times during her sets), but thanks to Claude's constructive intrusion into her life, she is no longer isolated, and she is not mad. The last we see of her, she is still playing the piano in the motel lounge and has attracted a following of regulars. Without the financial burden of the house, she is gainfully employed as a lounge singer, and she is no longer living isolated ten miles from her nearest neighbor. In contrast to Faulkner's narrator, who helps us to understand Emily Grierson but only after she is dead and it is too late to do anything that would improve her life, Claude's intrusion into Michelle Placervent's life has helped the victim, not just eased his own conscience. And in this story, Claude is not responsible in any way for Michelle's situation, again unlike Faulkner's narrator, who is part of the "we" who has watched Emily over the years and speculated about her various disappointments but *done nothing* to console her.

There are several stories in Gautreaux's collections in which characters go out of their ways to help others, even though they are not responsible for the plights of these victims: two examples are "Resistance" (also in *Welding with Children*), in which a retired man helps his alcoholic neighbor's child with her school science project; and "The Bug Man" (from *Same Place, Same Things*), another story in which a lonely woman's depression is noticed by a man, the exterminator, on a service call, who then tries to help her. In other stories, Gautreaux's characters recognize their own role in the problem at hand—however tangential their responsibility is—and act to make change. Usually, these characters are aging parents, realizing that their grandchildren's plights are a result of how they raised these children's parents. For example, in the title story of *Welding with Children,* a man realizes that his lack of involvement in the raising of his daughters (traditional though it may have been at the time for the fathers not to be involved) must have something to do with the fact that they all have had children out of wedlock. So he cleans up his own house—(and yard) literally—and swallows his pride in order to seek advice from one of the townsmen whose children live more "respectable" lives. Similarly, in "Little Frogs in a Ditch" and "The Courtship of Merlin LeBlanc" (both in *Same Place, Same Things*), grandfathers take on the responsibility of taking care of their grandchildren. In the former, the grandfather tries to make reparation to a victim of his grandson's con game (only to discover that the victim is another grandfather trying to improve *his* grandson's life). And in the latter, when the grandfather's efforts to find a wife to help him raise his dead daughter's baby go awry, *his* father and grandfather step in and advise him to just take responsibility for the child himself. All of these and many other Gautreaux characters share with the Faulkner prototype the sensitive conscience and social awareness that is so troubling to them, but Gautreaux's characters are not incapacitated with brooding over the situation. They *act*.

.   .   .

To a reporter for *The Daily Mississippian,* Tim Gautreaux "complained that so much of fiction written today is 'dark.' 'I refuse to believe that the only literary character worth writing about is going to blow his brains out,' he said" (Coleman). As has been seen in earlier chapters, it seems that, as they bring women out from the margins, Toni Morrison and Lee Smith are able to share this optimism, surprisingly, even as they bring out of the closet violence perpetrated against women by family and acquaintances. Even Ernest Gaines, whose last book, *A Lesson before Dying,* ends with a ray of hope not found in the earlier books, seems to be at least moving toward an optimistic attitude about the future of the South.[11]

In her 1976 essay, "Saving the Life That Is Your Own," Alice Walker makes a distinction between the writing of black and white Americans: "for the most part, white American writers tended to end their books and their characters' lives as if there were no better existence for which to struggle." Consequently, she says, "The gloom of defeat is thick." In contrast, she perceives black writers as "always involved in a moral and/or physical struggle, the result of which is expected to be some kind of larger freedom" (*In Search* 5).

Walker gives two reasons for this distinction between white and black writers: first, that the African-American "literary tradition is based on the slave narratives, where escape for the body and freedom for the soul went together," and second, that African-Americans "have never felt themselves guilty of global, cosmic sins" (*In Search* 5). Fred Hobson and Barbara Bennett have both noted that one change in contemporary southern literature is the absence of this guilt. In *The Southern Writer in the Postmodern World,* Hobson first reminds his reader of the "tragic sense" (4) that characterizes southern literature through the 1950s and then notes that "[i]n the South of the late 1960s positive thinking, not contrition, was dominant" (6). Bennett believes that women writers in particular "have once and for all turned away from the shame and guilt with which pre-1970 southern writers seemed preoccupied. Instead, they convey optimism and affirmation" (124). I perceive the same attitudes in the fiction of Tim Gautreaux, and I would suggest that over twenty-five years after the original publication of Walker's essay, gender and class have joined race as the central issues in southern literature. Distinguishing her fiction from traditional southern literature, Kentucky native and writer Bobbie Ann Mason notes the optimism of her characters: "I don't think the people I write about are obsessed with the past. I don't think they know anything about the Civil War, and I don't think they care. They're kind of naïve and optimistic for the most part: they think better times are coming, and most of them embrace progress" (Wendy Smith 425).

Notes

Introduction. Crossing the Tracks of the Dixie Limited: Overcoming Anxiety of Influence and Filling in the Blanks

1. I would add Ellen Gilchrist to the list of writers covered in this study, and direct readers to chapter 4 of my book *The Fiction of Ellen Gilchrist* for an examination of Gilchrist's recasting and re-visioning of *The Sound and the Fury* (1929) in her novel *The Annunciation* (1983). One might also read on this subject Marcel Arbeit's article on Faulkner's *The Reivers* (1962) and Padgett Powell's *Edisto* (1984), at the beginning of which Arbeit makes an observation similar to mine about the progression from anxiety of influence: "While in the 1950s and 1960s all Southern writers felt the urge to cope with Faulkner in one way or another, in the 1970s most of them gave up writing in Faulkner's mode and in the 1980s they even dared parody him" (276).

2. Yaeger also draws on O'Connor's Dixie Limited analogy, and I must credit Yaeger with calling my attention to the Hurston passage I use as an epigraph of this introduction (see Yaeger 34–35).

3. Most exemplary of what I mean about early Faulkner criticism is the way that readers of *Absalom, Absalom!* present within their analyses of the novel the "truth" about what exactly occurred between the characters whose stories Quentin and Shreve are trying to put together into a coherent narrative. Perhaps not until Robert Dale Parker's 1991 study of the novel has someone made so clear how much of the story is only the characters' conjecture and, indeed, not very plausible conjecture.

4. In *Dirt and Desire: Reconstructing Southern Women's Writing, 1930–1990*, Patricia Yaeger also notes how "the dominant critical machinery enshrines William Faulkner as *the* literary icon of southern studies. At issue is the fact that Faulkner is always defined not only at but *as* the nexus of southern literary history" (96). Later in her book, Yaeger remarks upon the similar complaint critics— feminist critics in particular—had against Richard King's 1980 *A Southern Renaissance: The Cultural Awakening of the American South, 1930–1955*, from which

"women were excluded . . . as were African Americans" (Yaeger 115). King's study exhibits the narrow focus on southern literature of some *critics*. As Yaeger points out, King acknowledges the presence of (even as he dismisses) such writers as Richard Wright, Ralph Ellison, Carson McCullers, Flannery O'Connor, and Katherine Anne Porter.

5. I'm paraphrasing here Beneatha Younger's expression of disgust with her brother ("Just look at what the New World hath wrought" [act 3]) toward the end of Lorraine Hansberry's *A Raisin in the Sun*.

6. Critical biographer David Minter discusses Faulkner's awareness of the "danger . . . of becoming enamored of imagination, prejudiced against facts" and his determination, in returning home to write, to "look again and again at the immediate" (75). Minter links Faulkner's concern with writing about "the actual" with his sense of displacement in Oxford after his return there: "Oxford was what Faulkner knew, and his return committed him to it. Yet it never became completely his home. After the war, he had come back to find that he was 'at home again in Oxford, Mississippi, yet at the same time . . . not at home'" (Minter 76). Turning to the source of this description of Faulkner's alienation—a letter from Faulkner to Malcolm Cowley—one finds that Faulkner continued his explanation of his alienation as "at least not able to accept the postwar world" (Cowley 74). Richard Gray interprets this reading of Faulkner's "equivocal stance to his 'native land'" as "naturally encourag[ing] a dual focus . . . drawn by a double agent, someone who knows what it is both to be an insider and an outsider" (171).

7. Patricia Yaeger disagrees with those critics (Yaeger mentions Richard King rather than Bryant) who would end the Southern Renascence in the mid-1950s: "For a southern renaissance to be said to be over in 1955 suggests that the best southern writers could not respond to the civil rights movement with any complexity—a benighted portrait of the South indeed." She argues that "[i]n 1955 the story of Anglo and African southern women's writing had just begun—or . . . started up again" (53). In any case, my study will show how southern women's stories have "started up" yet again.

8. In a chapter titled "Southern Regionalism," Bryant suggests that "[p]art of William Faulkner's popularity among northern and eastern readers after 1950 was due to a residual interest in southern literature as a species of exotica, which in turn was an outsider's response to the strong regional character of much of it" (117). One can see in the continued popularity of southern-set films as well as literature that Bryant's perception that regionalism "continues to be an important aspect of the work of many, if not most, of the writers who would come to prominence in the years following World War II" (117) is still valid thus far into the twenty-first century.

9. *Many Things Have Happened since He Died* was first published under the name Elizabeth Dewberry Vaughn, but the author has since dropped the name Vaughn from her byline.

10. Throughout this study (particularly in the chapters on Gaines, Smith, and Glasgow), I refer to Quentin Compson as the prototype of which Faulkner created various manifestations throughout his fiction because Quentin is the epitome of this character type in Faulkner's canon. Myra Jehlen suggests that the original manifestation of this Faulkner character type can be found in his very first novel, *Soldier's Pay* (1926), and certainly the character type precedes Faulkner's creation of Quentin in *The Sound and the Fury* with Bayard Sartoris of the original manuscript of *Flags in the Dust,* written before *The Sound and the Fury,* though published as *Sartoris* in the same year as Quentin's first appearance (Jehlen 26).

11. Daniel J. Singal argues that by the time Faulkner wrote his Snopes trilogy, "stereotypes dissolved. . . . Where before all Snopeses had looked exactly alike, they began showing up in many different flavors and varieties." Singal's summarizing descriptions of the different Snopeses, however, support my contention that they are still all negatively depicted, and while they may indeed be, as Singal argues, "agents of change" (245), the change Faulkner is prognosticating is a new New South no less corrupt than the Old South. Indeed, Singal illustrates this very point with his comparison and contrast of Ab Snopes, as referenced in *The Hamlet,* to Thomas Sutpen, both of whom were expected, as poor whites, to use the back door. Singal notes that Ab not only "'shoved right past the nigger' guarding the front door of the big house" but also "deliberately tracked horse manure onto a fancy rug." Then, Ab's son Flem seeks revenge for the insult upon his family by "earning enough money to acquire the de Spain house itself and hire his own black servants." Singal's analysis of Flem's plan to accomplish this goal, in contrast to Sutpen, "by reversing every facet of the Cavalier ethos, fashioning for himself an identity that is the precise opposite of the old planter ideal" (247), is accurate, but still it does not replace the Old Order with a more positive New Order. See also Elizabeth Spencer's essay written for the 1981 Faulkner and Yoknapatawpha conference, in which she expresses her concern that Faulkner blames Snopeses for all the corruption of the New South, that "[t]he Snopeses have been set up for us to despise." While she acknowledges that Jason Compson, a descendent of the aristocracy, "is a lot worse than any Snopes," she points out that "Faulkner didn't write whole trilogies about Jason Compson" (135).

12. Matthew Guinn points out the "near-monolithic record of southern experience viewed through the lens of the upper classes." He notes how "[w]hile black authors have augmented middle- and upper-class perceptions of the region, until recently poor whites have little input into the region's representation in literature—and thus the aristocratic agrarian mode has prevailed" (3). Similarly, Fred Hobson suggests that "of all the southerners who would tell their own stories but have been silenced—by race, class, or gender—the lower-class white has, until recently, been the most effectively silenced." He adds that "[p]rivileged, lettered southerners [including Faulkner] have written *about* and occasionally even for poor whites . . . [b]ut rarely did poor whites speak for themselves" (*But* 135).

Recognizing the emerging voices of "lower-class white" writers, Hobson includes discussion of several of their memoirs in his book *But Now I See: The Southern Racial Conversion Narrative.* Matthew Guinn's study of contemporary southern fiction includes several blue-collar writers but not Gautreaux, whose work has only recently started to receive critical notice.

13. As Patricia Yaeger does in *Dirt and Desire: Reconstructing Southern Women's Writing, 1930–1990,* I include Morrison as a contributor to the canon of southern literature (Yaeger includes her among a list of nonsouthern "black women who write in equally stirring ways about ancestral southern roots" [10]). For example, much of *Song of Solomon* is set in the South; and certainly the issues found in Morrison's fiction, particularly in *Song of Solomon* and *Beloved,* are the same issues that concern her contemporaries who were born in and or who write from the South. Yaeger argues that "Morrison is deeply absorbed by and in dialogue with an 'official' southern literary tradition; she is constantly rewriting Faulkner—changing Clytie's ragged body into Circe's rage [in *Song of Solomon*], rerouting Judith's and Rosa's tattered trousseau into Sethe's bold re-creation of a pieced-together wedding dress [in *Beloved*]" (55).

Chapter 1. Cross-Country Corpses in Faulkner, Barthelme, and McMurtry

1. Although he does not mention Faulkner in his reference to the influence of modernists on Barthelme's novel, Malmgrem's interpretation of the Dead Father as being "connected to our innate need to discover meaning" (36) echoes Irving Howe's focus on how Addie's death leads her children to ponder the meaning of life in the passage just quoted.

2. In the interview with Brans, Barthelme does not comment upon her comparison of the two novels, and Brans does not pursue the subject or provide reasons why she thinks "that *The Dead Father* was a lot like Faulkner's *As I Lay Dying*" (123). Barthelme's reticence to discuss the connection to Faulkner with Brans does seem to suggest some anxiety of influence. As alluded to in the previous note, Malmgren comments upon another source of anxiety-inducing influence that would include Faulkner (although Malmgren does not refer specifically to Faulkner) in his interpretation of the Dead Father as "the literary tradition in whose shadow Barthelme writes, with respect to whom he suffers no small anxiety of influence—the great modernists" (36). Perceiving more intent than anxiety on Barthelme's part, Jerome Klinkowitz suggests that "Barthelme uses the occasion of his second novel [*The Dead Father*] to carry modernism [represented by the Dead Father] to its grave" (13). Similarly, rather than a *reflection of* anxiety of influence, Richard F. Patteson calls *The Dead Father* "the definitive *meditation on* the anxiety of influence. The refusal either wholly to reject or wholly to embrace tradition is one of the most encompassing aspects of postmodern suspensiveness [*sic*]" (10; emphasis added).

3. Much more recently, Marc Hewson writes about "the difference between masculine stasis and feminine process . . . [t]he dichotomy between female activity and male inaction" depicted in this novel (553). While I agree that the novel favors activity over inaction and that Addie emerges as more admirable and sympathetic than her husband, and though I find *provocative* Hewson's argument regarding Addie's *positive* influence on her children, which he illustrates by reading their *acts* of love in a much more positive light than have other critics, the latter argument is not convincing in that it does not take into consideration, for example, the destructive rivalry between Darl and Jewel, which has resulted from their mother's favoring Jewel while seeming to blame Darl for the oppression of motherhood.

4. Again, I do not disagree with Marc Hewson's argument that "despite her initial anger at Anse for impregnating her again," she soon recognized that "the bond between her and Cash is not weakened by Darl's birth"—that the line "I was three now" (Faulkner, *As* 173) indicates a bonding with both of her sons (and then with her other children), as Hewson puts it, "proliferation without division" (557). However, I still contend that Addie is distressed by having children. The mother of one small child would already know that, like Addie's husband, children take their mother's presence for granted—until it is absent. She would know that a mother's interest in her children's lives is likely not to be reciprocated. Furthermore, Hewson's argument does not take into account Darl's perception of himself as being unloved and, again, his consequential rivalry with Jewel, whom he perceives to be favored by their mother.

5. In a recent article on Addie, Amado Chan interprets her motivations for both her burial request and her affair similarly and perceives them as acts of revenge and defiance more so than as assertions of her own needs and desires (Chan).

6. On the other hand, I find compelling Patricia McKee's reading of Darl's actions as indicative of his "desire for a reckoning," which McKee perceives in "the way he looks forward to Addie's death early in the novel, in his attempt to burn up the coffin, and in his vision at the flooding river [of] the distance between [the others] and him" ("*As*" 626). This reading of Darl is similar to my later discussion of Addie's belief in a judgment day, further illustrating the influence Addie had upon her children. Perhaps Darl's attempts to destroy his mother's corpse are acts of judgment against her rather than expressions of his love (trying to end her humiliation). Either reading supports the notion that Addie's treatment of her children had negative consequences.

7. See Colleen Donnelly's article on the novel, in which she notes the juxtaposition of the sections narrated by Darl and Vardaman and then argues that "Faulkner [thereby] assigned some special significance to the interplay of the two voices." She also points out that in the manuscript of the novel their narrative styles were remarkably similar (55). Gabriele Schwab also links the two characters and suggests that Vardaman may follow in Darl's footsteps: "Darl and Vardaman,

the two sons who share Addie's oversensitive state of mind, transform Addie's dead body in their fantasies in such an intense way that they live on the verge of psychotic breakdown" (215).

8. Frederick Karl's association of the Dead Father's son Edmund with the bastard son of Lear (*American* 386) suggests a comparison between Jewel's rebellious nature and that of Barthelme's Edmund.

9. Similarly, Paul S. Nielsen argues that "[a]s great truths go, [her father's words are] not much, and in some contexts it would be taken as a dismissal of all meaning [but] Addie cannot do that; it must mean, and it must be *made* to mean" (35). In contrast to McKee, Nielsen, and my readings of the significance of the repeated recollection of Addie's father's summary of the meaning of life, Amy Louise Wood argues that "[i]n rejecting her father's credo, she is, likewise, rejecting the Christian notion that one suffers during one's secular life for the promise of a better life in the afterworld; instead, Addie searches for passion and feeling in the world" (102). But I don't see where Addie "rejects" her father's words; they seem, rather, as I show, to motivate her to action.

10. One might compare this abrupt burial to the absence of a burial scene in Faulkner's novel. After all of the turmoil involved in getting the body to Jefferson to be buried, it may at first seem odd that we do not witness the event itself. Faulkner merely emphasizes with this gap in the narrative that, in fact, the burial was not the true purpose of the trip for Addie's survivors.

11. See Diana York Blaine's description of the various reader responses found in past criticism—and her assessment of women's different responses to these characters (425–26).

12. Jill Bergman notes that Faulkner only "allow[s Addie] to speak" after "[r]eturning her to her pre-sexual state by dressing her in her wedding dress, dragging her decaying body throughout the novel, [thereby] undermin[ing] the power he gives [her]" (405–6). Harriet Hustis shows how Faulkner's "[c]ompelling female characters such as Addie and Caddy are nevertheless absent presences influencing the lives and bonds of men" and how his more minor female characters (she lists Dewey Dell, Cora Tull, and Mrs. Compson) "offer little hope for a subjectivity that would transcend their role as 'object' of the masculine joke-activity operative in *As I Lay Dying* and *The Sound in the Fury*" (118).

13. The attitude about the West in the novel's sequel, *Streets of Laredo,* however, seems more compliant with Robert Brinkmeyer's theories about southern writers who set works in the West. Ultimately, that novel criticizes the violence, particularly as it is enacted against women and children; and the characters, led by women (Lorena and Maria Garza) struggle to get home, where such senseless and violent killing is less likely to occur. The novel comes to a pessimistic close, however. Although her children and her husband are safe, Lorena is "burdened" by the sense that she is only getting a "reprieve" from the violence: "Evil men or evil circumstances would come and prove stronger than all the good in her life. She had her husband back and would soon have her children with her, but in her

fear, she could not help feeling that the reprieve was only temporary. . . . She and her family were safe, but only for a time" (*Streets* 527).

14. It is interesting to note that the first casualty of the journey to Montana, young Sean O'Brien, dies from multiple snakebites after passing through a nest of water moccasins while crossing the first river the group comes to.

15. The reader learns in *Streets of Laredo* that "[o]nly after the boy's death, in Montana, had Call been able to admit that Newt had been his son." Only then, too, does Call allow himself to regret his treatment of his son: "Now, with the boy several years dead, it made Call sad to think of him. He had fathered a son, but had not been a father to him, although Newt had lived with the Hat Creek outfit most of his short life. He had lived with the outfit, but as an employee, not a son. Now it was too late to change any of that. The memory of it was a sore that throbbed every time his mind touched it" (*Streets* 165).

16. Mark Busby makes a similar point: "Although the traditional trail drive novel stressed the accomplishment of the mission—the purposeful journey—in *Lonesome Dove* McMurtry emphasizes that the end of the line is less important than the journey itself." Reminding the reader of the varying motivations for the journey in *As I Lay Dying*, Busby notes that "each character [of *Lonesome Dove*] ha[s] a different reason for the exercise. Call wants to further adventuring as long as possible, Gus to see Clara in Nebraska, Newt to participate in an adult activity, Jake to avoid July Johnson, Lorena to get to San Francisco" (195).

17. In her article on the novel, Ernestine P. Sewell also refers to Montana in Edenic terms: "a Garden of Eden where a man can have all the land he wants just for the taking" (219). So, too, do Richard Campbell and Jimmie L. Reeves in their article on the miniseries based on the novel: "Call believes in Montana as a wilderness Nirvana that can re-invigorate and purify him. And this vision of Montana as 'a cattleman's paradise,' as a place that makes men out of boys, as a place free from civilization, represents an outgoing, dying vision of the meaning of the West" (37).

18. Although they are given, rather than taken, Call's gifts to Newt are comparable to Thomas's expropriation of his father's belt, sword, and keys in *The Dead Father*. And as the Dead Father resists acknowledging his son's readiness to take on the role of father, so, too, is Call reluctant to acknowledge his son's relation to himself. Janis Stout's explanation of the scene in *Lonesome Dove* also calls to mind the earlier discussion of *The Dead Father*: "Call cannot bring himself to speak the word of acknowledgement that will pass authority on to his son and bring a new order into being. Aging and tired, the barren patriarch starts back to Texas, leaving his men leaderless and his herd ownerless. . . . *Lonesome Dove* has moved from a dissolving order to no order at all" (248).

19. This episode in the miniseries based on the novel includes a moving sequence of flashback images of the various deaths that occurred during Call's journey northwest.

20. Robert Brinkmeyer notes that as a consequence of "living with complete

individual freedom, one can become isolated and misanthropic" (86). Certainly Call is an isolated misanthrope. This scene suggests that Newt is on his way toward isolating himself from others in order to avoid further disappointment; one would not be surprised to find that his disillusionment with his father led to a misanthropic opinion of people in general. According to the narrator of *Streets of Laredo,* however, Newt does not have to live this lonely life very long. Actually, then, Call's gift of his horse ultimately condemns his son to an early death: the Hell Bitch falls on Newt, crushing his rib cage and, significantly, his heart. Somewhat contradicting the quotation cited from *Lonesome Dove* regarding Newt's immediate affinity with the Hell Bitch, the narrator of the sequel reports that "[i]t was the view of everyone who knew horses that, while an able ranch manager, Newt was much too inexperienced to trust with a horse as mean and as smart as the Hell Bitch. Still, the Captain had given Newt the horse, and Newt felt obliged to ride her" (*Streets* 30).

21. Steve Fore also suggests that Deets, the only African-American among the cowboys, is similarly two-dimensional. He calls Deets "a veritable saint among men" and argues that "here lies the 'problem' with Deets—there's no . . . personality to speak of except for his unfailing kindness, sunny disposition, generosity, and competence. In a narrative environment full of prickly, rounded, strikingly individualized characters, Deets is distinctive only in his utter blandness" (59).

22. Mark Busby notes, too, of "Blue Duck's evil" that "it is not a common evil like most human weaknesses"; however, Busby then refers to Blue Duck's actions as "almost superhuman evil" (187). I would argue, rather, that McMurtry suggests that Blue Duck's nature is *sub*human.

23. Lorena does play a central and quite heroic role in *Streets of Laredo,* as does another woman (a Mexican woman in fact), Maria Garza. In this novel, too, Call must face his own fallibility, and others must finish his job for him. Indeed, Maria Garza almost has to be the one to kill the outlaw whom Call has been hired to kill—even though this outlaw is her son. And Lorena saves Call's life. By novel's end, Call is missing a leg (cut off by Lorena to save his life) and an arm, and even more humiliating than having to allow people to wait on him, Call must endure Lorena helping him relieve himself. McMurtry may have balanced his treatment of men and women with this sequel, but since the sequel is not nearly the novel that *Lonesome Dove* is, the development of Lorena and Maria does not leave the lasting impression that his characterization of Call and Gus does after reading *Lonesome Dove.*

24. My reading of Call's secular focus goes along with Robert Brinkmeyer's contention that "[s]eeking the West means . . . stepping free from the fundamental ideologies of society and into the wilderness of unmediated confrontation *with the here and now*" (55; emphasis added). However, my conclusion reveals that here again McMurtry ultimately contrasts with the contemporary *southern* writers of the West in whose fiction Brinkmeyer sees "a streak of optimism" (105).

Chapter 2. Miss Jane Is Still Not in the History Books: Gender, Race, and Class Discrimination in the Fiction of Faulkner and Gaines

1. Gaines made this remark when guest-speaking at a class I took under Professor Bernice Webb at the University of Southwestern Louisiana (now the University of Louisiana at Lafayette) in the spring of 1986. More recently, Gaines refers to a similar, if not the same, episode in an interview with John Lowe: "Someone asked me when I wrote *The Autobiography of Miss Jane Pittman*, was I thinking about Dilsey in Faulkner's novel *The Sound and the Fury*. And I said, 'No, I did not have Dilsey in mind.' And by the way, the difference between Dilsey and Miss Jane Pittman is that Faulkner gets Dilsey talking her story from his kitchen; the young schoolteacher in my book gets Miss Jane's story from Miss Jane's kitchen. And it makes a difference" (Lowe, "Interview" 313). For a discussion of Faulkner's interest in the African-American woman as servant, see Diane Roberts's chapter on the "Mammy" in Faulkner's fiction in her book *Faulkner and Southern Womanhood*. And for a similar note of contrast between white and black *women* writers (Flannery O'Connor and Harriet Ann Jacobs, in particular), see Patricia Yaeger's *Dirt and Desire* (40).

2. Daniel J. Singal makes an interesting point regarding "critics deploring how women and black characters often receive insufficient opportunities to address the reader directly": "Admirable figures who carry Faulkner's key meanings often speak little but achieve an enormous impact when they do, while those less admirable (Horace Benbow and Gavin Stevens [two of Faulkner's liberal white males]) are given reams of dialogue with which to hang themselves." He notes, too, that "[m]any of those admirable characters . . . are women and blacks—. . . [Charles] Bon and Judith [Sutpen,] . . . Caddy Compson, Dilsey Gibson, Addie Bundren, Lucas Beauchamp." Singal concludes, then, that "adding up the column inches of 'voice' in Faulkner to measure whether or not he has endowed a character with an adequate amount of 'subjectivity' is a fruitless enterprise" (212). While Singal's point of contrast between the less admirable verbose and the more admirable characters of few words is valid, it is still the men with voice who dominate the text; it is still their perspective from which the stories (and their conflicts) develop and thus toward whom the reader's sympathy is often drawn.

3. Alvin Ramsey, however, is troubled by Jane's heroic act in the movie because of the contrast depicted between her (heroic) and the rest of the Black population (scared): "On television, the final image we were left with was of Jane walking *alone* up to the drinking fountain and taking a drink of water, *alone*. It was an image of individualistic behavior, with Jane emerging as the one courageous individual out in front of an assembly of scared Black onlookers" (35). He contrasts this scene with the final scene in the novel: "The novel ended in the midst of conflict. It was clear that the people of Samson were just beginning their struggle, and that Jane was acting *with* them as a vital part of the group and was

not acting *for* them as an individual. . . . Gaines' ending of the novel with a group of Black people *collectively* going into the struggle is the important image for us to remember" (36). Like Callahan, too, Ramsey complains about the "implicit message [in the movie's ending] that this [Jane's drink from the 'whites only' water fountain] was a triumphant act; that there was in the act some retribution for the enslavement, murder and oppression suffered by Black people in America. The message—the lie—was that Black people were making progress within the American system" (35). Similarly, Vilma Raskin Potter finds the ending to the movie troubling because "the effect of this alteration is to declare what the novel's epic design does not declare: that the drinking fountain is what the whole black experience since Emancipation has been all about; it is the *end* for which all this began. If Jane can drink at the fountain, then America is safe" (372).

4. It is interesting to note, however, that in Gaines's earlier novel *Of Love and Dust,* a male character, the narrator James Kelly, has this role. Like Jane, he tells the story of the central actor (another male character) after this character has died tragically while asserting his right to be a man. Michael Sartisky's description of James Kelly and characters like him in the Gaines canon sounds very much like Faulkner's Dilsey: "They are not all that deferential and not that servile and they are respected because they're not. But they don't really challenge the codes. He [James Kelly] has accepted the system. He's not the figure . . . who is going to change it, but he endures" (270). However, like Jane Pittman, he is also the chronicler of the hero's tragic story of defiance. Unlike Dilsey, then, he at least has a voice if not the courage to himself defy the system.

5. Recalling that I earlier grouped Big Laura with these men because of her courageous fight and heroic death, it is interesting to note here that Albert Wertheim calls her a "Moses figure" for leading her people out of slavery, as well as for establishing "moral laws" for the newly freed group (222). Thus, she, too, is almost, though not quite, a Christ-figure—that is, a Christ-*like* figure, just as she is man-*like*.

6. This horse's description in mythical terms is reminiscent of Faulkner's bear Old Ben, which the boy Ike McCaslin also dreamed about before ever actually seeing. As the stallion represents the character of the African-American people, as will be discussed subsequently, the bear is representative of a way of life, which involved slavery, that Ike paradoxically wishes both to preserve and to destroy (his ambivalent behavior is discussed in the next section of this chapter).

7. One might speculate that Gaines's development of the former horse tamer, Yank, in his later novel *A Gathering of Old Men* is a projection of Joe Pittman had he lived as long. Such an idea further identifies Gaines's technique with Faulkner's, for so, too, as has been argued most effectively by John T. Irwin, are Horace Benbow and Gavin Stevens manifestations of Quentin Compson. Faulkner, too, seems to have speculated in the development of events that plague these men what kind of issues Quentin might have had to struggle with later had he not chosen to

end his life at eighteen. Also intriguing is the comparison that can be made between Joe Pittman's death and the death of a white man, Walter Laurent, in Gaines's short story "Bloodline." The similarity in their deaths—both men are dragged by horses—might remind the reader that the white man, although the person against whose oppression the black man struggles to assert his rights, is not himself invincible.

8. In his article complaining about the movie version of the novel in which the horse's color is changed to white—in fact, the horse is an albino—Alvin Ramsey argues another interpretation of the significance of the horse's color in the novel: "This black horse symbolized Joe's own Black manhood, his Black youth, and Black strength—all of which he was trying as best he could to maintain." Therefore, he continues, "Joe Pittman died while in pursuit of a *black* horse [that] represented the essence of his life—seeking, struggling to maintain a grip on Black manhood" (33). Although Ramsey's reading may at first be more pleasing than the one I offer, its positive message is undermined by the fact that Joe is killed by this horse. Has he failed, then, to be the man that, according to Ramsey, taming the horse would prove him to be? With Ramsey's complaint about the horse's color change for the movie, however, I agree without reservation: "There was [as a result of the color change] no triumph in Joe's death. The image that was gotten across was one of a Black cowboy being destroyed by whiteness" (34).

9. Shortly after a similar reading of Dilsey as both "comfort[ing] . . . in . . . that she escapes the destruction visited upon the Compson family" but problematic in that she has no section of her own (Beavers 129), Herman Beavers remarks upon a different negative aspect of the "endurance narrative," as it is reflected in Gaines's *Catherine Carmier*; he suggests that this first Gaines novel's title character "dramatizes the entrapment of the endurance narrative: she becomes a symbol of deference, placing the needs of the patriarch before her own. Hence the roles of lover and daughter become tangled" (138).

10. In *A Gathering of Old Men,* Gaines more directly and fully develops the association between the black preacher and the white man. The preacher is the one black man who tries to talk the old men out of standing up to the white men. For further discussion of the connection between Madame Toussaint and African-Americans' "ancestral folk past," see Valerie Babb (21).

11. Gaudet's reading may remind the reader of events in Hurston's *Their Eyes Were Watching God.* As will be discussed in chapter 3, Tea Cake beats Janie after another man shows interest in her because "[b]eing able to whip her reassured him in possession" and in order to show the community "who is boss" in their house (140–41). A significant difference, of course, is that in Hurston's novel, the woman does not—literally—"ask for it." However, there are critics who (like Jack Hicks, also cited above) ignore or (like Gaudet) play down this beating in their arguments for Tea Cake as the perfect lover for Janie. Indeed, when I read an early version of the next chapter at the 1992 College Language Association conference in which I

took Tea Cake to task for this behavior, a woman in the audience defended him with the remark, "He only hit her once." On the other hand, in his reading of the story, Herman Beavers does critique Amy's attitude, perceiving it as evidence that "Amy has deeply internalized the conventions of a patriarchal household, where white women are imprisoned within the domestic sphere" (163).

12. An interesting comparison can be made between Gaudet's reading of this story and Joanne V. Creighton's discussion of Faulkner's "Was," the first story of *Go Down, Moses.* Creighton concludes that the tragedy (that of the thwarted relationship between Tomey's Turl and Tennie) hidden underneath the comedy (of the chase to recapture Tomey's Turl and elude the clutches of Sophonsiba Beauchamp) is "unimportant" and that "Tomey's Turl does not suffer under slavery" (90). However, Creighton goes on to qualify this reading, adding that when later stories of *Go Down, Moses* are read, the tragedy of Tomey's heritage, at least—the rape of his mother by Carothers McCaslin, who was also the woman's father—is realized. Still, Kiyoyuki Ono finds a flaw in Creighton's initial reading of "Was" by itself: "for the reader, as for Ike [McCaslin]," Ono argues, "Turl's and Tennie's feelings are not [quoting Creighton] 'unimportant because they are not described'; rather, they are all the more important because they are not described" (159).

13. Herman Beavers compares Gaines's Tee Bob Samson of *Autobiography of Miss Jane Pittman* to Isaac McCaslin: "Like Ike McCaslin, Tee Bob is a liminal figure, caught between the conventions of white male privilege and his desire to relinquish that privilege" (153). A comparison can be made between Ike and another character from this Gaines novel, Jane's adopted son, Ned. When Ike renounces his inheritance, he explains to McCaslin Edmonds the problem he perceives in the concept of owning land: "I cant [*sic*] repudiate it. It was never mine to repudiate. It was never Father's and Uncle Buddy's to bequeath me to repudiate because it was never Grandfather's to bequeath them . . . because it was never old Ikkemotubbe's to sell to Grandfather for bequeathment and repudiation . . . because on the instant when Ikkemotubbe discovered, realised, that he could sell it for money, . . . it ceased ever to have been his" (245–46). Man, according to Ike, is merely God's overseer (246). Frank Shelton equates this view of "ownership of the land [as] a crime against nature" with "ownership of people [as] a crime against humanity" ("Of" 25) and compares it to the ideas in the sermon preached by Gaines's Ned Douglass:

> "This earth is yours and don't let that man out there take it from you. . . . It's yours because your people's bones lays in it; it's yours because their sweat and their blood done drenched this earth. . . . Your people's bones and their dust make this place yours more than anything else. . . . *I'm not telling y'all men own the earth.* . . . *You don't own this earth, you're just here for a little while,* but while you're here don't let no man tell you the best is for him and you take the scrap. No, your people plowed this earth, your people chopped down the trees, your

people built the roads and built the levees. These same people is now buried in this earth, and their bones's fertilizing this earth." (*Autobiography* 107; emphasis added)

14. Similarly, Faulkner is much more interested in the effects of the rapes of Eunice and Tomey by Carothers McCaslin, who is Tomey's father, on Ike than on the women themselves. Also similar, in *In My Father's House,* as Marcia Gaudet points out: "Gaines's focus [with regard to the rape of Robert X's sister] is clearly on the brothers and how they react to the violence against their sister. In the foreground are the issues of family honor, duty, and justice as perceived by the brothers and the devastating effect of the rape *on them*" (154; emphasis added). Minrose Gwin concludes an essay on the African-American women in *Go Down, Moses* considering the women's missing perspectives on their various tragedies. Her "wondering" about the various women's thoughts ends with "I want to know the 'Delta Autumn' woman's name" ("Her" 96).

15. See Wagner-Martin, too, for a summary of the change in critical assessment of Isaac McCaslin over the years, from the perception of his renunciation as "noble" to the more recent criticism of it as "harmful" (Introduction 18).

16. The relative Frank Laurent refers to is a niece, and, considering the earlier discussion of Gaines's development of black women, it is interesting to note here his depiction of a white woman who is only *referred to* in the story; she never actually appears. Her characterization is limited to Felix's opinion that she is waiting for her uncle to go to the hospital for treatment or to die: "all she wanted was to get him out of that house so she could take over. After she did that, that was going to be the end of us. We was going to have to pay rent or we was going to have to leave. I doubt if half of the people on the place could do either one" (164). Thus, although Frank's "altruism" is severely limited, he is much less villainized than she is. Although Gaines develops other white women more fully than he does Frank's niece, he does not develop them much more positively, as will be shown of Candy Marshall in the last section of this chapter. For example, another white female character is Anne-Marie Duvall of "Just Like a Tree," who may go to pay her respects to the black woman who worked for her family and who is now getting ready to move away, but whose concern is still self-serving and patronizing. Anne-Marie brings a seventy-nine-cent scarf to pay Aunt Fe back for her many years of service, and ultimately she is "punished" for intruding into the black community's gathering: Gaines makes her walk part of the way on the cold, wet night; has her fall into a puddle; and then, when she finally makes it to the house, he emphasizes her not belonging. Mrs. Samson in *Autobiography of Miss Jane Pittman* may defend Tee Bob's black half-brother, the product of adulterous miscegeny between her husband and one of the women on the plantation, and plead with her husband not to send him away after he gets into a fight with a white man, but Gaines thereby supports the myth that southern white women did

not care very deeply about their husbands' miscegenous affairs. Gaines is, however, very sympathetic in his characterization of Louise in *Of Love and Dust,* although he also portrays her as somewhat simple-minded.

17. Timmy's eviction also recalls events in the title story/last chapter of *Go Down, Moses,* for its cause is similar to the reason that Samuel Worsham Beauchamp is evicted from the McCaslin plantation by Roth Edmonds: both boys have broken the rules. In contrast, whereas Faulkner's black character has stolen from the plantation store, Gaines's character has hit back when attacked by a white man. Gaines has further compounded the crime against the young black man in his work, having the man who evicts him be his own father. In this way he reminds the reader, too, of the white man's responsibility for bringing the black man into the very community that despises him.

18. In contrast to his development of Mathu, but comparable to Faulkner's development of Lucas, is Gaines's development of Raoul Carmier (in *Catherine Carmier*), who views himself superior to both African-Americans and Cajuns because of his Creole heritage. However, Raoul is not presented as an admirable or sympathetic character. Raoul's behavior and fate in the novel are also comparable to a Faulknerian character—this time the white man Thomas Sutpen: by coming between his daughter Catherine and her lover and rejecting their child, his grandson, Raoul loses, as Joseph Griffin puts it, "the very succession he longs for so intensely" ("Creole" 37).

19. Somewhat contrasting with Washington's reading and providing further support that Gaines does not go along with his characters' association of guns and manhood, Suzanne Jones notes that Clatoo and Mathu, two of the most highly respected of the old men, encourage the old men to go home, "pointing out that they have proven their manhood, just by standing up to Sheriff Mapes" (as Washington suggests), but also that they "have gained self-respect and the respect of *everyone there, black and white*" (53; emphasis added).

20. I do not, however, agree with Davis regarding Candy's achievement of insight by the end of the novel (143). Candy is not given a voice in the novel, and therefore her thoughts cannot be known; further, as will be shown, her words and actions do not support such a reading.

21. In contrast, remarking upon the fates of Jackson and Tee Bob in *Catherine Carmier* and *The Autobiography of Miss Jane Pittman,* respectively, Gaines talks about "someone else . . . pick[ing] up where they left off," a more traditional tragic ending. In this and other comments by both Gaines and his critics, Gaines's awareness of the elements of the genre of tragedy is made apparent, indicating that he consciously constructs his narratives in tragic form. For example, Gaines has remarked upon the limitations of space and time in Greek tragedy (O'Brien 29), and, except for its last section, *A Gathering of Old Men* takes place in the course of a single day. Indeed, Gaines has even said that "the sense of Greek tragedy . . . keeps coming back in [his] writing" (O'Brien 30). In addition, John Edgar

Wideman (78) and Valerie Babb (62) discuss *Of Love and Dust* in tragic terms; Frank Shelton argues that *In My Father's House* "fits the pattern of classical tragedy in its concern for determinism and free will and for excess pride and its consequences" ("*In*" 343); and William Parrill perceives in *In My Father's House* the "stark inevitability of Greek tragedy" (184).

22. In *Of Love and Dust*, in contrast, however, Gaines aligns a white woman with a black man in conflict against her Cajun husband.

23. For a discussion of the role of Candy in the novel as "a role traditionally reserved for white males" and of her relationship with Mathu, see the article on this novel by Charles J. Heglar and Annye L. Refoe (66).

24. In "Bloodline," Frank Laurent expresses similar annoyance when one of his tenants checks with Amalia before following his orders to bring Copper to him: "Who the hell's running this place, me or Amalia?" (173). Felix then points out to Frank how his power has come to be reduced, like Candy's, through the sharecropping system (to be discussed later in connection to this novel).

25. After remarking upon Candy's "public humiliation" of being "carried off under her boyfriend's arm—at the sheriff's insistence and with the approval of all the black men"—and being "thrown, kicking and screaming, into her car," Mary Helen Washington points out the "strange coalition" in this novel between "these elderly black men and a brutal white sheriff—bitter lifetime enemies—suddenly united in their antipathy for a strong woman" ("House" 24).

26. Sederberg echoes Joseph Gold who, after comparing Ike with Pontius Pilate (63), contrasts him with Christ: "Christ gave up his woodworking tools to undertake work with men, while Ike gives up men in order to become a carpenter" (66). Other critics who have remarked on Ike's failure as a Christian or as a Christ figure, respectively, include John Lewis Longley Jr., who points out, "At the end of his long life it appears that . . . he who saves himself cannot save others" (98), and David Minter, who calls him a "reductive . . . imitation of Jesus. He protects his purity by living a life that is less than human. Without entanglements, including those introduced by ownership, sex, and progeny, too little of life is left" (189).

27. See Jerry Bryant for a similar discussion of the declining power of the aristocracy in *The Autobiography of Miss Jane Pittman*. He argues that Robert Samson, head of the white plantation in that novel, "represents a dead culture. He is one of the last of a long line of white Southerners who have maintained an inflexible resistance to change and growth" ("From" 118).

28. Jones compares Gil to Faulkner's Bayard Sartoris, who also "takes the fictional step for his social class [in Sartoris's case, the aristocracy] in *The Unvanquished* (1938) when he withstands both family and community pressure to kill his father's murderer" (49).

29. Thus Gaines has created another Christ figure, and he develops still another one in his most recent novel, *A Lesson Before Dying* (1994). One might contrast Gaines's very positive Christ figures (besides those I've mentioned, Joseph Griffin

argues a sound case for Marcus from *Of Love and Dust* ["Ernest" 82–83]) with Faulkner's Christ figures, who fall far short of the original: for example, Benjy, Miss Quentin, and Caddy of *The Sound and the Fury*; Joe Christmas of *Light in August*; and Ike McCaslin of *Go Down, Moses*.

30. Valerie Babb remarks on this conflict as it appears in "A Long Day in November" when she suggests that Eddie's "car becomes a symbol of those aspects of a technological culture which further draw society away from humanistic values" (17). In burning the car, then, Eddie not only saves his marriage but also destroys a part of the "technological culture" that is causing trouble for the black sharecropper, as revealed in much of Gaines's fiction, including *A Gathering of Old Men*.

31. In an essay entitled "Of Machines and Men: Pastoralism in Gaines's Fiction," Frank Shelton explains the transition that took place early in the twentieth century when the landowners began "parceling out their land to the Cajuns, pushing the blacks who had previously sharecropped the land off the most fertile areas and finally off the land altogether," and when the tractor, the "machine in the garden," which is also associated with the Cajuns, arrived ("Of" 21). Still, Shelton does not confirm the validity of Gaines's vision of a pastoral life for the African-Americans *before* this period, although he does note a "dichotomy between [the African-Americans'] kinship with the southern land and the oppression blacks experienced on that land" that exists in the works of many African-American writers (13), and he points out the paradox in Gaines's fiction of "the plantation [being] at the same time a source of strength and continuity for his black characters" and "a force for entrapment and dehumanization that must be changed" (14).

32. Talking with Marcia Gaudet and Carl Wooton about his love for the home of his childhood, Gaines inadvertently confirms this reading: "I suppose as children we loved the quarters. I mean we loved it more than the people who owned it loved it, but we were limited. See, I could love that patch of land. . . . [W]e could love that very much, because that's where everything was for us." Interesting for how appropriate it is to my point above, Gaines concludes his explanation for his attachment to the land he writes about with the remark that he is "not trying to preserve the Old South, for damned sure" (Gaudet and Wooton 75).

33. Valerie Babb has also noted Lou's two names: "His . . . formal name," she argues, "is that of a white man, one the parish expects will uphold its social rules" (117). I would further qualify this denotation—not just "that of a white man" but, more accurately, "that of a *Cajun*." The "social rules" of the Cajuns, as various Gaines's scholars have pointed out, have been a source of conflict throughout Gaines's canon. For example, in *Of Love and Dust* these rules keep white men and black women from any deeper relationship than a sexual one and black men and white women from any relationship at all. In that novel, although Sidney Bonbon loves his black mistress, he cannot marry her or openly acknowledge his children

by her, whom he also loves very much. Also, he is forced to kill Marcus, a black man who is sexually involved with his wife (whom he does not love) because, as the novel's narrator explains, "If he hadn't killed Marcus, he would have been killed himself. *The Cajuns on the river would have done that*" (277; emphasis added).

34. Of course, as Suzanne Jones (53), as well as Milton and Patricia Rickels point out, the "battle scene" is also told in somewhat comic tones, reflective, however, as the Rickels put it, of "the exultation of liberation" (224) rather than of a condescending narrator. David C. Estes remarks upon Gaines's use of humor in his fiction: "the humor directly foregrounds issues of racism, so that through incongruities and ironic reversals, Gaines uses laughter as a weapon to retrieve the dignity of African Americans" ("Gaines's" 228). Comparable to my argument that the tragic conclusions of events in *A Gathering of Old Men* are not undermined, are perhaps even underscored, by the comic elements in the novel are Estes's remarks upon the combination of comedy and tragedy in *Of Love and Dust*: "Despite abundant comedy, the narrative pessimistically portrays racial conflict and the inevitable, violent reaffirmation of white supremacy, which finally drowns out the sound of laughter" ("Gaines's" 231). In *A Gathering of Old Men,* one should note that there is no humor in the tone of Dirty Red's account of Charlie's death, which brings the (previously comically rendered) battle to a tragic end.

35. Carl E. Rollyson Jr. believes that "Parts Four and Five of 'The Bear' and 'Delta Autumn' all read like possible conclusions to the book which are super-seded, each in its turn, by another attempt at closure," including the actual ending story, "Go Down, Moses" (115). Similarly, the closing sections of *A Gathering of Old Men* present several possible conclusions: Charlie achieving his manhood, the battle between the African-Americans and the Cajuns, and the trial that restores the aristocracy to power. Gaines apparently rejected the first two conclusions as possible endings to such a day, knowing that ultimately the community would not tolerate such insurrection for long. Commenting on the "double ending" she perceives ("first a shootout and then a trial"), Suzanne Jones suggests that "the second [ending] reaffirms what Gaines has already proven in the novel—that talking can produce results" (55). While I agree with her perception of Mapes's change as he listened to Charlie's story, I do not agree that the talking during the trial brought about any (progressive) *communal* change to speak of: if the talking during the trial is perceived to be humorous by the open-minded, supposedly liberal Lou Dimes, it is probably not taken seriously by many of the other witnesses either. Indeed, as Lou points out, given the laughter in the courtroom, "people passing by out on the street must have thought [they] were showing a Charlie Chaplin movie in there" (213). On the other hand, airing their stories as they "gathered" seems to have been cathartic. Thus, I do not disagree with Jones's thesis that Gaines is ultimately favoring talk over revenge/violence.

36. For a less critical reading of Lou's final section and a more optimistic perception of the novel's conclusion, see Herman Beavers (172–73).

37. In this light, though, the ending can still be viewed as *comedic*; as Robert W. Corrigan points out, "comedy tends to be more concerned with the fact that despite all our individual defeats, life does nonetheless *continue on* its merry way" (353; emphasis added).

38. Craig Werner makes a direct, brief comparison between Lou and Gavin in *Intruder in the Dust* and while doing so notes that "his insights, like those of Gavin Stevens, are rendered nearly useless by his inability to take action" (43). Werner does not, however, note the apparent limitations to Lou's insights.

39. A parallel can be found between Polk's comparison of Gavin's experience with the deputy in "Pantaloon in Black" and the experiences of Lou and Mapes in Gaines's novel. Referring to Gavin and the deputy, Polk writes, "Both become privy to grief, to human passion, where they had least expected it, in a Negro. The deputy tries to understand it; Stevens is arrogantly sure that he understands 'The Negro' completely. It is thus much more likely to be that redneck deputy who will, one of these days, be able to meet black men and women as individual human beings" (150). Similarly, while Mapes acknowledges Charlie's "manhood" at the end of the long day of the gathering, Lou describes the old men in stereotypical terms (as minstrel figures) even after such a day. Except for how his humiliation in court might affect his memory, Mapes, like Faulkner's "redneck deputy," seems to show more potential than Gavin for changing his views of African-Americans.

40. David Smith also views Gaines's fiction more optimistically than his books warrant. In his essay on Gaines and Faulkner, Smith argues that a significant contrast between the two writers' vision is that "Faulkner's characters . . . look constantly backward, overwhelmed by past events and trapped by their tragic inability to make meaningful change," while "Gaines's characters [who] are also deeply bound by the past . . . recognize that change is possible if one is willing to pay the price" (48). At the end of *Of Love and Dust* (the novel Smith is writing about when he makes these remarks), James Kelly leaves after Marcus Payne "pays the price" because he sees no change in attitude evident in the community that witnessed the sacrifice.

Chapter 3. The Sterile New South: Hurston's Contemporaneous Deconstruction of the Paradigm

1. It is interesting to note that in his book on *William Faulkner and Southern History*, Joel Williamson remarks upon the simultaneous writing and then close publication dates of and *Absalom, Absalom!* and *Gone with the Wind* (244–45), but he does not make any reference to Zora Neale Hurston or her writings in his book.

2. A number of critics have commented on Starks's emulation of the successful white man. In a 1938 review of the novel, W. A. Hunton agrees that Hurston is criticizing "the Negro's endeavor to pattern his life according to white bourgeois standards" but credits Starks with less egocentric motives than my reading allows:

"Joe Starks believed, as does a large section of the Negro middle class, that the race could only prove itself by rising to power, a power exactly like that of the white man, through self-segregation and self-help" (71). A reference is made to Starks's "white values" by James R. Giles (52). Cyrena N. Pondrom calls Starks "[a] cutting satire on white 'go-getters' who become wealthy on their own initiative and salesmanship and treat their wives as the paramount emblem of their status and potency" (190). Gay Wilentz says that Starks "is an example of the 'Black Bourgeoisie' who believed that the acquisitions of wealth and status would in some way make them closer to the white culture which thought them inferior" ("Defeating" 287). And James Krasner notes that Starks "surrounds himself with emblems of white authority and power" (121). In contrast to these critics, Mary Katherine Wainwright argues that "Janie's second marriage to Jody Starks represents the oppression of middle-class *black* women, who are expected to function only as symbols of their husbands' status and wealth without any regard for their own needs as human beings (238; Wainwright's emphasis).

3. Darryl Hattenhauer poses the provocative argument that Janie is as attracted to Starks's whiteness as he is to hers ("Death" 53) and makes a convincing case that Janie is as "influenced by white America" as I argue Starks is ("Death" 50).

4. Mary Helen Washington discusses Nancy's similar "white" dream for Janie, "based on being as much as possible like that white woman she used to have to bow and scrape to." According to Washington's reading, however, Nancy's motive is much less egocentric than that of Starks: "Even more important than mimicking whites was the status of being able to protect one's self from degradation to which a slave was subjected" ("Black" 70). Darwin T. Turner's description of Nanny's motive is reminiscent of the inspiration for Sutpen's design: "Feeling that life cheated her by enslaving her, Nanny vows that her granddaughter will enjoy the happiness she herself has never known" (106). Sutpen, too, the reader recalls, wanted to provide for people like himself, a poor sharecropper's son, a plantation where they would be welcomed in at the front door and cared for.

5. Here, one might apply Darryl Hattenhauer's case regarding Janie's "white" values ("Death" 50–51, 53) as another point of comparison with Henry.

6. Repeatedly in *Absalom, Absalom!* Sutpen's obsession with mating with various women in order to continue his line, as well as the mating of his slaves, is compared to the mating of animals. For example, in chapter 3, we are told that "the wild blood which he had brought into the country [he] tried to mix, blend, with the tame which was already there, with the same care and for the same purpose with which he blended that of the stallion and that of his own" (67). One might recall here Susan Willis's assessment of Starks's treatment of Janie as a "domestic pet," and thus one can see another comparison between Starks and Sutpen, in spite of Starks's lack of concern about mating and propagating.

7. Darryl Hattenhauer's explanation for Tea Cake biting Janie as he died is

also reminiscent of the behavior of Starks: "Tea Cake bites Janie to take her with him" ("Death" 48); one might compare that to the way that Starks started tearing Janie down about her looks when he noticed his own aging, "as if he didn't want her to stay young while he grew old" (Hurston 73). Susan Willis notes, too, the similarity between the "dying moments" of Tea Cake and Starks. She believes that Hurston is showing in these two instances "that women cannot hope to have themselves fully realized in their husbands." Surprisingly, although she notices this similarity, Willis still states that "Tea Cake and Joe Starks are worlds apart and in no other way comparable in their treatment of Janie" (*Specifying* 51).

8. See Robert Haas's article arguing that Janie believes in the end that she is dying of rabies and Darryl Hattenhauer's similar article, arguing that Janie has contracted rabies but is in denial about dying (both to be discussed subsequently). Haas enumerates the doctor's repeated warnings to Janie to stay away from Tea Cake and his concern about Tea Cake's danger to Janie (212–14). Hattenhauer provides other examples of Janie's "unconscious self-destructiveness," mainly remaining in the house after finding, first, the pistol and then the revolver, which she doesn't unload completely. Hattenhauer argues that she is "trying to arrange things so that she might die with him" ("Death" 47). Similarly, Pat Carr and Lou-Ann Crouther call Janie "a heroic martyr" who is not, in the end, "ready to start a subversive life [in Eatonville]; she is instead preparing herself as a willing sacrifice for Tea Cake and for the God that demanded blood sacrifices." Thus, they argue, "Hurston is not attempting merely to show the simple, liberated blossoming of a mature woman; she is instead examining the tragic sacrifice that is somehow demanded by our best and brightest" (56). In contrast, Ronald F. Anderson cites passages from the novel's end that he believes "[do] not sound like someone contemplating a wretched, violent death in the near future" (89).

9. My discussion of the possibility of Janie having been infected with rabies when bitten by Tea Cake has been updated since this chapter was published as an article in 1993. Here I incorporate the recent criticism discussing whether Janie is dying at the end of the novel. At the time I first surveyed the criticism on *Their Eyes Were Watching God* for the article that was eventually published in the *College Language Association Journal,* only Bernard W. Bell had mentioned (though not discussed) the possibility that "Janie is probably dying from Tea Cake's biting her" (Bell 127). The year before my article appeared (but after its acceptance for publication), Darryl Hattenhauer published a note and coauthors Pat Carr and Lou-Ann Crouther published an article posing the argument that Tea Cake had infected Janie with rabies; then, the same year that my article appeared, the *Marjorie Kinnan Rawlings Journal of Florida Literature,* which had published Carr and Crouther's article, ran Ronald Anderson's short refutation of their thesis; and later, just after my article appeared, Hattenhauer published a second, this time full-length article arguing again that Janie would die of rabies. Most recently, in an essay published in the 1997 book *Haunted Bodies: Gender and Southern Texts,*

Catherine Gunther Kodat brings up the issue, arguing that Janie must have been infected by the bite and noting the absence of any reference to her being treated (but mistakenly stating that still only Bernard Bell had noticed [320]).

10. Ronald Anderson disagrees with this reading, pointing out that "[t]he day before, [the doctor] had told [Janie] that the serum would be there the next morning (the day she was bitten), if not before" and that since it was "standard medical procedure to inoculate any person exposed to the rabies virus," one can assume that he gave Janie the serum (88).

11. Robert Haas refutes convincingly Ronald Anderson's case against human to human infection (and thus against the possibility that Janie has been infected), which Anderson bases on 1980 and 1989 articles in medical journals, with the statement, "the novel was written in 1937, not 1980 or 1989, and the medical risk of a human rabies bite was not established or known to Hurston, her characters, or her readers." Haas subsequently shows that "Janie's final feelings of satisfaction, peace, and joy are not incommensurate with [anticipating] death [or] with having for another day outlived possible death" (209). He makes two poignant points regarding the significance of Tea Cake biting Janie. First, whether she's going to die or not (and Haas himself notes that "a fully documented case of human-human transmission by saliva has never occurred" [214]), Janie *believes* she has been infected, which Haas supports with Janie's own thoughts (Haas 208): "that big old dawg . . . had killed her after all . . . through Tea Cake" (Hurston 169) and "He [Tea Cake] would be thinking up new songs to play to her *when she got there*" (Hurston 180; emphasis added). Second, after detailing the role the doctor who treats Tea Cake plays in establishing the risk to Janie of infection if Tea Cake bit her, Haas argues emphatically (that is, the italics are his) that "*it does not really matter*" if Dr. Simmons's worries are invalid. He shows how "Hurston builds Dr. Simmons up within the world of her novel as a source of authoritative truth, certainly as far as Janie is concerned. Even if by some more remote and sophisticated standard he is wrong, that has no bearing on how Janie acts and feels" (214).

12. Although Hortense J. Spillers "is not certain of how these images of loss and labor should be read, nor why they strike with such finality, . . . this rolling in of fish nets and cleaning of meshes," she actually explains the reason this is so in her reading of this passage: "If we take Janie as a kind of adventurer, as a woman well familiar with the rites of burial and grief, then we read this closure as a eulogy." In this explanation, Spillers, perhaps unintentionally, supports the argument that Janie has come to die. However, Spillers specifies that this passage is "a eulogy for the living," explaining that "Janie has been 'buried' along with Tea Cake" and thus, apparently, Spillers does not interpret the ending as suggesting that Janie is dying (196).

13. Mary Jane Lupton's reading of these seeds contrasts with mine. She believes that they represent "survival," for "in planting them Janie remains committed to growth" (41). I wonder, though, when did she plant them, and if she did, who is

going to water them if she dies? However, Lupton's reading might be applied to the earlier reference in the novel to Tea Cake himself "seeding the garden for [Janie]" (105).

14. Patricia Felisa Barbeito also views Janie's childlessness "metaphorically [as] her rejection of traditional codified roles." She connects the childlessness to Janie's "refus[al] to reproduce the female legacy described and embodied by her grandmother" and suggests that "Janie's procreative capabilities find expression within another type of female genealogy or heritage; she gives voice to her grandmother's frustrated desire to preach a great sermon" (385).

15. Hurston herself reminds us in the very beginning of the novel that "women forget all those things they don't want to remember, and remember everything they don't want to forget. The dream is the truth" (1); thus, as Anita M. Vickers points out, "The prose that follows [this passage] will not be an historical representation of the events" (305–6). Such a perception of Truth as being in the mind of the beholder is also reminiscent of Faulkner.

Chapter 4. Resounding Truths in *Absalom, Absalom!* and *Song of Solomon*: Exploring Epistemology with Faulkner and Morrison

1. Recalling that Gaines ended up finding familiar agricultural, peasant communities in the works of Russian writers like Turgenev, it is interesting that in a 1981 interview Morrison described her work as "village literature, fiction that is really for the village, for the tribe. Peasant literature for *my* people" (LeClair 120). And just as Gaines did find at least a *version* of his own people in the literature of Faulkner, Morrison acknowledges in this same interview that "Faulkner wrote what I suppose could be called regional literature [that is] good—and universal—because it is specifically about a particular world," which, she says, is also "what I wish to do" (LeClair 124). And in another interview, when asked how she feels about how authors like Faulkner depict African-Americans in their work, she responds, "Faulkner was brilliant at it" (Schappell 100).

2. Duvall repeats these concerns and qualifications in a later essay titled "Toni Morrison and the Anxiety of Faulknerian Influence" (3). Morrison herself cautions against "merely trying to place [a] book into an already established literary tradition" (Claudia Tate 161).

3. Several critics have noted the similarities between Faulkner's Clytie of *Absalom, Absalom!* and Morrison's Circe of *Song of Solomon,* including Nancy Ellen Batty in the only other extended pairing of these two works to date. I agree with Batty that "Quentin's encounter with the Sutpens' house servant, Clytie, [is similar to] Milkman's encounter with the Butler's servant, Circe" (84), but I also find Milkman's visit with Circe comparable to Quentin's with Rosa Coldfield and similarities between these two women as well, particularly in their unrelenting outrage over the insults against them and their determination to avenge them-

selves against those who insulted them. Speaking of Circe's outrage, Chiara Spallino contrasts her with Faulkner's Dilsey, "who continues lovingly to serve her white masters even after their decline and death. Revenge and not endurance animate Circe's ghost" (520).

Surprisingly, Susan Willis has compared Pilate to Thomas Sutpen, calling both "mythic heroes" ("Eruptions" 39) but then contrasting Morrison's utopian vision with Faulkner's dystopian one ("Eruptions" 41). Willis also notes the parallels between Morrison's household of three women—Pilate, Reba, and Hagar—and the three-woman household (Clytie, Judith, and Rosa) in *Absalom, Absalom!* during the Civil War, but she again points out a significant distinction: "Sutpen, even in his absence, is still the center of the household" in the Faulkner novel ("Eruptions" 41). Finally, Andrea Dimino has also compared Circe and Clytie, in much the same way that I compared Gaines's Jane Pittman and Dilsey: "For Morrison, Clytie's silence is symptomatic of the role that black people play in the classics of American literature. . . . It is vital, then, that in *Song of Solomon* Morrison gives Circe a voice of her own with which to recount the history of both blacks and whites" (35). Like this chapter's reading of *Song of Solomon* with *Absalom, Absalom!*, Dimino finds that "[t]hese works [and she adds "The Bear"] all depict young men undergoing initiations into adulthood by way of a quest to understand the past" (35).

4. Linda Hutcheon acknowledges briefly this similarity between these two novels when she points out that *Song of Solomon* "parod[ies] both the structures and theme of the recoverability of history in Faulkner's *Absalom, Absalom!*" to illustrate her argument that a "parodic mix of authority and transgression, use and abuse, characterizes intra-American intertextuality" (131).

5. His first two questions are quoted from Dick Higgins's *A Dialectic of Centuries* (101).

6. One reviewer of Morrison's later novel *Jazz* has remarked on Morrison's tendency to send her characters South—"if need be . . . all the way back to antebellum"—in her novels (Leonard 48).

7. Bertram Wyatt-Brown traces this mimicry of the white man back to slavery in Africa where slaves imitated masters in order to "raise their own low self-esteem and create a distance between themselves and others whose own position in society was not so lofty." Wyatt-Brown sees this practice repeated by American slaves who "belonged to 'quality folks' [and] often disdained the so-called 'po' white trash'" (31)—like Thomas Sutpen's family of origin.

8. Philip M. Royster explains perhaps best the association between the peacock and Milkman:

The white color of the peacock suggests Milkman's name; the bird's name itself puns on two vulgar names associated with the male penis (Just before Milkman leaves town his sister, Magdelene, attacks him for urinating on her life as well as that of her sister [and says he feels he has the right to "pee" on them because of his "cock"]); the peacock's tail as well as its strut suggests the vain sex-role determined behavior that characterizes the way Milkman treats Hagar, his mother, and his sisters; most of all, the bird cannot fly because of its tail. (437–38)

9. Apparently, the first Macon Dead, who was earlier compared to Thomas Sutpen, differs from Sutpen in that he values his wife, whereas wives, to Sutpen, are merely part of his design.

10. This hunting trip might be compared to the hunting trip in *Absalom, Absalom!* during which General Compson learns much of Thomas Sutpen's history. And Milkman's loss of the symbols of his inherited materialism, one by one, is reminiscent of how the young Isaac McCaslin must leave behind his gun, compass, and watch before the bear will allow him to get a glimpse of itself. Doreen Fowler reads this part of "The Bear" as Ike "stripping himself of all symbols of power and authority, outwardly signing his willingness to relinquish the 'I'" (138), and Linda Hutcheon, who has also noted this "intertextual echo" of "The Bear" in *Song of Solomon,* argues that Milkman "must be stripped of his physical symbols of the dominant white culture and submit to a trial by endurance in order to be accepted" by the black men of Shalimar (134).

11. I must credit Philip Weinstein's *What Else But Love?* with calling my attention to this quotation. Weinstein also poses a similar view to mine regarding how Morrison perceives "the Faulknerian syndrome of outraged innocence": he argues that she has the black men of her work "outgrow" this "adolescent complaint" (*What* 149).

12. Morrison's objectivity, therefore, provides another argument against the character Jules Raynard's theory regarding the shared guilt of whites and blacks in Gaines's *Autobiography of Miss Jane Pittman.* Similar to my argument against Raynard's theory that both races are to blame for supporting the system that led Tee Bob to commit suicide, Morrison shows in *Beloved* that it is the system that is corrupt. Her view of black complicity in the consequential violence is that this corrupt system of oppression leads not only to white on black violence but also to black on black violence.

13. Gay Wilentz points out that, "when Hagar sets out to kill Milkman after being humiliated and dropped by him, the community comments that he's getting what he deserves for 'messing with his own cousin.'" Wilentz notes how Pilate "foreshadows the disastrous end to their relationship by referring to Milkman as Hagar's brother rather than cousin" and explains the importance of exogamy "in most African societies [because it] insures that the children from an upcoming marriage will be healthy, productive members of society." Thus, Wilentz argues, "The sexual relationship between Milkman and his cousin Hagar is doomed at the start since it breaks this African cultural practice" ("Civilizations"

67). It is interesting to note that, in contrast to African incest taboos, Henry Sutpen and Quentin Compson try to defend their incestuous desires for their sisters by drawing on their European roots. Even after discovering that Charles Bon is their brother, Henry condones Bon's marriage to Judith with the assertion that "kings have done it! Even dukes!" (273). Quentin's view of himself as a more suitable choice for Caddy than Dalton Ames is related to historical allowances for incest in *Western* civilization, as listed by Constance Hill Hall, including "a privilege . . . reserved for royalty" (6; see also Bauer, "'I'" 87 n. 7).

14. While I credit Craig Werner with pointing out to me Rosa's distinction as a female narrator, I do not agree entirely with his assessment of her: yes, she is "a static figure," but her depiction is too derisive to allow her to come across as "the enduring saint" (48). Indeed, I am surprised by critics' failure to perceive the comedic in Rosa's characterization.

15. Daniel Singal examines this issue "of whether Quentin's progress [in *Absalom, Absalom!*] is enough to save him" but concludes that "we cannot overlook Quentin's morbid complaint on the novel's penultimate page of how he is 'older at twenty than a lot of people who have died,' followed by the entry in the genealogy that has his life end later that year in Cambridge" (219). Still, Singal's exploration of Quentin's development in *Absalom, Absalom!*, reflected in his "heroic act" of going in to see what is hidden in the Sutpen house, is quite provocative: Singal believes that this

> decision to pursue knowledge whatever the cost is no small matter, qualifying as an act of Faulknerian heroism [that] would strongly suggest that the Quentin of *Absalom, Absalom!* has undergone a substantial transformation from the pathetic soul who committed suicide in *The Sound and the Fury.* . . . By contrast, this new Quentin displays no obsession with purity and, thanks to his alliance with Shreve, is able to comprehend and accept the fluid medium of history, even making his peace with the fact that things never finish themselves. (218)

16. Catherine Carr Lee makes a provocative case for Milkman's survival: "this leap may not bring Milkman's death at all. Many critics have failed to note that just before Milkman leaps off the plateau, Guitar sets his rifle aside" (120).

17. But Hutcheon also suggests that "[t]he questioning of the universal and totalizing in the name of the local and particular does not automatically entail the end of all consensus." Quoting Victor Burgin, she argues, "*Of course* moralities and histories are 'relative,' but this does not mean they do not *exist*" (12). One might employ this understanding to support Daniel Singal's argument against the reader of *Absalom, Absalom!* being "free to arrive at any narrative that he or she might wish. . . . *Absalom, Absalom!* was crafted with painstaking care to perpetuate a specific 'scratch'—the fictional history of an antebellum southern family *as it*

existed within William Faulkner's imagination, along with the moral and cultural meanings that history carried for him" (215).

Chapter 5. No Mere Endurance Here: The Prevailing Woman's Voice in Lee Smith's *Oral History*

1. It is interesting to consider how this Appalachian novel, in which social class is more divisive than race (there not being many nonwhites in the region), develops the passionate/dispassionate dichotomy one finds between traditional Old Southern perceptions of black and white women: as slave women were used as concubines and sold away should their sexual relationships become inconvenient to their masters, so, too, is Red Emmy treated in this novel. Similarly, the more suitable, "ladylike" wives are characterized romantically but not depicted as passionate.

2. One might note that Red Emmy is not given a voice either—or even a section of her own. In an interview with Edwin T. Arnold, Lee Smith explained that she did, in fact, write "a section from Red Emmy's point of view," but her editor advised her to leave it out in order "to leave a central mystery at the core of the novel, which is whether Emmy was a witch or not and whatever happened to her" (Arnold 254). A related benefit of this omission is that Red Emmy achieves legendary stature like the other larger-than-life characters of this novel—Almarine, Pricey Jane, and Dory. Association with these characters is appropriate for Red Emmy, a woman who inspired such passion in Almarine. According to Smith, the deleted section reveals Emmy to be "not a witch at all, but completely crazy" and is therefore written in what she calls "bad Benjy" (referring to Faulkner's Benjy Compson). Had it been included, Red Emmy would be more comparable to the very unromantic Rose Hibbitts and Pearl than to Almarine, Pricey Jane, and Dory.

3. I don't say marry because, as Granny Younger points out, in this community, "Young folks just gets them a roof and moves under it and when the circuit rider comes around he makes it legal by saying the words, or they don't fool with it one way or the other" (62).

4. In spite of Granny Younger's highly romantic descriptions of Almarine and Pricey Jane, Linda Byrd reminds the reader that Almarine did trade a mule for Pricey Jane, which Byrd interprets as "an early hint that he views her as a possession" and contrasts with his passion for Red Emmy (127). While this interpretation of Almarine's attitude goes along with my comparison between him and Sutpen, I disagree with Byrd's description of Pricey Jane as "a sexually passionate wife" (128); as I have noted, the only evidence of the sexual nature of this couple's relationship is the existence of their children. We witness no passionate scenes like those between Almarine and Red Emmy.

5. Anne Goodwyn Jones addresses the speciousness of "[w]riterly texts" in

Oral History, citing as the first example Jennifer's pompous diary, "which she keeps, ironically, for a course in oral history." She also contrasts the "genuineness" of the oral narratives with "the rhetorical prose" of Richard's journal (119). With her third example of the inferiority of the written word, the Hardyesque failure of Richard's note to reach Dory, Jones concludes: "So it is written language that is limited and fragile: divested of sound, separated from its body, rendered merely visible, reified into ink on paper, it can be manipulated or lost or silenced or misinterpreted almost at will. The power of the written word in this oral culture is attenuated and almost inhuman" (136).

6. Richard's confidante in Hoot Owl Holler, the Methodist minister Aldous Rife, who, like Richard, escapes his profession at the Smith Hotel, is reminiscent of another Faulkner character, Reverend Hightower in *Light in August,* who is the confidant and advisor of Byron Bunch and who disapproves of Byron's infatuation with Lena Grove. The echoes from *Light in August* continue with Lena Grove, a poor white woman whose sexuality, like Dory's, Byron (like Richard) finds both attractive and repelling. In contrast to these obsessive and destructive sexual relationships (in both novels), Aldous enjoys a passionate but not destructive sexual relationship with the hotel proprietor, Justine Poole. Theirs is one of only two healthy relationships in the novel, the other being the marriage between Sally and Roy, which will be discussed later. As with Sally and Roy, the key to Aldous and Justine's success is that Justine's enjoyment of sex does not frighten or intimidate Aldous. One hears another echo from *Light in August* in the postcoital conversations like the one discussed above between Aldous and Justine, but especially those Sally describes that occur between herself and Roy, which are reminiscent of the salesman of *Light in August,* as Joel Williamson describes him, "settled in bed with his wife telling her about Lena and Byron between episodes of making love" (367).

7. Richard has also been "successful" with a student in his class, Jink Cantrell, Dory's younger brother. Jink's section reveals the lessons Richard has taught him about the importance of proper grammar and particular moral values, the first of which will be useless to Jink except to help him escape from his environment, and the second of which is limited to the issues of slavery and the treatment of African-Americans, a subject also not applicable to his life in Hoot Owl Holler, since, according to Granny Younger, there are no black people in this community and Jink remarks that he's seen only one black man in his life. But Jink is a smart pupil and has begun to apply the term "immoral" to rumors surrounding his sister Dory, who, like Caddy following Dalton Ames's desertion of her, has apparently been promiscuous since Richard's departure. Jink even begins to echo Quentin Compson, again, the prototype for the character of Jink's mentor. Similar to Quentin's wish that he and Caddy and Benjy could run off together (rather than have Caddy marry Herbert Head), Jink says, "Sometimes I wished it was just Dory and Mary [his younger, frail sister] and me and him [Richard or Little

Luther; it's not clear which man he means] off someplace, someplace pretty, and all the rest of them dead. . . . I wished it was Dory and Mary and me and him in a little house in that grassy bald where the fine grass grows all around in a perfect circle, up top of Hurricane Mountain. I wished it was me and them" (193–94). Unlike Quentin, who fantasizes running off with Caddy before she can marry Herbert Head, though, Jink would settle for Dory marrying Little Luther if it would only stop the rumors. He shares Quentin's sensitivity about his sister's honor but is not obsessed with her.

Finally, Jink's section may also remind one somewhat of the sections of *As I Lay Dying* from Vardaman's point of view. Like Vardaman, Jink is a young boy trying to understand the activities of those around him, particularly the sudden departure of someone—in this case, Richard's desertion of himself and Dory.

8. Given the similarity between Sally's mother, Dory, and Eula Varner Snopes, one might compare Sally to Eula's daughter, Linda, who, as Daniel Singal points out, quoting Gavin Stevens in *The Mansion,* "does not go around saying 'I must do something to help, I've got to do something, I can't just sit here idle' [*Mansion* 200]." Given my discussion of how Sally rejects cultural superstitions that curse her family and goes to Pearl's aid when called, one might apply Singal's reading of Linda to Sally: "Freed of that paralyzing ambivalence born of conflicting cultural values that destroys characters like Bayard [Sartoris] and Quentin, Linda displays the capacity for direct, immediate action that Faulkner had long been seeking in his protagonists." As I argue regarding Sally's emergence by the end of the novel as a prevailing voice, Singal perceives Linda as "[t]he vehicle [Faulkner] needed to realize his ideal self [which] would not be a male Sartoris or Compson or McCaslin but a maimed female Snopes" (290).

9. As I noted in chapter 2, although I find provocatively appealing Philip Dubuisson Castille's argument that Dilsey does not get involved with the librarian's scheme to rescue Caddy because by this time she is free of the Compsons (429–30), at the same time I believe it is too optimistic a reading. After all, Dilsey does ask what Jason said about the photograph.

10. One might think of this quotation when reading Barbara Bennett's conclusions regarding the ultimately optimistic vision of contemporary southern women writers (like Lee Smith): "hope [for good] surfaces regularly in the writing of southern women. . . . What remains after the laughter is, more often than not, affirmation and optimism about the future" (124–25).

Chapter 6. Rape Fantasies vs. Rape Realities: More Skeletons Coming Out of Southern Closets

1. This discussion leaves out perhaps the most "infamous" rape in southern literature, the homosexual rape of Bobby Trippe by a mountain man in James Dickey's *Deliverance* (1970). As for the most "famous" rapes in southern literature,

I would say that there is actually a tie for "most famous" between the scene often referred to as a "rape" in *Gone with the Wind* and the less ambiguous rape in Tennessee Williams's 1947 *A Streetcar Named Desire*. There, too, it is interesting to note that the charisma of the rapist somewhat glamorizes the rape, while the manipulative personality of the victim leads to an attitude (at least in the early responses to the play) that she got what she deserved. Laura and Edward Morrow note that "the audience of 1947 no doubt blamed Blanche partially, if not primarily, for her rape. . . . Blanche has been acting seductively toward Stanley, and when he advances on her, she does not scream." The Morrows infer that "Williams intends us, at least in part, to blame the victim, to conclude that, with horrible irony, Blanche's attempted seduction of Stanley ultimately succeeds" (67).

2. An interesting parallel can be made between the silence of such "gentlemen"—silent largely, one might argue, in the interest of maintaining the social order—and Horace Benbow, as he is read by Sondra Guttman. Guttman argues that Horace's disgust with the way that Temple tells the story of her rape and subsequent lifestyle suggests that he "cannot tolerate the idea of Temple resisting attack, exercising her agency by attempting to alter the social order so that she will not be victimized" (102).

3. In her essay on incest in southern women's fiction, Minrose Gwin makes the same point of contrast with Faulkner: "What Allison, Smith, and Walker do that Faulkner does not is to reveal and dramatize the effects of incestuous abuse on the female victim/survivor *from her perspective* ("Nonfelicitous" 420; Gwin's emphasis).

4. One might do a similar reading of Thomas Thompson's East Texas (and very southern) novel *Celebrity,* in which a rape leads to the destruction of a friendship and the downfall of three promising men. The victim of this rape is in that novel, too, treated as a mere plot device, first to break the three boys up and send them on individual paths and then to bring final justice to the one of them who actually raped her. In between the rape, which occurs in chapter 3, and her murder of her rapist in the novel's second-to-last chapter, the focus of this over six-hundred–page novel is on these three men, trying to reconcile their burdened consciences with their various successes on their individual roads to "celebrity."

5. It is interesting to note the echo here of a passage in Faulkner's *The Hamlet,* in which Faulkner writes that Jack Houston "proved that at least you cannot escape either past or future with nothing better than geography" and then continues parenthetically, "(Geography: that paucity of invention, that fatuous faith in distance of man who can invent no better means than geography for escaping; himself of all, to whom, so he believed he believed, geography had never been merely something to walk upon but was the very medium which the fetterless to- and fro-going required to breathe in.)" (214–15).

6. Remembering the reference earlier to *Streetcar Named Desire,* it is interesting to note here Mark Royden Winchell's theory that "[f]or much of her life,

Blanche's difficulties stemmed from the lack of a forceful patriarchy," including both her male relatives and her gay husband (140). One might add Mitch to Winchell's list, as he ultimately deserts her as well. Sadly, when she finally meets a man who demands his role as head of the house (Stanley), he rapes rather than protects her.

Chapter 7. Don't Just Sit There; Do Something: Frustration with Faulkner from Glasgow to Gautreaux

1. In her biography of Glasgow, Goodman points out an echo of this Faulkner story in Glasgow's *life*—or rather, Glasgow "lore." According to one Glasgow legend, a Franciscan monk from Florence who served as an interpreter for Glasgow's party during their 1908 trip to Italy later "became one of Glasgow's suitors, last seen trying to gain entrance to One West Main [her address in Richmond]. People wondered if he, like Homer Baron in Faulkner's 'A Rose for Emily,' had also been murdered and entombed by the woman he jilted" (*Ellen* 108).

2. Pamela R. Matthews perceives the tone of *The Sheltered Life* as angry and suggests that Glasgow's anger is not only directed at the theme of evasive idealism but also "targets a cultural norm that, as it elevated heterosexuality, negated a tradition of female bonding Glasgow had discovered for herself." I would add the romantic idealist as another aspect of her culture that Glasgow takes issue with in her novel and add her impatience with this character type as further corroboration for Matthews's assessment of "the novel's anger" (179).

3. This description also echoes the opening of Faulkner's "That Evening Sun" (first published in 1931 as "That Evening Sun Goes Down"): "The streets are paved now, and the telephone and electric companies are cutting down more and more of the shade trees" (*Collected* 289).

4. I therefore disagree with Renee R. Curry's view that the story's narrator "remains too embedded in the construct of the community to interrogate his neighbors, a reflection again of a Faulkner who remains too much embedded in the construct of patriarchy to see a great distance beyond it" (398). However, I do agree with the rest of Curry's reading, which argues that the community was all along aware of—and indeed covered for—Emily's crime. My reading of the narrator's awareness of Emily's oppression, as reflected in the way that he evokes the reader's sympathy for this woman before revealing the extent of her madness, is more akin to Isaac Rodman's reading of the narrator "as isolated as Miss Emily herself, or as Faulkner himself as a young man" and who may speak "as the voice of the town" but who does not identify with the other members of the community (4).

I would add to Rodman's reading that it is interesting to note how the narrator, who speaks in first-person plural for most of the story, including himself in his narration of the community's reaction to Emily (except when referring to the views of the town's women or of the men "of Colonel Sartoris' generation" [*Collected* 120]), switches abruptly from first- to third-person plural before narrating the story's horrifying conclusion: "Already *we* knew that there was one room in that region above the stairs which no one had seen in forty years, and which would have to be forced. *They* waited until Miss Emily was decently in the ground before they opened it" (129; emphasis added). The use of "they" indicates that the narrator apparently does not want to be perceived as being a party to this intrusion into Emily's private life rather than his actual absence from the scene because at the end of the story he does say that, upon entering the room and surveying its contents, "*we* noticed that in the second pillow was the indention of a head" (130).

5. Robert Crosman argues similarly, "deprived of her father, she had found a suitor outside the limits of respectability for a woman of her class and background; threatened with his loss as well she found a way to keep him, and then she remained true to him all the days of her life" (209).

6. While I would be hesitant to suggest that Delia and Homer's common last name is evidence that Glasgow had "A Rose for Emily" consciously in mind when she wrote *The Sheltered Life*, the echo does call attention to the two characters' similar roles: the disappearance of both characters, Delia from the ball when she goes outside with George, and Homer from the town, reveals a "crime"—George's adultery and Emily's murder of Homer—but in both works the community ignores the evidence and allows the crimes to go unpunished (although Glasgow finally allows Eva to "punish" her husband).

7. Glasgow's description of the young David Archbald's reaction to witnessing the death of a deer anticipates in tone and imagery Faulkner's descriptions of Isaac McCaslin of *Go Down Moses*. Glasgow writes:

> For the eyes of the hunted had looked into his at the end; and that look was to return to him again and again, as a childish fear of the dark returns to the grown man when his nerves are unstrung. In how many faces of men, women, children, and animals, all over the world, had he seen that look of the hunted reflected? A look of bewilderment, of doubt, of agony, of wondering despair; but most of all a look that is seeking some God who might, but does not, show mercy. (104)

Like Isaac, the general would remain haunted by "the look in the eyes of the dying buck," which "now . . . was everywhere" (109).

8. Like me, Isaac Rodman has difficulty believing "the seeming inability of the townspeople to associate the smell of decaying meat with the disappearance of Homer Baron" and argues that, "[a]s surely as a gentleman does not tell a lady she smells . . . a closed Southern town does not send its venerable idol to jail or asylum for murdering a Yankee" (7). Renee Curry also points out that "when Miss Emily clearly continues to live, the community refuses to invest in an alternative inter-

pretation about the arsenic. They simply forget it or suppress it. This druggist and the community members thus house information that our narrator could pursue, but he or she does not" (397). See also Lawrence R. Rodgers's reading of "A Rose for Emily" as a detective story. Rodgers believes Judge Stevens's explanation for the bad smell is "ignoring a murder" and "a conveniently calculating means on his part of preserving order" (126).

9. *All the King's Men,* published a decade after *Absalom, Absalom!* and only four years after *Go Down, Moses,* includes a chapter on Burden's Civil War–era ancestor, Cass Mastern. Burden's interest in his ancestor echoes Quentin's interest in the Sutpen history, and the story itself, left to his descendents in his papers, may remind readers of Isaac McCaslin finding out about the sexual escapades of his ancestor Old Carothers. Clearly, Warren, like Faulkner, perceived the Civil War era as continuing to play a role in the character development of his twentieth-century protagonists.

10. Mary Arensberg and Sara E. Schyfter find another way to view Emily's murder of Homer as triumphant: perhaps she "killed her lover before [a sexual] encounter was possible; by maintaining her virginity, she is able to prevent Homer from either leaving her or triumphing over her" (129).

11. A former student of mine, Karen W. Warren, traces this progression toward a more optimistic vision in her thesis, "Masculinity and Communal Change in the Fiction of Ernest J. Gaines." And in his article on *A Lesson Before Dying,* Ed Piacentino looks at the role of Paul Bonin, noting "his genuine sensitivity and humanity" (76). He compares Paul to the "white Southerner with liberal and open-minded racial views, views contrary to racial attitudes of the white majority during the era of segregation [which] has a basis in Southern autobiography," as examined by Fred Hobson in *But Now I See: The White Southern Racial Conversion Narrative* (Piacentino 74). One might *contrast* this white Gaines character, whom Piacentino reads in heroic terms, with the Faulkner prototype who shares these liberal views but is not optimistic about others coming to his way of thinking.

Bibliography

Allison, Dorothy. *Bastard Out of Carolina.* New York: Dutton, 1992.

Anderson, Ronald F. "Zora Neale Hurston's *Their Eyes Were Watching God.*" *Marjorie Kinnan Rawlings Journal of Florida Literature* 5 (1993): 87–90.

Arbeit, Marcel. "Coming of Age in Faulkner's *The Reivers* and Padgett Powell's *Edisto.*" In *Faulkner, His Contemporaries, and His Posterity,* edited by Waldemar Zacharasiewicz, 276–83. Transatlantic Perspectives series 3. Tübingen: Francke, 1993.

Arensberg, Mary, and Sara E. Schyfter. "Hairoglyphics in Faulkner's 'A Rose for Emily': Reading the Primal Trace." *Boundary 2* 15, no. 1–2 (1986–1987): 123–34.

Arnold, Edwin T. "An Interview with Lee Smith." *Appalachian Journal* 11 (1984): 240–54.

Babb, Valerie. *Ernest Gaines.* Twayne's United States Authors series 584. Boston: Twayne, 1991.

Barbeito, Patricia Felisa. "'Making Generations' in Jacobs, Larsen, and Hurston: A Genealogy of Black Women's Writing." *American Literature* 70 (1998): 365–95.

Barthelme, Donald. *The Dead Father.* New York: Farrar, 1975.

Batty, Nancy Ellen. "Riff, Refrain, Reframe: Toni Morrison's Song of Absalom." In *Unflinching Gaze: Morrison and Faulkner Re-Envisioned,* edited by Carol A. Kolmerten, Stephen M. Ross, and Judith Bryant, 77–90. Jackson: University Press of Mississippi, 1997.

Bauer, Margaret D. *The Fiction of Ellen Gilchrist.* Gainesville: University Press of Florida, 1999.

———. "'I have sinned in that I have betrayed the innocent blood': Quentin's Recognition of His Guilt." *Southern Literary Journal* 32, no. 2 (2000): 70–89.

Beavers, Herman. *Wrestling Angels into Song: The Fictions of Ernest J. Gaines and James Alan McPherson.* Penn Studies in Contemporary American Fiction series. Philadelphia: University of Pennsylvania Press, 1995.

Bell, Bernard W. *The Afro-American Novel and Its Tradition.* Amherst: University of Massachusetts Press, 1987.

Bennett, Barbara. *Comic Visions, Female Voices: Contemporary Women Novelists and Southern Humor.* Southern Literary Studies series. Baton Rouge: Louisiana State University Press, 1998.

Bergman, Jill. "'this was the answer to it': Sexuality and Maternity in *As I Lay Dying.*" *Mississippi Quarterly* 49 (1996): 393–407.

Blaine, Diana York. "The Abjection of Addie and Other Myths of the Maternal in *As I Lay Dying.*" *Mississippi Quarterly* 47 (1994): 419–39.

Bleikasten, André. "Fathers in Faulkner." In *The Fictional Father: Lacanian Readings of the Text,* edited by Robert Con Davis, 115–46. Amherst: University of Massachusetts Press, 1981.

———. "Faulkner in the Singular." In *Faulkner at 100: Faulkner and Yoknapatawpha, 1997,* edited by Donald M. Kartiganer and Ann J. Abadie, 204–18. Jackson: University Press of Mississippi, 2000.

Boyd, Valerie. *Wrapped in Rainbows: The Life of Zora Neale Hurston.* New York: Scribner, 2003.

Bradley, David. "Lee Smith's Home Truths." Review of *Oral History,* by Lee Smith. *Village Voice,* 2 August 1983, 39.

Brans, Jo. "Embracing the World: An Interview with Donald Barthelme." *Southwest Review* 67 (1982): 121–37.

Brinkmeyer, Robert, Jr. *Contemporary Southern Writers and the West.* Lamar Memorial Lectures series 42. Athens: University of Georgia Press, 2000.

Broughton, Panthea Reid. "Faulkner's Cubist Novels." In *A Cosmos of My Own: Faulkner and Yoknapatawpha, 1980,* edited by Doreen Fowler and Ann J. Abadie, 59–94. Jackson: University Press of Mississippi, 1981.

Bryant, J. A., Jr. *Twentieth-Century Southern Literature.* New Perspectives on the South series. Lexington: University Press of Kentucky, 1997.

Bryant, Jerry H. "Ernest J. Gaines: Change, Growth, and History." *Southern Review* n.s. 10 (1974): 851–64.

———. "From Death to Life: The Fiction of Ernest J. Gaines." *Iowa Review* 3, no. 1 (1972): 106–20.

Busby, Mark. *Larry McMurtry and the West: An Ambivalent Relationship.* Texas Writers series 4. Denton: University of North Texas Press, 1995.

Busch, Frederick. "Voices of Hoot Owl Holler." Review of *Oral History,* by Lee Smith. *New York Times Book Review,* 10 July 1983, 15.

Byerman, Keith E. "Afro-American Folklore and the Shape of Contemporary Black Fiction: The Example of Ernest Gaines's *The Autobiography of Miss Jane Pittman.*" In *Design, Pattern, Style: Hallmarks of a Developing American Culture,* edited by Don Harkness, 49–50. Charleston: American Studies Press, 1983.

———. *Fingering the Jagged Grain: Tradition and Form in Recent Black Fiction.* Athens: University of Georgia Press, 1985.

Byrd, Linda. "The Emergence of the Sacred Sexual Mother in Lee Smith's *Oral History.*" *Southern Literary Journal* 31, no. 1 (1998): 119–42.

Callahan, John. "Image-Making: Tradition and the Two Versions of *The Autobiography of Miss Jane Pittman.*" *Chicago Review* 29, no. 2 (1977): 45–62.

Campbell, Richard, and Jimmie L. Reeves. "Resurrecting the TV Western: The Cowboy, the Frontier, and *Lonesome Dove.*" *Television Quarterly* 24, no. 3 (1990): 33–41.

Canby, Henry Seidel. "The School of Cruelty." Review of *Sanctuary,* by William Faulkner. *Saturday Review of Literature,* 21 March 1931, 673–74. Reprinted in *William Faulkner: The Contemporary Reviews,* edited by M. Thomas Inge, 56–59. American Critical Archives series 5. Cambridge: Cambridge University Press, 1995.

———. "Youth and Age." Review of *The Sheltered Life,* by Ellen Glasgow. *Saturday Review of Literature,* 27 August 1932, 63. Reprinted in *Ellen Glasgow: The Contemporary Reviews,* edited by Dorothy M. Scura, 328–29. American Critical Archives series 3. Cambridge: Cambridge University Press, 1992.

Carr, John. *Kite-Flying and Other Irrational Acts: Conversations with Twelve Southern Writers.* Baton Rouge: Louisiana State University Press, 1972.

Carr, Pat, and Lou-Ann Crouther. "Pulling in the Horizon: Death, Sacrifice, and Rabies in Zora Neale Hurston's *Their Eyes Were Watching God.*" *Marjorie Kinnan Rawlings Journal of Florida Literature* 4 (1992): 51–57.

Cash, W. J. *The Mind of the South.* New York: Knopf, 1941.

Castille, Philip Dubuisson. "Dilsey's Easter Conversion in Faulkner's *The Sound and the Fury.*" *Studies in the Novel* 24 (1992): 423–33.

Chan, Amado. "Stereotypical, but Revengeful and Defiant: Addie Bundren in Faulkner's *As I Lay Dying.*" *Journal of Evolutionary Psychology* 22, no. 3–4 (2001): 118–22. North Carolina Libraries for Virtual Education (NCLIVE) <http://web5.infotrac.galegroup.com/itw/infomark/796/106/61256110w5/purl=rc1_ITOF_0_A83038238&dyn=6!xrn_8_0_A83038238?sw_aep=ncliveecu>.

Christian, Barbara. *Black Feminist Criticism: Perspectives on Black Women Writers.* New York: Pergamon, 1986.

Coleman, Courtney. "Gautreaux Settles into Fall's Writer-in-Residence Position." *Daily Mississippian,* 28 August 1996 <http://dm.olemiss.edu/archives/96/9608/960828/960828Ewriter.html>.

Conroy, Pat. *The Great Santini.* New York: Houghton Mifflin, 1976.

———. *The Lords of Discipline.* New York: Houghton Mifflin, 1980.

———. *The Prince of Tides.* New York: Houghton Mifflin, 1986.

Corrigan, Robert W. "Aristophanic Comedy: The Conscience of a Conservative." In *Comedy: Meaning and Form,* edited by Corrigan, 353–62. San Francisco: Chandler, 1965.

Cowley, Malcolm. *The Faulkner-Cowley File: Letters and Memories, 1944–1962.* New York: Viking, 1966.

Creighton, Joanne V. *William Faulkner's Craft of Revision: The Snopes Trilogy, "The Unvanquished," and "Go Down, Moses."* Detroit: Wayne State University Press, 1977.

Crosman, Robert. "How Readers Make Meaning." *College Literature* 9 (1982): 207–15.

Curry, Renee R. "Gender and Authorial Limitation in Faulkner's 'A Rose for Emily.'" *Mississippi Quarterly* 47 (1994): 391–402.

Dale, Corinne. "The Power of Language in Lee Smith's *Oral History.*" *Southern Quarterly* 28, no. 2 (1990): 21–34.

Davis, Thadious M. "Ernest J. Gaines, 1933–." In *African American Writers,* edited by Valerie Smith, Lea Baechler, and A. Walton Litz, 129–45. New York: Scribner's, 1991.

Denard, Carolyn. "Toni Morrison and the American South: Introduction." *Studies in the Literary Imagination* 31, no. 2 (1998): i–vii.

Dewberry, Elizabeth. *Many Things Have Happened since He Died, and Here Are the Highlights.* New York: Doubleday, 1990.

Dickey, James. *Deliverance.* Boston: Houghton Mifflin, 1970.

Dimino, Andrea. "Toni Morrison and William Faulkner: Remapping Culture." In *Unflinching Gaze: Morrison and Faulkner Re-Envisioned,* edited by Carol A. Kolmarten, Stephen M. Ross, and Judith Bryant Wittenberg, 31–47. Jackson: University Press of Mississippi, 1997.

Dixon, Thomas. *The Clansman, An Historical Romance of the Ku Klux Klan.* New York: Doubleday and Page, 1905.

Donaldson, Susan V., and Anne Goodwyn Jones. "Haunted Bodies: Rethinking the South through Gender." In *Haunted Bodies: Gender and Southern Texts,* edited by Anne Goodwyn Jones and Susan V. Donaldson, 1–19. Charlottesville: University Press of Virginia, 1997.

Donnelly, Colleen. "The Syntax of Perception in *As I Lay Dying.*" *CEA Critic* 53, no. 2 (1991): 54–68.

Doyle, Mary Ellen. "*The Autobiography of Miss Jane Pittman* as a Fictional Edited Autobiography." In *Critical Reflections on the Fiction of Ernest J. Gaines,* edited by David C. Estes, 89–106. Athens: University of Georgia Press.

———. "A *MELUS* Interview: Ernest J. Gaines—'Other Things to Write About.'" *MELUS* 11 (1984): 59–81. Reprinted in *Conversations with Ernest Gaines,* edited by John Lowe, 149–71. Jackson: University Press of Mississippi, 1995.

———. *Voices from the Quarters: The Fiction of Ernest Gaines.* Southern Literary Studies series. Baton Rouge: Louisiana State University Press, 2002.

Duncan, Todd. "Scene and Life Cycle in Ernest Gaines' *Bloodline.*" *Callaloo* 1, no. 3 (1978): 85–101.

Duvall, John D. "Doe Hunting and Masculinity: *Song of Solomon* and *Go Down, Moses.*" *Arizona Quarterly* 47 (1991): 95–115.

———. "Toni Morrison and the Anxiety of Faulknerian Influence." In *Unflinching Gaze: Morrison and Faulkner Re-Envisioned,* edited by Carol A. Kolmerten, Stephen M. Ross, and Judith Bryant Wittenberg, 3–16. Jackson: University Press of Mississippi, 1997.

Ellison, Ralph. "American Humor." Appendix to "Comic Elements in Selected Prose Works by James Baldwin, Ralph Ellison, and Langston Hughes," by Elwyn Ellison Breaux, 146–57. PhD diss., Oklahoma State University, 1971.

———. *Shadow and Act.* New York: Random, 1953.

Estes, David C., "Gaines's Humor: Race and Laughter." In *Critical Reflections of the Fiction of Ernest J. Gaines,* edited by Estes, 228–49. Athens: University of Georgia Press, 1994.

Fabre, Michel. "Bayonne ou le Yoknapatawpha d'Ernest Gaines." *Recherches Anglaises et Américaines* 9 (1976): 208–22. Translated by Melvin Dixon and Didier Malaquin. *Callaloo* 1, no. 3 (1978): 110–23.

Faulkner, William. *Absalom, Absalom!* 1936. First Vintage International edition. New York: Random, 1990.

———. *As I Lay Dying.* 1930. First Vintage International edition. New York: Random, 1990.

———. *Collected Stories.* 1934. Vintage Books edition. New York: Random, 1977.

———. *Essays, Speeches and Public Letters.* Edited by James B. Meriwether. New York: Random House, 1965.

———. *Flags in the Dust.* New York: Random, 1973.

———. *Go Down, Moses.* 1942. First Vintage International edition. New York: Random, 1990.

———. *The Hamlet.* New York: Random, 1940.

———. *Intruder in the Dust.* New York: Random, 1948.

———. *Light in August.* New York: Random, 1932.

———. *The Mansion.* New York: Random, 1959.

———. *The Portable Faulkner.* Edited by Malcolm Cowley. New York: Viking, 1946.

———. *The Reivers.* New York: Random, 1962.

———. *Requiem for a Nun.* New York: Random House, 1951.

———. *Sanctuary.* New York: Random, 1931.

———. *Sartoris.* New York: Random, 1929.

———. *Soldier's Pay.* New York: Boni and Liverwright, 1926.

———. *The Sound and the Fury.* 1929. First Vintage International edition. New York: Random, 1990.

———. *The Town.* New York: Random, 1957.

———. *The Unvanquished.* New York: Random, 1938.

Ferguson, SallyAnn. "Folkloric Men and Female Growth in *Their Eyes Were Watching God.*" *Black American Literature Forum* 21 (1987): 185–97.

Figes, Eva. *Tragedy and Social Evolution.* London: Calder, 1976.

Fitzgerald, Gregory, and Peter Marchant. "An Interview with Ernest J. Gaines." *New Orleans Review* 1 (1969): 331–35. Reprinted in *Conversations with Ernest Gaines,* edited by John Lowe, 3–15. Jackson: University Press of Mississippi, 1995.

Flores, Toni. "Claiming and Making: Ethnicity, Gender, and the Common Sense in Leslie Marmon Silko's *Ceremony* and Zora Neale Hurston's *Their Eyes Were Watching God.*" *Frontiers* 10, no. 3 (1989): 52–58.

Fore, Steve. "The Same Old Others: The Western, *Lonesome Dove,* and the Lingering Difficulty of Difference." *Velvet Light Trap* 27 (1991): 49–62.

Fowler, Doreen. *Faulkner: The Return of the Repressed.* Charlottesville: University Press of Virginia, 1997.

Fox-Genovese, Elizabeth. "To Write My Self: The Autobiographies of Afro-American Women." In *Feminist Issues in Literary Scholarship,* edited by Shari Benstock, 161–80. Bloomington: Indiana University Press, 1987.

Gaines, Ernest. *The Autobiography of Miss Jane Pittman.* New York: Dial, 1971.

———. *Bloodline.* 1968. New York: Norton, 1976.

———. *Catherine Carmier.* New York: Atheneum, 1964.

———. *A Gathering of Old Men.* 1983. First Vintage Contemporaries edition. New York: Random, 1992.

———. *In My Father's House.* 1978. New York: Norton, 1983.

———. *A Lesson Before Dying.* New York: Knopf, 1993.

———. "Miss Jane and I." *Callaloo* 1, no. 2 (1978): 23–38.

———. *Of Love and Dust.* 1967. New York: Norton, 1979.

Gaudet, Marcia. "Black Women: Race, Gender, and Culture in Gaines's Fiction." In *Critical Reflections on the Fiction of Ernest J. Gaines,* edited by David C. Estes, 139–57. Athens: University of Georgia Press, 1994.

Gaudet, Marcia, and Carl Wooton. *Porch Talk with Ernest Gaines: Conversations on the Writer's Craft.* Southern Literary Studies series. Baton Rouge: Louisiana State University Press, 1990.

Gautreaux, Tim. *Same Place, Same Things.* New York: St. Martin's, 1996.

———. *Welding with Children.* New York: St. Martin's, 1999.

Gilchrist, Ellen. *The Annunciation.* Boston: Little, Brown, 1983.

———. *In the Land of Dreamy Dreams.* 1981. Boston: Little, Brown, 1985.

Giles, James R. "The Significance of Time in *Their Eyes Were Watching God.*" *Negro American Literature Forum* (1972): 52–53, 60.

Glasgow, Ellen. *A Certain Measure: An Interpretation of Prose Fiction.* New York: Harcourt, Brace, 1938.

———. *The Deliverance.* New York: Doubleday, Page, 1904.

———. *The Sheltered Life.* 1932. Edited by Carol Manning. Charlottesville: University of Virginia Press, 1994.

Godbold, E. Stanly, Jr. *Ellen Glasgow and the Woman Within.* Baton Rouge: Louisiana State University Press, 1972.

Gold, Joseph. *William Faulkner: A Study in Humanism from Metaphor to Discourse.* Norman: University of Oklahoma Press, 1966.

Goodman, Susan. *Ellen Glasgow: A Biography.* Baltimore: Johns Hopkins University Press, 1998.

———. "Memory and Memoria in *The Sheltered Life.*" *Mississippi Quarterly* 49 (1996): 241–54.

Gordon, Lois. *Donald Barthelme.* Twayne's United States Authors series 416. Boston: Twayne, 1981.

Gray, Richard. *Writing the South: Ideas of an American Region.* Cambridge Studies in American Literature and Culture series. Cambridge: Cambridge University Press, 1986.

Grenier, Cynthia. "The Art of Fiction: An Interview with William Faulkner, September 1955." *Accent* 16 (1956): 167–77. Reprinted as "1955 Interview with Cynthia Grenier" in *Lion in the Garden: Interviews with William Faulkner, 1926–1962.* Edited by James B. Meriwhether and Michael Millgate, 215–27. New York: Random, 1968.

Gresset, Michel. *A Faulkner Chronology.* Jackson: University Press of Mississippi, 1985.

Griffin, Joseph. "Creole and Singaleese: Disruptive Caste in *Catherine Carmier* and *A Gathering of Old Men.*" In *Critical Reflections on the Fiction of Ernest J. Gaines,* by David C. Estes, 30–45. Athens: University of Georgia Press, 1994.

———. "Ernest J. Gaines's Good News: Sacrifice and Redemption in *Of Love and Dust.*" *Modern Language Studies* 18, no. 3 (1988): 75–85.

Guinn, Matthew. *After Southern Modernism: Fiction of the Contemporary South.* Jackson: University Press of Mississippi, 2000.

Guttman, Sondra F. "Representing Rape, Revising America: Sexual Violence in American Modernist and Proletarian Literatures." PhD diss., State University of New Jersey-Rutgers, New Brunswick, 1999.

Gwin, Minrose. "Her Shape, His Hand: The Spaces of African American Women in *Go Down, Moses.* In *New Essays on "Go Down Moses,"* edited by Linda Wagner-Martin, 73–100. Cambridge: Cambridge University Press, 1996.

———. "Nonfelicitous Space and Survivor Discourse: Reading the Incest Story in Southern Women's Fiction." In *Haunted Bodies: Gender and Southern Texts,* edited by Anne Goodwyn Jones and Susan V. Donaldson, 416–40. Charlottesville: University Press of Virginia, 1997.

Gwynn, Frederick L., and Joseph L. Blotner, eds. *Faulkner in the University: Class Conferences at the University of Virginia, 1957–58.* Charlottesville: University of Virginia Press, 1959.

Haas, Robert. "Might Zora Neale Hurston's Janie Woods Be Dying of Rabies?: Considerations from Historical Medicine." *Literature and Medicine* 19 (2000): 205–28.

Hall, Constance Hill. *Incest in Faulkner: A Metaphor for the Fall.* Ann Arbor: UMI Research Press, 1983.

Hansberry, Lorraine. *A Raisin in the Sun: A Drama in Three Acts.* New York: Random, 1959.

Harper, Mary T. "From Sons to Fathers: Ernest Gaines' *A Gathering of Old Men.*" *College Language Association Journal* 3 (1988): 299–308.

Hattenhauer, Darryl. "The Death of Janie Crawford: Tragedy and the American Dream in *Their Eyes Were Watching God.*" *MELUS* 19, no. 1 (1994): 45–56.

———. "Hurston's *Their Eyes Were Watching God.*" *Explicator* 50 (1992): 111–12.

Heglar, Charles J., and Annye L. Refoe. "Survival with Dignity": The Elderly African American in the Novels of Ernest Gaines." *Cross Roads* 3, no. 1 (1994–95): 57–68.

Hewson, Marc. "'My children were of me alone': Maternal Influence in Faulkner's *As I Lay Dying.*" *Mississippi Quarterly* 53 (2000): 551–67.

Hicks, Jack. *In the Singer's Temple: Prose Fictions of Barthelme, Gaines, Brautigan, Piercy, Kesey, and Kosinski.* Chapel Hill: University of North Carolina Press, 1981.

Higgins, Dick. *A Dialectic of Centuries: Notes Towards a Theory of the New Arts.* New York: Printed Editions, 1978.

Hobson, Fred. *But Now I See: The White Southern Racial Conversion Narrative.* Baton Rouge: Louisiana State University Press, 1999.

———. *The Southern Writer in the Postmodern World.* Mercer University Lamar Memorial Lectures series 33. Athens: University of Georgia Press, 1991.

Holman, C. Hugh, and William Harmon. *A Handbook to Literature.* 5th ed. New York: Macmillan, 1986.

Howe, Irving. *William Faulkner: A Critical Study.* 3rd ed. Chicago: University of Chicago Press, 1975.

Hubbard, Dolan. "In Quest of Authority: Toni Morrison's *Song of Solomon* and the Rhetoric of the Black Preacher." *College Language Association Journal* 35 (1992): 288–302.

Hunton, W. A. "The Adventures of the Brown Girl in Search for Life." Review of *Their Eyes Were Watching God,* by Zora Neale Hurston. *Journal of Negro Education* 7, no. 1 (1938): 71–72.

Hurston, Zora Neale. *Jonah's Gourd Vine.* 1934. New York: HarperCollins, 1990.

———. *Their Eyes Were Watching God.* 1937. New York: HarperCollins, 1990.

Hustis, Harriet. "Masculinity as/in Comic Performance in *As I Lay Dying* and *The Sound and the Fury.*" *Faulkner Journal* 15, no. 1–2 (1999–2000): 107–23.

Hutcheon, Linda. *A Poetics of Postmodernism: History, Theory, Fiction.* New York: Routledge, 1988.

Irwin, John T. "Horace Benbow and the Myth of Narcissa." *American Literature* 64 (1992): 543–66.

Jackson, Blyden. "Jane Pittman through the Years: A People's Tale." In *American Letters and the Historical Consciousness: Essays in Honor of Lewis P. Simpson*, edited by J. Gerald Kennedy and Daniel Mark Fogel, 255–73. Baton Rouge: Louisiana State University Press, 1987.

Jehlen, Myra. *Class and Character in Faulkner's South*. New York: Columbia University Press, 1976.

Jones, Anne Goodwyn. "The World of Lee Smith." *Southern Quarterly* 22 (1983): 115–39.

Jones, Suzanne W. "Reconstructing Manhood: Race, Masculinity, and Narrative Closure in Ernest Gaines's *A Gathering of Old Men* and *A Lesson Before Dying*." *Masculinities* 3, no. 2 (1995): 43–66.

Jordan, Jennifer. "Feminist Fantasies: Zora Neale Hurston's *Their Eyes Were Watching God*. *Tulsa Studies in Women's Literature* 7 (1988): 105–17.

Kael, Pauline. "The Current Cinema: Cicely Tyson Goes to the Fountain." Review of *The Autobiography of Miss Jane Pittman* [CBS made-for-television movie]. *New Yorker*, 28 January 1974, 73–75.

Karl, Frederick R. *American Fictions, 1940–1980: A Comprehensive History and Critical Evaluation*. New York: Harper and Row, 1983.

———. *William Faulkner: American Writer*. New York: Random, 1989.

Kerr, Walter. *Tragedy and Comedy*. New York: Simon and Schuster, 1967.

King, Richard H. *A Southern Renaissance: The Cultural Awakening of the American South, 1930–1955*. New York: Oxford University Press, 1980.

King, Sigrid. "Naming and Power in Zora Neale Hurston's *Their Eyes Were Watching God*." *Black American Literature Forum* 24 (1990): 683–96.

Klinkowitz, Jerome. *Donald Barthelme: An Exhibition*. Durham: Duke University Press, 1991.

Kodat, Catherine Gunther. "Biting the Hand That Writes You: Southern African-American Folk Narrative and the Place of Women in *Their Eyes Were Watching God*." In *Haunted Bodies: Gender and Southern Texts*, edited by Anne Goodwyn Jones and Susan V. Donaldson, 319–42. Charlottesville: University Press of Virginia, 1997.

Kolmerten, Carol A., Stephen M. Ross, and Judith Bryant Wittenberg, eds. *Unflinching Gaze: Morrison and Faulkner Re-Envisioned*. Jackson: University Press of Mississippi, 1997.

Krasner, James. "The Life of Women: Zora Neale Hurston and Female Autobiography." *Black American Literature Forum* 23 (1989): 113–26.

Kreyling, Michael. *Inventing Southern Literature*. Jackson: University Press of Mississippi, 1998.

Kubie, Lawrence S. Review of *Sanctuary*, by William Faulkner. *Saturday Review of Literature*, 20 October 1934, 218, 224–25. Reprinted as "William Faulkner's *Sanctuary*: An Analysis," in *Twentieth-Century Interpretations of "Sanctuary": A*

Collection of Critical Essays, edited by J. Douglas Canfield, 25–31. Englewood Cliffs, N.J.: Prentice-Hall, 1982.

Laney, Ruth. "A Conversation with Ernest Gaines." *Southern Review* 10 (1974): 1–14. Reprinted in *Conversations with Ernest Gaines,* edited by John Lowe, 56–68. Jackson: University Press of Mississippi, 1995.

LeClair, Thomas. "The Language Must Not Sweat: A Conversation with Toni Morrison." *New Republic,* 21 March 1981, 25–29. Reprinted in *Conversations with Toni Morrison,* edited by Danille Taylor-Guthrie, 119–37. Jackson: University Press of Mississippi, 1994.

Lee, Catherine Carr. "The South in Toni Morrison's *Song of Solomon*: Initiation, Healing, and Home." *Studies in the Literary Imagination* 31, no. 2 (1998): 110–23.

Lee, Harper. *To Kill a Mockingbird.* New York: Lippincott, 1960.

Leonard, John. Review of *Jazz,* by Toni Morrison. *Nation,* 25 May 1982. Reprinted in *Toni Morrison: Critical Perspectives Past and Present,* edited by Henry Louis Gates Jr., 36–49. New York: Amistad, 1993.

Longley, John Lewis, Jr. *The Tragic Mask: A Study of Faulkner's Heroes.* Chapel Hill: University of North Carolina Press, 1963.

Lowe, John, "An Interview with Ernest Gaines." In *Conversations with Ernest Gaines,* edited by Lowe, 297–328. Jackson: University Press of Mississippi, 1995.

———. Introduction to *The Future of Southern Letters,* edited by Jefferson Humphries and Lowe, 3–19. New York: Oxford University Press, 1996.

Lupton, Mary Jane. "Black Women and Survival in *Comedy American Style* and *Their Eyes Were Watching God.*" *Zora Neale Hurston Forum* 1 (1986): 38–44.

Luscher, Robert M. "The Pulse of *Bloodline.*" In *Critical Reflections on the Fiction of Ernest J. Gaines,* edited by David C. Estes, 62–88. Athens: University of Georgia Press, 1994.

Malin, Irving. Review of *The Dead Father,* by Donald Barthelme. *Commonweal* 4 June 1976: 379–80.

Malmgren, Carl D. "Exhumation: *The Dead Father.*" In *Narrative Turns and Minor Genres in Postmodernism,* edited by Theo D'haen and Hans Bertens, 25–40. Amsterdam: Rodopi, 1995.

Malory, Barbara. "Barthelme's *The Dead Father.*" *Linguistics in Literature* 2 (1977): 44–111.

Matthews, Pamela R. *Ellen Glasgow and a Woman's Traditions.* Charlottesville: University Press of Virginia, 1994.

McCorkle, Jill. *Ferris Beach.* Chapel Hill, N.C.: Algonquin, 1990.

McDonald, Walter R. "'You Not a Bum, You a Man': Ernest J. Gaines's *Bloodline.*" *Negro American Literature Forum* 9 (1975).

McDowell, Frederick P. W. *Ellen Glasgow and the Ironic Art of Fiction.* Madison: University of Wisconsin Press, 1960.

McHale, Brian. *Postmodernist Fiction.* New York: Methuen, 1987.

McKay, Nellie. "An Interview with Toni Morrison." *Contemporary Literature* 24, no. 4 (1983): 413–29. Reprinted in *Conversations with Toni Morrison,* edited by Danille Taylor-Guthrie, 138–55. Jackson: University Press of Mississippi, 1994.

McKee, Patricia. "*As I Lay Dying*: Experience in Passing." *South Atlantic Quarterly* 90 (1991): 579–632.

———. *Producing American Races: Henry James, William Faulkner, Toni Morrison.* Durham: Duke University Press, 1999.

McMurtry, Larry. *Dead Man's Walk.* New York: Simon and Schuster, 1995.

———. *Lonesome Dove.* New York: Simon and Schuster, 1985.

———. *Streets of Laredo.* New York: Simon and Schuster, 1993.

Mencken, H. L. "The Sahara of the Bozart." In *Prejudices, Second Series.* New York: Knopf, 1920.

Millgate, Michael. *The Achievement of William Faulkner.* Athens: University of Georgia Press, 1989.

Milton, John. *Paradise Lost.* In *Complete Poems and Prose,* edited by Merritt Y. Hughes, 207–469. New York: Macmillan, 1985.

Minter, David. *William Faulkner: His Life and Work.* Baltimore: Johns Hopkins University Press, 1980.

Mitchell, Margaret. *Gone with the Wind.* New York: Macmillan, 1936.

Moore, Robert R. "Desire and Despair: Temple Drake's Self-Victimization." In *Faulkner and Women: Faulkner and Yoknapatawpha, 1985,* edited by Doreen Fowler and Ann J. Abadie, 112–27. Jackson: University Press of Mississippi, 1986.

Morrison, Toni. *Beloved.* New York: Knopf, 1987.

———. "Faulkner and Women." In *Faulkner and Women: Faulkner and Yoknapatawpha 1985,* edited by Doreen Fowler and Ann J. Abadie, 295–302. Jackson: University Press of Mississippi, 1986.

———. *Playing in the Dark: Whiteness and the Literary Imagination.* New York: Vintage, 1993.

———. *Song of Solomon.* New York: Knopf, 1977.

———. *Sula.* New York: Knopf, 1973.

———. *Tar Baby.* New York: Knopf, 1992.

Morrow, Laura, and Edward Morrow. "The Ontological Potentialities of Anti-chaos and Adaptation in *A Streetcar Named Desire.*" In *Confronting Tennessee Williams's "A Streetcar Named Desire": Essays in Critical Pluralism,* edited by Philip C. Kolin, 59–70. Contributions in Drama and Theatre Studies series 50. Westport, Conn.: Greenwood, 1993.

Nielsen, Paul S. "What Does Addie Bundren Mean, and How Does She Mean It?" *Southern Literary Journal* 25, no. 1 (1992): 33–39.

Nilon, Charles H. *Faulkner and the Negro: An Analysis of Faulkner's Treatment of Negro Characters in His Novels and Short Stories.* New York: Citadel, 1965.

O'Brien, John. "Ernest J. Gaines." In *Interviews with Black Writers,* edited by

O'Brien, 79–93. New York: Liveright, 1973. Reprinted in *Conversations with Ernest Gaines,* edited by John Lowe, 25–38. Jackson: University Press of Mississippi, 1995.

O'Connor, Flannery. *Mystery and Manners: Occasional Prose.* Edited by Sally and Robert Fitzgerald. New York: Farrar, 1961.

O'Connor, John J. "TV: Splendid 'Jane Pittman' Relates Black History." Review of *The Autobiography of Miss Jane Pittman* [CBS made-for-television movie]. *New York Times,* 31 January 1974, 67.

O'Donnell, Patrick. "Faulkner in Light of Morrison." In *Unflinching Gaze: Morrison and Faulkner Re-Envisioned,* edited by Carol A. Kolmerten, Stephen M. Ross, and Judith Bryant Wittenberg, 219–27. Jackson: University Press of Mississippi, 1997.

———. "Remarking Bodies: Divagations of Morrison from Faulkner." In *Faulkner, His Contemporaries, and His Posterity,* edited by Waldemar Zacharasiewicz, 322–27. Transatlantic Perspectives series 3. Tübingen: Francke, 1993.

Ono, Kiyoyuki. "The Secret of 'Was' Is." In *Faulkner Studies in Japan,* edited by Thomas L. McHaney, 148–73. Athens: University of Georgia Press, 1985.

Parker, Betty Jean. "Complexity: Toni Morrison's Women." In *Sturdy Black Bridges: Visions of Black Women in Literature,* edited by Roseann Bell, Bettye J. Parker, and Beverly Guy-Sheftall, 251–57. Garden City: Doubleday, 1979. Reprinted in *Conversations with Toni Morrison,* edited by Danille Taylor-Guthrie, 60–66. Jackson: University Press of Mississippi, 1994.

Parker, Robert Dale. *"Absalom, Absalom!": The Questioning of Fictions.* Twayne's Masterworks Studies series 76. Boston: Hall, 1991.

Parrill, William. "An Interview with Ernest Gaines." *Louisiana Literature* 3, no. 2 (1986): 17–44. Reprinted in *Conversations with Ernest Gaines,* edited by John Lowe, 172–99. Jackson: University Press of Mississippi, 1995.

Patterson, Laura S. "Ellipsis, Ritual, and 'Real Time': Rethinking the Rape Complex in Southern Novels." *Mississippi Quarterly* 54 (2000–2001): 37–58.

Patteson, Richard F. Introduction to *Critical Essays on Donald Barthelme,* edited by Patteson, 5–21. New York: Hall, 1992.

Piacentino, Ed. "'The common humanity that is in us all': Toward Racial Reconciliation in Gaines's *A Lesson Before Dying.*" *Southern Quarterly* 42, no. 3 (2004): 73–85.

Pilkington, John. *The Heart of Yoknapatawpha.* Jackson: University Press of Mississippi, 1981.

Polk, Noel. "Man in the Middle: Faulkner and the Southern White Moderate." In *Faulkner and Race: Faulkner and Yoknapatawpha, 1986,* edited by Doreen Fowler and Ann J. Abadie, 130–51. Jackson: University Press of Mississippi, 1987.

Pondrom, Cyrena N. "The Role of Myth in Hurston's *Their Eyes Were Watching God.*" *American Literature* 58 (1986): 181–202.

Potter, Vilma Raskin. "*The Autobiography of Miss Jane Pittman*: How to Make a White Film from a Black Novel." *Literature/Film Quarterly* 3 (1975): 371–75.

Powell, Padgett. *Edisto*. New York: Farrar, Straus, Giroux, 1984.

Putzel, Max. "What is Gothic about *Absalom, Absalom!*?" *Southern Literary Journal* 4 (1971): 3–19.

Ramsey, Alvin. "Through a Glass Whitely: The Televised Rape of Miss Jane Pittman." *Black World,* August 1974, 31–36.

Raper, Julius Rowan, ed. *Ellen Glasgow's Reasonable Doubts: A Collection of her Writings*. Baton Rouge: Louisiana State University Press, 1988.

Raper, Julius Rowan. *From the Sunken Garden: The Fiction of Ellen Glasgow, 1916–1945*. Baton Rouge: Louisiana State University Press, 1980.

Reilly, Rosalind B. "*Oral History*: The Enchanted Circle of Narrative and Dream." *Southern Literary Journal* 23, no. 1 (1990): 79–92.

Rickels, Milton, and Patricia Rickels. "'The Sound of My People Talking': Folk Humor in *A Gathering of Old Men*." In *Critical Reflections on the Fiction of Ernest J. Gaines,* edited by David C. Estes, 215–27. Athens: University of Georgia Press, 1994.

Roberts, Diane. *Faulkner and Southern Womanhood*. Athens: University of Georgia Press, 1994.

Roberts, James L. "The Individual and the Family: Faulkner's *As I Lay Dying*." *Arizona Quarterly* 16 (1960): 26–38.

Roberts, John W. "The Individual and the Community in Two Short Stories by Ernest J. Gaines." *Black American Literature Forum* 18 (1984): 110–13.

Rodgers, Lawrence R. "'We all said, "she will kill herself"': The Narrator/Detective in William Faulkner's 'A Rose for Emily.'" *Clues* 16 (1995): 117–29.

Rodman, Isaac. "Irony and Isolation: Narrative Distance in Faulkner's 'A Rose for Emily.'" *Faulkner Journal* 8, no. 2 (1993): 3–12.

Rollyson, Carl E., Jr. *Uses of the Past in the Novels of William Faulkner*. Studies in Modern Literature series 37. Ann Arbor: UMI Research Press, 1984.

Rouse, Blair. *Ellen Glasgow*. Twayne's United States Authors series 26. Boston: Hall, 1962.

———, ed. *Letters of Ellen Glasgow*. New York: Harcourt, 1958.

Rowell, Charles H. "'This Louisiana Thing That Drives Me': An Interview with Ernest J. Gaines." *Callaloo* 1 (1978): 38–51. Reprinted in *Conversations with Ernest Gaines,* edited by John Lowe, 86–98. Jackson: University Press of Mississippi, 1995.

Royster, Philip M. "Milkman's Flying: The Scapegoat Transcended in Toni Morrison's *Song of Solomon*." *College Language Association Journal* 24 (1982): 419–40.

Rubin, Louis. *Writers of the Modern South: The Faraway Country*. Seattle: University of Washington Press, 1963.

Rushdy, Ashraf H. A. "Daughters Signifyin[g] History: The Example of Toni Morrison's *Beloved*." *American Literature* 64 (1992): 567–97.

Saeta, Elsa, and Izora Skinner. "Interview with Ernest Gaines." *Texas College English* 23, no. 2 (1991): 1–6. Reprinted in *Conversations with Ernest Gaines,* edited by John Lowe, 241–52. Jackson: University Press of Mississippi, 1995.

Sartisky, Michael. "Writing about Race in Difficult Times: An Interview with Ernest J. Gaines." In *Conversations with Ernest Gaines,* edited by John Lowe, 253–75. Jackson: University Press of Mississippi, 1995.

Schappell, Elissa, with Claudia Brodsky Lacour. "Toni Morrison: The Art of Fiction CXXXIV." *Paris Review* 129 (1993): 83–125.

Schultz, Elizabeth. "'Free in Fact and at Last': The Image of the Black Woman in American Fiction." In *What Manner of Woman: Essays on English and American Life and Literature,* edited by Marlene Springer, 316–44. New York: New York University Press, 1977.

Schwab, Gabriele. "The Multiple Lives of Addie Bundren's Dead Body: On William Faulkner's *As I Lay Dying.*" In *The Other Perspective in Gender and Culture: Rewriting Women and the Symbolic,* edited by Juliet Flower MacCannell, 209–41. New York: Columbia University Press, 1990.

Sederberg, Nancy B. "'A Momentary Anesthesia of the Heart': A Study of the Comic Elements in Faulkner's *Go Down, Moses.*" In *Faulkner and Humor: Faulkner and Yoknapatawpha, 1986,* edited by Doreen Fowler and Ann J. Abadie, 79–96. Jackson: University Press of Mississippi, 1986.

Sewell, Ernestine P. "McMurtry's Cowboy-God in *Lonesome Dove.*" *Western American Literature* 21 (1986): 219–25.

Shannon, Sandra G. "Strong Men Getting Stronger: Gaines's Defense of the Elderly Black Male in *A Gathering of Old Men.*" In *Critical Reflections on the Fiction of Ernest J. Gaines,* edited by David C. Estes, 195–214. Athens: University of Georgia Press, 1994.

Shelton, Frank W. "Ambiguous Manhood in Ernest J. Gaines's *Bloodline.*" *College Language Association Journal* 19 (1975): 200–209.

———. "*In My Father's House*: Ernest Gaines after Jane Pittman." *Southern Review* n.s. 17 (1981): 340–45.

———. "Of Machines and Men: Pastoralism in Gaines's Fiction." In *Critical Reflections on the Fiction of Ernest J. Gaines,* edited by David C. Estes, 12–29. Athens: University of Georgia Press, 1994.

Singal, Daniel J. *William Faulkner: The Making of a Modernist.* Chapel Hill: University of North Carolina Press, 1997.

Smith, David Lionel. "Bloodlines and Patriarchs: *Of Love and Dust* and Its Revisions of Faulkner." In *Critical Reflections on the Fiction of Ernest J. Gaines,* edited by David C. Estes, 46–61. Athens: University of Georgia Press, 1994.

Smith, Lee. *Black Mountain Breakdown.* New York: Putnam's, 1980.

———. *Oral History.* New York: Putnam's, 1983.

Smith, Wendy. "*PW* Interviews: Bobbie Ann Mason." *Publisher's Weekly,* 30 August 1985, 424–25.

Spallino, Chiara. "*Song of Solomon*: An Adventure in Structure." *Callaloo* 8 (1985): 510–24.

Spencer, Elizabeth. "Emerging as a Writer in Faulkner's Mississippi." In *Faulkner and the Southern Renaissance: Faulkner and Yoknapatawpha, 1981,* edited by Doreen Fowler and Ann J. Abadie, 120–37. Jackson: University Press of Mississippi, 1982.

Spillers, Hortense J. "A Hateful Passion, A Lost Love." In *Feminist Issues in Literary Scholarship,* edited by Shari Benstock, 181–207. Bloomington: Indiana University Press, 1987.

Stout, Janis P. "Cadillac Larry Rides Again: McMurtry and the Song of the Open Road." *Western American Literature* 24 (1989): 243–51.

Styron, William. *Lie Down in Darkness.* Indianapolis: Bobbs-Merrill, 1951.

Sundquist, Eric J. *Faulkner: The House Divided.* Baltimore: Johns Hopkins University Press, 1983.

Swiggart, Peter. *The Art of Faulkner's Novels.* Austin: University of Texas Press, 1964.

Tanner, Laura E. *Intimate Violence: Reading Rape and Torture in Twentieth-Century Fiction.* Bloomington: Indiana University Press, 1994.

Tate, Claudia. "Toni Morrison." In *Black Women Writers at Work,* edited by Tate, 117–31. New York: Continuum, 1983. Reprinted in *Conversations with Toni Morrison,* edited by Danille Taylor-Guthrie, 156–70. Jackson: University Press of Mississippi, 1994.

Tate, Linda. *A Southern Weave of Women: Fiction of the Contemporary South.* Athens: University of Georgia Press, 1994.

Taylor-Guthrie, Danille, ed. *Conversations with Toni Morrison.* Literary Conversations series. Jackson: University Press of Mississippi, 1994.

Taylor, Walter. *Faulkner's Search for a South.* Urbana: University of Illinois Press, 1983.

Thompson, Thomas. *Celebrity.* New York: Doubleday, 1982.

Thornton, Jerome E. "'Goin' on de muck': The Paradoxical Journey of the Black American Hero." *College Language Association Journal* 31 (1988): 261–80.

Turner, Darwin T. *In a Minor Chord: Afro-American Writers and Their Search for Identity.* Carbondale: Southern Illinois University Press, 1971.

Twain, Mark. *The Tragedy of Pudd'nhead Wilson and The Comedy/Those Extraordinary Twins.* Hartford, Conn: American, 1894.

Vickers, Anita M. "The Reaffirmation of African-American Dignity through the Oral Tradition in Zora Neale Hurston's *Their Eyes Were Watching God.*" *College Language Association Journal* 37 (1994): 303–15.

Vickery, Olga. *The Novels of William Faulkner: A Critical Interpretation.* Rev. ed. Baton Rouge: Louisiana State University Press, 1964.

Vigderman, Patricia. "Fast Times in Hoot Owl Holler." Review of *Oral History,* by Lee Smith. *Nation,* 1 October 1983, 282.

Vinson, Audrey L. "Pilate Dead: Conjuress." In *The World of Toni Morrison,* edited by Bessie W. Jones and Vinson, 63–77. Dubuque, Iowa: Kendall/Hunt, 1985.

Volpe, Edmond L. *A Reader's Guide to William Faulkner.* New York: Farrar, 1964.

Waggoner, Hyatt H. *William Faulkner: From Jefferson to the World.* Lexington: University of Kentucky Press, 1959.

Wagner[-Martin], Linda W. *Ellen Glasgow: Beyond Convention.* Austin: University of Texas Press, 1982.

Wagner-Martin, Linda. Introduction to *New Essays on "Go Down Moses,"* edited by Linda Wagner-Martin, 1–20. Cambridge: Cambridge University Press, 1996.

Wainwright, Mary Katherine. "The Aesthetics of Community: The Insular Black Community as Theme and Focus in Hurston's *Their Eyes Were Watching God.*" In *The Harlem Renaissance: Reevaluations,* edited by Amritjit Singh, William S. Shiver, and Stanley Brown, 233–43. New York: Garland, 1989.

Walker, Alice. *The Color Purple.* New York: Harcourt, 1982.

———. *In Search of Our Mothers' Gardens: Womanist Prose.* New York: Harcourt, 1983.

Warren, Karen W. "Masculinity and Communal Change in the Fiction of Ernest J. Gaines." Master's thesis, East Carolina University, 1999.

Warren, Robert Penn. *All the King's Men.* New York: Harcourt, Brace, 1946.

———. "Faulkner: The South, the Negro, and Time." In *Faulkner: A Collection of Critical Essays,* edited by Warren, 251–71. Englewood Cliffs, N.J.: Prentice-Hall, 1966.

Washington, Mary Helen. "The Black Woman's Search for Identity." *Black World,* August 1972, 68–75.

———. "The House Slavery Built." Review of *A Gathering of Old Men,* by Ernest J. Gaines. *Nation,* 14 January 1984, 22–24.

Weinstein, Philip M. "David and Solomon: Fathering in Faulkner and Morrison." In *Unflinching Gaze: Morrison and Faulkner Re-Envisioned,* edited by Carol A. Kolmerten, Stephen M. Ross, and Judith Bryant Wittenberg, 48–74. Jackson: University Press of Mississippi, 1997.

———. *What Else But Love?: The Ordeal of Race in Faulkner and Morrison.* New York: Columbia University Press, 1996.

Werner, Craig. "Minstrel Nightmares: Black Dreams of Faulkner's Dreams of Blacks." In *Faulkner and Race: Faulkner and Yoknapatawpha, 1986,* edited by Doreen Fowler and Ann J. Abadie, 35–57. Jackson: University Press of Mississippi, 1987.

Wertheim, Albert. "Journey to Freedom: Ernest Gaines' *The Autobiography of Miss Jane Pittman* (1971)." In *The Afro-American Novel since 1960,* edited by Peter Bruck and Wolfgang Karrer, 219–35. Amsterdam: Grüner, 1982.

White, Daniel. "'Haunted by the Idea': Fathers and Sons in *In My Father's House* and *A Gathering of Old Men.*" In *Critical Reflections on the Fiction of Ernest J.*

Gaines, edited by David C. Estes, 158–79. Athens: University of Georgia Press, 1994.

Wideman, John Edgar. "*Of Love and Dust*: A Reconsideration." *Callaloo* 1, no. 3 (1978): 76–84.

Wilentz, Gay. "Civilizations Underneath: African Heritage as Cultural Discourse in Toni Morrison's *Song of Solomon.*" *African American Review* 26 (1992): 61–76.

———. "Defeating the False God: Janie's Self-Determination in Zora Neale Hurston's *Their Eyes Were Watching God.*" In *Faith of a (Woman) Writer,* edited by Alice Kessler Harris and William McBrien, 285–91. Contributions in Women's Studies series 86. Westport, Conn.: Greenwood, 1988.

Williams, David. *Faulkner's Women: The Myth and the Muse.* Montreal: McGill-Queen's University Press, 1977.

Williams, Tennessee. *A Streetcar Named Desire.* New York: New Directions, 1947.

Williamson, Joel. *William Faulkner and Southern History.* Oxford: Oxford University Press, 1993.

Willis, Susan. "Eruptions of Funk: Historicizing Toni Morrison." *Black American Literature Forum* 16 (1982): 34–42. Reprinted in *Critical Essays on Toni Morrison,* edited by Nellie McKay, 308–29. Boston: Hall, 1988.

———. *Specifying: Black Women Writing the American Experience.* Madison: University of Wisconsin Press, 1987.

Wilson, James D. *The Romantic Heroic Ideal.* Baton Rouge: Louisiana State University Press, 1982.

Winchell, Mark Royden. "The Myth Is the Message, or Why *Streetcar* Keeps Running." In *Confronting Tennessee Williams's "A Streetcar Named Desire": Essays in Critical Pluralism,* edited by Philip C. Kolin, 132–45. Contributions in Drama and Theatre Studies series 50. Westport, Conn.: Greenwood, 1993.

Wood, Amy Louise. "Feminine Rebellion and Mimicry in Faulkner's *As I Lay Dying.*" *Faulkner Journal* 9, no. 1–2 (1993–94): 99–112.

Wyatt-Brown, Bertram. "The Mask of Obedience: Male Slave Psychology in the Old South." In *Haunted Bodies: Gender and Southern Texts,* edited by Anne Goodwyn Jones and Susan V. Donaldson, 23–55. Charlottesville: University Press of Virginia, 1997.

Yaeger, Patricia. *Dirt and Desire: Reconstructing Southern Women's Writing, 1930–1990.* Chicago: University of Chicago Press, 2000.

Young, Stark. *So Red the Rose.* New York: Scribner's, 1934.

Zeitlin, Michael. "Father-Murder and Father-Rescue: The Post-Freudian Allegories of Donald Barthelme." *Contemporary Literature* 34 (1993): 182–203.

Zoglin, Richard. "Poetry on the Prairie." Review of *Lonesome Dove* [CBS television miniseries]. *Time,* 6 February 1989: 78.

Index

Schultz, Elizabeth, 106
Schwab, Gabriele, 197–98n.7
Schyfter, Sara E., 224n.10
Sederberg, Nancy B., 79, 207n.26
Sewell, Ernestine P., 199n.17
Sexuality: female, 17, 97–99, 106–7, 198n.12; oppression of, 8, 98–99, 134, 138–39, 141–42
Shannon, Sandra G., 80
Shelley, Percy Bysshe, 140–41
The Sheltered Life (Glasgow), 222n.2; *Absalom, Absalom!* parallels to, 179, 180, 184; *Go Down, Moses* parallels to, 184, 223n.7; impotence themes and, 10, 178–81, 183–84; romanticism themes in, 182–83; "A Rose for Emily" parallels to, 178–85, 223n.6; *Sanctuary* parallels to, 179, 184
Shelton, Frank, 56, 71, 74, 207n.21, 208n.31
Singal, Daniel J., 120, 151, 163, 174, 191, 195n.11, 201n.2, 217n.15, 217–18n.17; 220n.8
Skinner, Izora, 48
Slavery, 134; literature influenced through, 191–92; sin themes regarding, 29, 110, 136
Smith, David, 57–58, 210n.40
Smith, Lee, 95, 165, 172, 220n.10; Faulkner revisions by, 2, 8–9, 28, 134, 221n.3; innocence themes by, 151–52; oppression and, 134, 155–56; optimism by, 191; southern themes by, 134; women's treatment and, 140, 159. *See also Oral History*
Smith, Wendy, 192
Social status: *Absalom, Absalom!* and, 96–101; oppression and, 9–11, 82–87, 208n.33; *Their Eyes Were Watching God* and, 96–101
Song of Solomon (Morrison), 6, 95, 112,

215–16n.8, 217n.16; *Absalom, Absalom!* parallels to, 6–8, 114–32, 215n.4, 216n.9–10; "The Bear" parallels to, 216n.10; epistemological aspects of, 114–17, 123–25; form of, 115; incest in, 216n.13; *Go Down, Moses* parallels to, 113–14; misogyny and, 127–28; Old South perspective in, 7–8; romanticism in, 123; summary of, 123; themes of, 115; women's voices in, 127–28
So Red the Rose (Young), 179
The Sound and the Fury (Faulkner), 63–64, 116, 172, 208n.29, 220n.9; *Autobiography* parallels to, 47–54, 201n.1; heroism perspectives in, 53–54; narrative structure of, 134–35; themes of, 119, 121; women's marginalization in, 27, 40, 47–49; women's strength representations in, 49–52
The Sound and the Fury/Oral History parallels: character journal, 150, 219n.5; character prototype, 144, 195n.10; endurance, 134, 155–56; land possession, 158; narrative structure, 134–35, 140, 218n.2, 219–20n.7
South, the: Glasgow themes on, 178–79, 181; literary perspectives on, 3; optimism and, 191–92; romanticism of, 7–9, 29, 42; transformation of, 8, 158, 172–73, 195n.11; western parallels to, 39–40, 198n.13. *See also* New South; Old South; Oppression; Romanticism
Southern Renascence: ending of, 8–9, 194n.7; New South depiction in, 110; Old South depiction in, 28, 110; rape perspectives in, 165–67
Spallino, Chiaro, 215n.3
Spencer, Elizabeth, 195n.11

Louisiana native Margaret Donovan Bauer is the
Ralph Hardee Rives Chair of Southern Literature at
East Carolina University and, since 1997, the editor
of the *North Carolina Literary Review*, published by
East Carolina University and the North Carolina
Literary and Historical Association. Her previous
book is *The Fiction of Ellen Gilchrist* (University Press
of Florida, 1999), and she has published articles on
southern writers in such periodicals as the
Mississippi Quarterly and the *Southern Literary Journal*
and in several edited collections of essays.